INTERNAL SECURITY PROBLEMS IN NORTHEAST INDIA INSURGENCY AND COUNTER INSURGENCY

INTERNAL SECURITY PROBLEMS IN NORTHEAST INDIA INSURGENCY AND COUNTER INSURGENCY

Insurgency And Counter Insurgency In Assam Since 1985

Onkar Sadashiv Pawar

KALPAZ

ISBN 978-93-5128-297-6
Price : ₹ 990

First Published, 2016

Published by

Kalpaz Publications
C-30, Satyawati Nagar,
Delhi-110052
Ph. : 9212142040
E-mail: kalpaz@hotmail.com

Printed at : G. Print Process, Delhi

Cataloging in Publication Data—DK
Courtesy: D.K. Agencies (P) Ltd. <docinfo@dkagencies.com>

Pawar, Onkar Sadashiv, author.
Internal security problems of Northeast region of India : insurgency and counter insurgency in Assam since 1985 / Onkar Sadashiv Pawar.
pages cm
Running title: Internal security problems of North-East region of India.
Includes bibliographical references.
ISBN 9789351281976 (invalid)

1. Internal security—India, Northeastern. 2. Insurgency—India, Northeastern. 3. Insurgency—India—Assam. 4. Counterinsurgency—Government policy—India, Northeastern. 5. Counterinsurgency—Government policy—India—Assam. I. Title. II. Title: Internal security problems of North-East region of India.

HV6295.I4P39 2016 DDC 355.021809541 23

Dedicated

This book to my beloved late grandfather
Mr. Krishnaji Govind Pawar

Contents

List of Maps

List of Tables

List of Sketch

Forward

At the outset I would like to appreciate Shree Onkar Pawar as, he his publishing his Ph.D research work in a book form and I am very pleased to write about "Forward" for his book entitled "Internal Security Problems in North-East India: Insurgency and Counter Insurgency.", which is being subject of vital importance and timely.

The strategic development which has been taking place in the era of global village, which ultimately resulted in revolutionary changes in the concept of security. Therefore, in this globalised world the goal of national security is not only to defend the country from external aggression but also to assure the well being of citizens of the country. This suggests that proper efforts must be taken to maintain the territorial integrity and to utilize available resources for the prosperity of the people of the country. However, the failure of maintenance of territorial integrity often makes a nation vulnerable to the external threats. This creates a link between internal and external security environment which is always crucial in this changing international scenario. The challenges to India's national security have to be seen in this perspective which suggests that the internal environment holds a key position for the security and stability of the country. There is also a difference between Defence and Security. A nation may be well defend but may not be secure.

The author Onkar Pawar has rightly attempted to study the problem that we confront in Northeast regionof India from this perspective. However, he does not have simplistic and development centric approach. The author argues that to understand the phenomenon of insurgency, one has to understand the genesis of this problem. He has carefully drafted the genesis of the insurgency problem and explains the other factors that sustain insurgency and it related violence in the region. Moreover, he has examined the complex nuances and dynamics that make insurgent groups formidable. While doing so he empirically analyzed the ground situation with the help of material, historical and geographical facts. He has carefully described the role played by the inimical neighbours in fomenting the insurgency in the region and their wider implication on India's national security.

The book provides bibliography and reference which would be valuable for students and research scholar too. The book which is an outcome of PhD research work is a good attempt of author. He has made earnest endeavour to answer the questions that he had set for himself. The author has written a descriptive book which I commend alike to the academician and general readers. This book will also be useful to policy formulations and those who implement the policies.

Lt. General (Dr.) **D. B. Shekatkar** (Retd.)
PVSM, AVSM, VSM

****

Lt. Gen. (Dr.) D. B. Shekatkar (Retd.), PVSM, AVSM, VSM, is a M.Sc., M.Phil., and Ph.D in Defence and strategic Studies. He has served in the Indian Army for four decades. He has extensive experience in combat insurgency and anti-terror operation in Jammu and Kashmir and Northeast region of India. He is currently the President at Forum for Integrated National Security, Mumbai.

Acknowledgements

This book is the outcome of research pursued for Ph.D degree from the Dept. of Defence and Strategic Studies, Savitribai Phule Pune University.

At the outset, I would like to take the opportunity to express my sincere thanks to my guide, Dr. Priyanath Adinath Ghosh, for his continuous illuminating guidance from the beginning till the end of this work. It is because of him that I could complete the research.

It gives me immense pleasure to thank faculty members of Department of Defence and Strategic Studies Professor A. S. Dalvi, Head, Professor S. B. Paranjape, Director, Yashwantrao Chavan National Centre of International Security and Defense Analysis (YC-NISDA), and Professor V. S. Khare for their support in the difficult times during the research. I would also like to convey my gratitude to the staff of the Department of Defense and Strategic Studies, Savitribai Phule Pune University, Pune for providing the facilities and helping to ease formalities.

Besides this, I would like to express my gratefulness to my teacher Dr. M. L. Sali Former Head, Department of Defence and Strategic Studies, Bhonsala Military College and now Principal of NDVP's Vani College, Dist. Dindori, Tal. Nashik, in persuading and timely guidance me to publish this research work in a book form. I express my special thanks to Lt. Gen. Dr. D. B. Shekatkar (Retd.) who has accepted to write the foreword for this book. I would like to express my deep sense of gratitude to Prof. Dr. Sudhir U. Meshram, Hon'ble Vice Chancellor North Maharashtra University, Jalgaon, for providing me excellent academic environment and support while pursing this research. I also appreciate Dr. (Mrs.) Suchita H. Kochargaonkar, Principal, Bhonsala Military College, Nashik who extended her good wishes for the completion of this research. I need to acknowledge the considerable assistance and cooperation received from Dr. V. Y. Jadhav former Head, Department of Defence and Strategic Studies, G. T. P. College, Nandurbar and now Principal of Arts College, Thalner, Tal. Jalgaon, Dr. J. A. Khan, Head, Mr. Ramesh I. Raut, Asst. Professor, Mr. Vikrant J. Kawale, Lecturer, Dept. of Defence and Strategic Studies, Mr. Bharat Gugane, Assistant Professor, Dept. of English, Bhonsala Military College, Nashik which has also shaped and made this study practically possible.

I would also like to express my profound gratitude to Dr. Tukaram R. Borse, I/C Director, School of Arts and Humanities and Librarian, Prof. Dr. Archana P. Degaonkar, Director, School of Social Sciences, Prof. Dr. R. H. Gupta, former Director School of Social Sciences, Dr. Shantaram Badgujar, former Director, Dept. of Adult and Continuation Education and Extension Services, Mr. Tushar Raysing, Asst. Professor, Department of Defence and Strategic studies, and Mr. Umesh Gogadia, Asst. Professor, Department of Political Science, and other colleagues of the School of Social Sciences, North Maharashtra University, Jalgaon who has supported and encouraged consistently to pursue this research.

My sincere thanks also goes to Mr. Sunil Deodhar founder of My Home India NGO as, he facilitated my visit to Northeast Region of India. I would also like to thank Mr. Shushant Talukdar for making all the arrangements for my field tours with in Assam, which made my visit very easy.

I gratefully acknowledge the kindness and time given to me by Mr. Wasbir Hussain, Executive Director and Secretary, Centre for Development and Peace Studies, Guwahati, Assam, Mr. H. K. Deka, former DGP of Assam, Mrinal Talukdar, Secretary, Nanda Talukdar Foundation, Guwahati, Assam, Mr. Sunil Nath, Surrender ULFA cader and the then Publicity Secretary, ULFA, Dr. Samujjal Bhattachariya, the then President of All Assam Students Union (ASSU) now Advisor (ASSU), Dr. Dilip Gogoi, Assistant Professor, Dept. of Political Science, Cotton College, Guwahati, and Mr. Ray, Bureau Chief Hindustan Samachar, Guwahati for sharing their valuable knowledge and discussing practical aspects about insurgency which provided some important inputs on the research topic.

I would also like to express my appreciation to the Librarian and library staff of OMEO KUMAR DAS Institute of Social Change and Development, Guwahati, University of Mumbai, Rambhau Mhalgi Prabhodhini, Mumbai, North Maharashtra University, Jalgaon, Bhonsala Military College, Nashik. I further place my honor to those, whose works has been referred by me while pursuing this research.

I am also obliged to Mr. K. Binu, Librarian, Bhonsala Military College, and Mr. Ashok Kudhale for their cooperation and assistance in editing the thesis. I also would like to acknowledge the assistance provided by my friends Mr. Tushar Mogre, Mr. Sachin Ghadigaonkar and Mr. Dattatrey Sapkal for finalizing the sketches.

The acknowledgement would be incomplete without mentioning my Parents, wife and brother. I would like to acknowledge the encouragement and support that was extended by my parents Mr. Sadashiv Krishnaji Pawar and Mrs. Sweta Sadashiv Pawar, my wife Ojaswi, brother Rishikesh and other family members throughout this endeavor.

I am extremely grateful to Mr. Amit Garg, Director, Kalpaz Publication, New Delhi, for accepting the manuscript for the publication of this work.

Lastly, I also would like to thank all those people who directly or indirectly helped me during the research.

Date: 30/11/2015
Place: Pune **Onkar Sadashiv Pawar**

Preface

Insurgency in Northeast region of India is one of the core challenges which India is facing today as a threat to her national security. The North East Region of India comprising of eight states namely Arunachal Pradesh, Assam, Meghalaya, Manipur, Mizoram, Nagaland, Sikkim and Tripura connects to the main land of India through a Siliguri corridor, a narrow passage of foothill land in North Bengal, which is 33 km in width on the eastern side and 20 km on the western side. This passage has been popularly known as Chicken's neck. Geo-strategic importance of the Siliguri corridor lies in the fact that it is the only way to enter into the North east region from mainland India. Moreover, Assam is the gateway to other states of Northeast region as it establishes a link between these States and rest of the country through Silliguri corridor only. All the roads and railway tracks of Northeast region passes through the state of Assam. If China and Bangladesh blocks the Silliguri corridor in case of a war, India will have to face very critical situation and may lose its connectivity with the Northeast region. The region is encircled by five countries viz. Bangladesh, Bhutan, Myanmar, Nepal and China. It is apparent that directly and indirectly these immediate neighbours indulge in anti Indian activities. This becomes a cause for concern especially in light of the three wars which India fought with Pakistan and one with China in 1962. Moreover, China's military infrastructural development in Tibet which is very close to the Line of Actual Control (LAC) in Arunachal Pradesh increases its geostrategic significanc. Another factor that increases the geostrategic significance of the region is the availability of vast natural resources such as tropical forest, potentials of Brahmaputra and its tributaries, tea, coal, timber, silk and jute. Moreover, it has a capacity of producing hydro power. It also has huge deposits of strategic minerals. Besides this, the region has more than one–third of the country's total biodiversity. The region is also rich in terms of genetic and ecosystem diversity. Varieties of medicinal plants with high international value are found in this region.

Insurgency prone in the North East region has been the source of serious concern for our national security since independence of the country. Since then, attempts have been made to deal with insurgency problem vigorously along with various aspects and dimensions. In view of this geopolitical connections and geostrategic significance this area has been crucial one from national development as well as security point of view. The views expressed and work carried out in this book is academic in nature while being a student of the subject Defence and Strategic Studies I accept the responsibility for any error due to incompetence and inadequacy. It is an attempt to contribute towards the required literature.

Dr. Onkar Sadashiv Pawar

List of Abbreviations

A

AASU	All Assam Students' Union
ABSU	All Bodo Students' Union
AAGSP	All Assam Gana Sangram Parishad
AFSPA	Armed Forces Special Powers Act
AGP	Aassm Gana Parishad
AIMLF	All India Muslim Liberation Front
AMULFA	All Muslim United Liberation Forum of Assam
ARNO	Arakan Rohingya National Organisation
ATTF	All Tripura Tiger Force
ANVC	Achik National Volunteer Council
ATTF	All Tripura Tribal Front
ADC	Autonomous District Council
AATSU	All Assam Tribal Students' Union
ASDC	Autonomous State Demand Committee

ADSO	All Dimasa Student Organisation
AS	Adam Sena

B

BAC	Bodo Autonomous Council
BTAD	Bodoland Territorial Area District
BTC	Bodoland Territorial Council
BIM	Bangladesh Islamic Manch
BLT	Bodo Liberation Tiger
BNLF	Bru National Liberation Force
Bodo SF	Bodo Security Force
BSF	Border Security Force
BNLF	Bru National Liberation Front
BVF	Bodo Volunteer Force
BPAC	Bodo People Action Committees
BNA	Bhutanese National Assembly
BOPs	Border Out Posts

C

CNA	Chin National Army
CHT	Chittagong Hill Tracts
CI	Counter Insurgency
CPO	Central Police Organisation

CEM	Chief Executive Member
CRPF	Central Reserve Police Force
CAPFs	Central Armed Police Forces
CPFs	Central Para-Military Forces

D

DGFI	Director General Forces Intelligence (Bangladesh)
DHD	Dima Halim Daoga
DNSF	Dimasa National Security Force
DFI	Defence Forces Intelligence (Bangladesh)
DSP	District Superintendent of Police

G

GNLF	Gurkha National Liberation Front

H

HUJI – B	Harkat –ul-Jihad-al-Islami of Bangladesh
HUM	Harkat-ul-Mujahideen
HNLC	Hynniwtrep National Liberation Council
HPC	Hamar Peoples' Conference
HuJI	Harkat-ul-Jihad-al-Islami of Bangladesh

I

IBRF	Indo-Burma Revolutionary Front
ICS	Islamic Chatra Shibir

IM (DT)	Illegal Immigrants (Determination Tribunal)
ILA	Islamic Liberation Army
ILAA	Independent Liberation Army of Assam
ISFI	Islamic Security Force of India
ISI	Inter Services Intelligence
ISS	Islamic Sevak Sangh
IURPI	Islamic United Reformation Protest of India
IB	Intelligence Bureau
IRDP	Integrated Rural Development Programme

J

JIC	Joint Intelligence Committee
JEI	Jamaat-e-Islami
JUUEH	Jamaat-ul-Ulema-e-Hind
JuM	Jamma'atul Mujahideen

K

KNV	Karbi National Volunteers
KLO	Kamatpur Liberation Organisation
KNA	Kuki National Army
KLA	Kuki Liberation Army
KNF	Kuki National Front
KYKL	Kanglei Yawol Kungla Lup

KSA	Karbi Student Association
KLNLF	Karbi Longri National Liberation Front
KIA	Kachin Independent Army
KPF	Karbi People's Front
KNPR	Karbi Long NC Hills Peoples' Resistance Force

L

LC	Line of Control
LAC	Line of Actual Control
LTTE	Liberation Tigers of Tamil Eelam
LITF	Liberation Islamic Tiger Force

M

MFO	Muslim Fundamentalist Organisation
MNF	Mizo National Front
MNFF	Mizo National Famine Front
MNP	Manipur Nationalist Party
MISA	Maintenance of Internal Security Act
DoNER	Ministry of Development of North Eastern Region
MULTA	Muslim United Liberation Tigers of Assam
MULFA	Muslim United Liberation Front of Assam
MSF	Muslim Security Force
MVF	Muslim Volunteer Force

MPLF	Manipur People's Liberation Front
MPA	Manipur Peoples Army
MoS	Memorandum of Settlement
MSCA	Muslim Security Council of Assam
MHA	Ministry of Home Affairs (Government of India)

N

NEC	North East Council
NSCN (I-M)	National Socialist Council of Nagaland (Muivah and Issaac Swu)
NSCN (K)	National Socialist Council of Nagaland (Khaplang)
NNC	Naga National Council
NFG	Naga Federal Government
NDFB	National Democratic Front of Bodoland
NEFA	North East Frontier Agency
NLFT	National Liberation Front of Tripura
NLFA	National Liberation Front of Arunachal

P

PLF	People's Liberation Front
PLA	Peoples' Liberation Army
PTCA	Plain Tribal Council of Assam
PMF	Para Military Forces

POTA	Prevention of Terrorist Act
POCA	Prevention of Organised Crime Act
PREPAK	Peoples Revolutionary Party of Kangleipak
POL	Petrol, Oil and Lubricants
PCG	People's Consultative Group
PSTD	Post Traumatic Stress Disorder

R

RPF	Revolutionary Peoples' Front
RAW	Research and Analysis Wing
RBA	Royal Bhutan Army
RSRE	Reimbursement of Security Related Expenditure

S

SSP	Sipahi-i-Sahab Pakistan
SIO	Student Islamic Organisation
SIMI	Student's Islamic Movement of India
SoO	Suspension of Operation
SF	Security Forces
SULFA	Surrender United Liberation Front of Assam
SIB	Subsidiary Intelligence Bureau
SPOs	Special Police Officers
SSB	Sashastra Seema Bal

T

TNV	Tripura National Volunteers

U

ULFA	United Liberation Front of Assam
UNLF	United National Liberation Front
UPVA	United Peoples Volunteers of Arunachal Pradesh
UTNLF	United Tribal National Liberation Front
UBNLF	United Bodo National Liberation Front
UMNC	United Mikir and North Cachar Hills District
UPDS	United Peoples' Democratic Solidarity
ULMA	United Liberation Militia of Assam
URPA	United Reformation Protest of Assam
UMFLA	United Muslim Liberation Front of Assam

V

VBIG's	Valley Based Insurgent Groups
VDPs	Village Defence Parties
VGs	Village Guards

1

Introduction

An attempt has been made in this chapter to discuss the long-standing notion of national security and emerging trends in the orb of national security. While making this attempt, the present study has explained how the notion of state security has moved towards the concept of security of people. An analytical approach has been pursued in this chapter. This chapter also consists of significance of the study, objectives, literature reviews, hypotheses, methodology, limitations of the study and a scheme of chapters.

1.1 Changing Concept of National Security

Different scholars understand the concept of national security in a different way at different points of time in the world. The concept has been changing according to the events that take place at international relations as it impacts on behaviour of nations in the world. For example, many power blocks were emerged due to the power politics between United States of America and Union of Socialist Soviet Republic during the cold war. Consequently, the then scholars began to believe in 'power politics' with states as the main actors and gave stress on obtaining more and more military power.[1] Due to this, policy-makers and experts both strongly believed that war is the only solution because conflict is inevitable in international relations. Thus, military-oriented security remained as a dominant model throughout the cold war.[2] State security remained primary concern and objective for the followers of military-oriented security. National security and state survival are the core values of military-oriented security; foreign policy of any state is formulated based on these two basic values. The threat to the national security of the country was largely influenced by international power structure during the cold war. Therefore, nations followed different means to ensure their national security in the period of cold war.[3] These include mainly alignments with the power-blocks, which dominated international politics. The bipolar system provided nation states an option to join coalition and ensure their national security.[4] Such explanation implies that security has been considered as security of territory from external attack, protection of national interest in foreign policy and global security from the threat of a nuclear war.[5] The concept has been related more to nation states than to people. It has been defined in geo-political terms, which encompasses different facets such as prevention, power balancing and military strategy in a state-centric area. In this way, the protection of the state from foreign attack, either real or imagined, has been the core of national security, which stimulated building-up of military power.[6] However, the change in understanding of the concept of security was noticed after the end of cold war era. The military-oriented concept which had emphasised the "centrality of state as centre of political life"[7] or state-centric security was questioned during the cold war era. However, the concept was believed to be somewhat unlikely and indefensible during post cold war period.[8] The concept became a leading subject of discussion, analysis and dialogue not only among the scholars but also among the strategists, policy-makers and economists. For example, Bary Buzan and his companies argued for expanding the scope of security by including issues, such as, politics, economy, society and ecology within the scope of security studies. Buzan argues that the issue of security is better appreciated if a holistic approach is adopted reintegrating the three levels, i.e. international system, the nation-state and individual.[9] He invented the term 'systemic security' to incorporate all security concerns at all levels.[10] Thus, the scope of concern for security has been widened through inclusion of three levels of international relations. The second important aspect of Buzan's argument is to concentrate on the interaction among various sources of insecurity, take a broad view of security, and develop a long-term approach.[11] Consequently, it is evident that the concept of national security has brought key issues to the forefront that were never a part of the security dialogue. For instance, issues like environment, food, social, political and cultural rights of individuals, which were not included in the military-oriented concept of external security threats, are to be incorporated in the security discourse. At the same time, it was also noted that application of military power is inevitable when and where required in the pursuit of national security. Many non-traditional issues related to security became a focus in international relations after the end of cold war. Moreover, it also created favourable environment for a complete re-evaluation of the whole concept of security. Even though the realist and neo-realist view has been that the goal of security is the survival of the state, it has become clear that most victims of both traditional and non-traditional security threats are the individual people who live in a certain country.[12] This is mainly because the traditional security theory does not deal with the rapidly growing non-traditional threats to security like, "the struggle for resources in the pursuit of energy, environmental degradation, forced migration, international terrorism, insurgency, dominance of non-state actors in drugs, arms, money laundering and financial crime organisation."[13]

Thus, the goal of national security is not just the protection of geographical periphery but also the prosperity of people living in the country. This includes the maintenance of the full autonomy of one's own resources and territorial integrity, freedom to develop advanced technology and the safeguarding of core values.[14] However, the threat to these core values originating from within the state makes a nation vulnerable to the external threats. India's core values are democratic rules, fundamental rights, social and economic equality, secularism and federalism. These values themselves are subjective in nature. Arnold Wolfers has suggested that, 'National security in the subjective sense is the absence of fear that such values will be attacked by others but in an objective sense it measures the absence of threat to the acquired values'. Thus, these core values must be reflected in the process of nation building. The wearing down of any one of these values is bound to erode the legitimacy of the state and consequently create a threat to its security. However, core values would require a protective ring of capabilities related to the maintenance of social unity and building up of techno-economic strength. Military capability is a crucial factor although it must be kept at the minimum sufficient level to provide convincing prevention against challenges to the topmost core. It implies that the major objective of national security is the creation of national consensus on common values of the society. The internal political and social stability, normal order of development and all-inclusive national strength of the country are very important factors in protecting and maintaining our national values. A rational society and national integration[15] are the basic conditions of survival (*see Figure* 1.1). Thus, national security comprises every action through which a society looks for the assurance of its survival and realises its objective internationally.

However, last two decades have witnessed an alarming and disastrous situation in the relationship among the people, communities and countries. In reality, most of the nation-states have been dealing with serious internal problems, which have been reflected in their external behaviour and position. The connection between internal and external setting of a nation is a requisite part of national security in a system, which is dominated by nation states. The internal environment of a nation is essential for security and stability of a nation. However, most of the states in the third world in general, and India in particular, lack complete national unity and solidity. Therefore, it would not be wrong to state that particularly India and generally third world states are dividable and insecure in nature. Therefore, all issues related to national security from domestic and external dimensions are required to be reviewed due to an

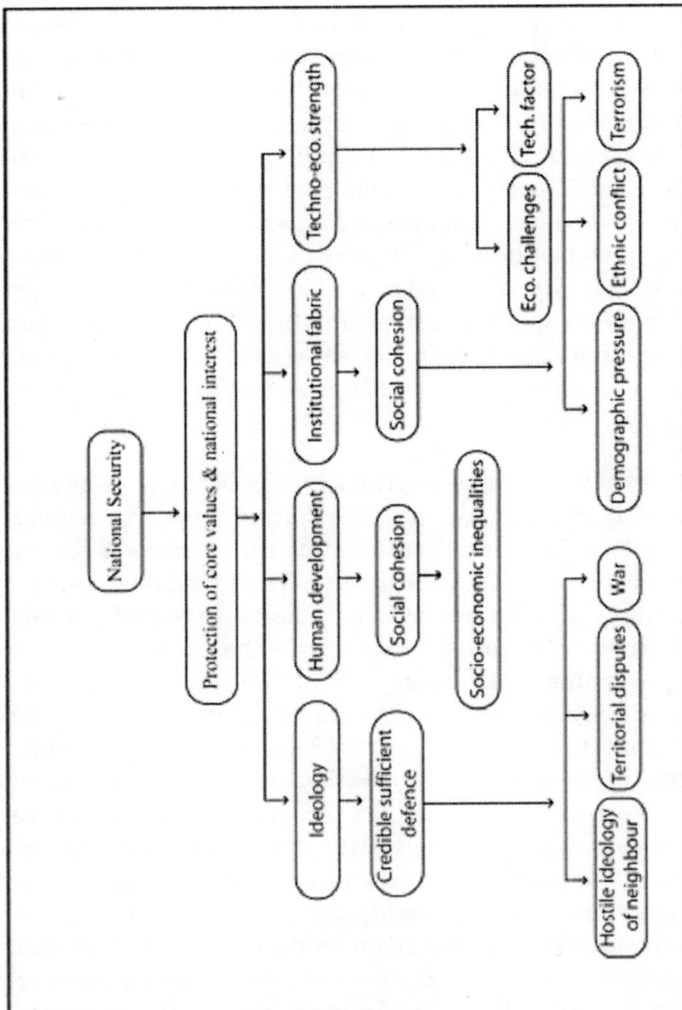

Figure 1.1 : Hypothetical Representation of National Security.

insubstantial nature of India's internal security and its impact on the power dynamics at regional levels.

Therefore, it is essential to state that the phrase 'national security' has to be used in a broad sense. At the national level, security is an integrated strategy, which means identifying and safeguarding crucial national interests. The real strength of national security lies with the overall strength or combination of various elements of national power. It also means that the leaders and policy-makers bear in their minds and co-ordinate all those elements in a proper direction in order to achieve national security. As stated by Indian scholar K. Subramanyam in his well-accepted definition of national security, "we should achieve the status of egalitarian society that can derive enough strength and moral to protect our sovereignty and territorial integrity".

Moreover, security is primarily the security of people in their daily life from the people's point of view.[16] A feeling of insecurity arises more from worries that relates to the daily life of people. This could be about job security, environmental security or security from crime.[17] Therefore, security needs to be oriented more towards the people than towards territory and government. In other words, the approach put more emphasis on ensuring security of the people in different aspects. The term 'human security' does not replace with the conventional concept of national security; rather, it increases the scope of the concept. It is more and more recognised that augmentation of human security maximises the range of national security. Human security and national security are mutually strengthening.[18] Thus, it is quite apparent that security is always considered as multidimensional, multilevel and multi-sectoral. Thus, it has expanded from the security of nations to security of groups and individuals. In other words, it has extended downwards from national level to individual level.[19] Emma Rothschild searches the current description of 'extended security' (of which human security is one element) in its theoretical background in European political thought. In this way, according to her, a newer approach to security has extended the concept of national security, which immediately preceded and coexists with it in four directions:

1. From the security of nations to the security of groups and individuals: It has extended downwards from nations to individuals.

2. From the security of nations to the security of international system, or of a super national physical environment: It has extended upwards, from the nation to the biosphere. The extension, in both cases, is in the sorts of entities whose security is to be ensured.

3. Extended horizontally, or to the sorts of security that are in question. Different entities such as individuals, nations, and systems cannot be expected to be secure or insecure in the same way. Therefore, the concept of security is extended from military to political economic, social environmental, or human security.

4. It is spread in all directions from nation states, including upwards to international institutions, downwards to regional or local government, and sideways to nongovernmental organisations, to public opinion and press, and to the abstract force of nature or of the market.[20] Thus, Political responsibility for ensuring security or for invigilating all these, 'concept of security' is extended in all directions.

In the light of the above interpretations about the changing concept of national security, generally, the problems of national security in India may be divided into two broad categories; secessionist and non-secessionist. The first type includes act of violence that come up from demands in proportion for territorial secession from India. The second type includes violence that steams from internal political issues but has no plan of separatist objective; both are considered as a threat to the integrity of the Indian union. At one hand, secessionist movement suggests the segmentation of India and at the other non-secessionist violence suggests danger of internal political, economic and social disintegration. Both acts are extremely dangerous to the government as it that would create a danger for national integrity and make the normal conduct of government difficult. In fact, this been observed in Northeast region of India since independence. These secessionist and non-secessionist movements are known as insurgency movements of the region.

1.2 Significance of the Study

It is believed that the any issue which disturbs social harmony of any part of the country is considered as a threat to India's internal security and ultimately to the national security of the country. Moreover, the threat to the country's national security is a threat to the country's autonomy. Thus, any kind of threat to the country's national security would lead the path to lose the sovereignty of the country. The issues of Northeast region in general and Assam in particular are studied in this view. Thus, the present study is certainly significant due to the following reasons:

1. The study is based on the idea that since independence of India, Northeast region of India have suffered insurgency severely. In this view, an attempt has been made to understand nature and different dimensions of insurgency at different times. This has helped to explain the reasons behind the prolonged insurgency in the region in general and Assam in particular. The specific issues have been dealt with in the present study to find out whether insurgency has transformed over the years in the Northeast region in general and Assam in particular and review the changes that have been occurring in insurgency.

2. The study has dealt with various counter-insurgency policies implemented by central and state governments of India. It examines relevant questions whether insurgency problem has resolved or not after the implementation of these policies. This helped to find out the advantages and disadvantages of the policies, which were implemented to

control the insurgency. The study also suggests certain policies to curb insurgency in order to maintain peace for sustainable development of the region.

1.3 Objectives of the Study

The objectives of the present study are as follows:

1. To study the geographical, historical and socio-economic aspects of the people of Northeast region in the perspective of national security of the country.

2. To find the origin of insurgency movement in Assam and to examine the role of neighbouring countries in the internal security of the region and thereby to study the prevailing situation in Assam since 1985.

3. To study the various counter-insurgency measures taken by both central and state governments of India in Assam.

4. To study the impact of insurgency and counter-insurgency measures on the Northeast region and particularly on the state of Assam.

5. To suggest a feasible strategy by which insurgency may be curbed.

1.4 Literature Review:

Since the last six decades, attempts have been made to adequately describe and analyse the historical background, core reasons of the conflict and the role of state and central governments in dealing with conflict. While making such attempt, different persons from different areas have put their views through their writings on this core issue. Thus, extensive literature is available on the subject from the different viewpoints of the historians, the political scientists, academicians and commentators at different points of time. These, wide ranging literature are well articulated in publications, both in print form and now increasingly on the internet. Some of the important works done by the scholars on the various issues of Northeast Region are reviewed as follows:

The geography and history is one of the perspective to study the prevailing situation of Northeast Region in general and Assam in Particular. Joysankar Hazarika (1996), Swaran Barua (1997), Chandrika Singh (2004), N. N. Bhattacharyya (2005), argues that geography, history and politics have the correlation and all these factors determine present and future developments of the region. Similarly, Monirul Hussain (1993), Sanjib Baruah (1999), Sajal Nag (2002), J. R. Mukharjee (2005), discussed about the root causes of the turmoil by presenting the historical and political facts. They also challenge colonial, nationalistic and regional historiography and its marginalization of the region by analyzing how nationalistic discourse has filtered down to regional and ethnic communities and thereby ignited divisive tendencies. Baruah argues that in multiethnic politics, loose federations not only make better democracies, in the era of globalization they make more economic sense as well. Historical and geographical perspective is crucial to understand the root causes of the conflict Udayon Misra (1993), emphasis that movement for Swadhin Asom and independent Nagalim are the challenges to the sovereignty of the Indian union. Sanjoy Hazarika (1994) (2000), argues that inhabitants of the region are grappling with the changes that the modern age persistently brings. It is these changes and alienation that are at the root of the militancy, the insurgencies, the desperation and the growing violence. However, in V. K. Nayar's (2005) perspective the core of the problems rests on external influence and spread of arms and drugs aggravating the situation. Besides these, deteriorating political ethos, fermenting religious and ethnic divide and lack of responsive and effective governance worsened the situation.

Dipankar Sengupta and Sudhir Kumar Singh (2004), Jaideep Saikia (2004) criticizes the role of Bangladesh and Pakistan. They argue that these two states are currently busy in fermenting trouble in this region. Saikia also argues that even after sixty years of independence, integration with the rest of India has eluded the eight states of the Northeast region. He raises the questions; does the Indian government understand the complexity of the forces that impair the region? Is it aware of the Northeast's feeling of alienation from the rest of India? What are the shortfalls in security in this region laid waste by relentless violence? In its quest to zealously guard the nation's frontiers, has New Delhi unconscionably ignored concerns of development? As it is the question about the development of the region Baruah (2005) urges for a reorientation of India's policy towards the Northeast region and to link it to a new foreign policy initiatives towards South East Asia. He believes that the economic integration of Northeastern states with the ASEAN region could go long way in bringing about stability, peace and prosperity. C. Joshua Thomas (2006) calls for accelerating the engagement process with the government of the neighbouring countries viz. Bangladesh, Bhutan, China, Myanmar, and Nepal and opening of the borders for trade to develop people to people contact. However, Monirul Hussain (1993), Anindita Dasgupta (2003), Renaud Egreteau (2006) all of them have criticized about the Indian government policies to curb the conflict. Hussain argues that the Indian state was not interested in resolving the crucial issue raised by the Assam movement and thereby the situation aggravated. Anindita Dasgupta in her paper while criticizing government policies highlights that civilians in the region have made psychological arrangements to put up with reckless violence and threat of violence. Similarly Renaud Egreteau while stating, that, various insurgent outfits have transformed into criminalized outfits in order to sustain their movements, he argues that due to the draconian laws enforced by the security forces, the insurgents too have become radicalized and more ruthless. However, while assessing the roots of the conflict, government policies over the conflict the measures suggested by them are somewhere illusionary as some are seems practical and some academically correct but practically incorrect.

1.5 Methodology

In view of the objectives of the study, the researcher has followed a descriptive method where insurgency situation in Assam has been described systematically. Researcher has adopted historical and geographical approach to focus on the past events that led to the evolution of the present insurgent situation. The present study also discusses the approaches of the central and state governments towards the Northeast issue. The researcher has gone through various official government documents, as a secondary data source, regarding counter-insurgency policies of both Central Government of India and State Government of Assam. The secondary source contains various governmental policies for eliminating the insurgency from the state of Assam. The researcher adopted an unstructured approach in order to obtain different views, approaches and opinions of the scholars, academicians, activist, surrendered insurgent cadre, ex-police officers, and locals regarding various aspects of insurgency in the Northeast through informal discussions and interviews which took place during the field trip. The researcher has the information collected through these discussions to understand various issues involved in the problem of conflict. Through inductive approach, the researcher has discussed various aspects of insurgency problem in different dimensions.

For the present study, the researcher carried out an extensive literature survey on the subject. The researcher visited various libraries of institutes like OMEO Kumar Das Institute of Social Change and Development, Guwahati, University of Mumbai, Rambhau Mhalgi Prabhodhini, Mumbai, North Maharashtra University Jalgaon and Bhonsala Military College, Nashik for data collection and referred to various reference books, periodicals, theses, reports and e-journals. Bibliography has been prepared based on secondary sources of information. The secondary sources of information consisted various official documents of Government of India like annual reports of Ministry of Home Affairs, various annual reports of Ministry of Development of Northeast region, Statistical Profile of Scheduled Tribes in India 2010- Ministry of Tribal Affair, Planning Commission Task Force reports, 12th Finance Commission Report, various five-year plan documents, Economic Survey of Assam, Directorate of Economics and Statistics, seventh and fifteenth report of State and District Administration-

Second Administrative Reforms Commission-India, North East Resources Databank, Census Report of India and official website of Government of Assam. Various governmental reports provided detailed information to understand different aspects of various issues of the Northeast region. Secondary source of information also includes various books, both authored and edited, journals, web information, magazines and paper clippings on related subject. All this information gathered through secondary source has enabled the researcher to understand the existing concepts of national security, insurgency and counter- insurgency. The researcher has compiled and verified the information collected from current and contemporary material to ensure its authenticity wherever possible. Accordingly, the researcher has organised and assembled the data for analysis. The researcher has analysed the data from socio-economic, historical, sociological and geo-political points of view. This has helped the researcher to understand and find out different aspect of various issues involved in the insurgency problem of Northeast. The hypotheses stated below have been tested on the basis of the information collected and subsequent interpretation of data compiled. The present study has followed qualitative method along with descriptive, historical and analytical approaches.

1.6 Hypothesis

The hypotheses formulated for the study are as follows :

1. The continued reliance on the security forces for maintenance of law and order inside Assam and short-term peace settlement for narrow political gains has not produced the desired environment or results.

2. The neighbouring states of Northeast region of India have not ceased instigation of violence as a state policy against India.

1.7 Limitations of the Study

The major limitation of the study is access the information from military sources due to various security problems in the Northeast. Consequently, the researcher has followed an unstructured approach and has made extensive use of secondary source of information to collect the information. Moreover, even though internal security problems of Northeast region have been studied, the present study is limited particularly to insurgency and counter-insurgency in Assam and its impact on national security.

1.8 Scheme of Chapters

The present study has been organised into seven chapters, which includes introduction as first chapter and conclusion as the final chapter of the thesis.

Chapter One: Introduction

This chapter discusses the traditional concept of national security and emerging trends in the sphere of national security. While making this attempt, the present study has explained how the notion of state security has moved towards the concept of security of people. This chapter has followed an analytical approach. It also consists of significance of the study, objectives, hypotheses, methodology, reviews of literature, limitations of the study and a scheme of chapterisation.

Chapter Two: Profile of North East Region

In the second chapter, an attempt has been made to understand the Northeast Region of India. The chapter is divided into two sections. The first section contains a profile of Northeast region. This section discusses the present racial and geographical status of the region. The second section highlights the past political and socio-cultural development, which has shaped the present Northeast region. The descriptive and analytical approach has followed for this chapter.

Chapter Three: Insurgency: An overview

In this chapter, an attempt has been made to understand the various 'insurgency movements'[21] of the Northeast region of India. For this purpose, this chapter has been divided into two sections. The first section discusses various definitions of insurgency. Section two describes the origin of insurgency movement and discusses the growth of insurgency in the states of this region. While exploring the origin and growth of insurgency movement, an attempt has been made to highlight those events that have made a significant impact over the Northeast region. It also deals with the reasons behind the prolonged insurgency in the region. In this chapter, the historical and analytical approach has been followed.

Chapter Four: Insurgency in Assam Since 1985

In this chapter, the researcher has attempted to explore and analyse certain key factors, which are responsible for the disorder and prolonged violent outbreak in the state of Assam. For this purpose, the chapter has been divided into four sections. The first section gives a brief summary of the state of Assam. This section covers geographical, demographical, linguistic and ethnic aspects of the state. In section two, various factors responsible for the outbreak of insurgency movement in the state and its rising hierarchies have been explained. The falling situation after the Assam agreement has been discussed in the third section. This section also gives a brief profile of major insurgent groups operating in the state. The fourth section explains the role of neighbouring countries in encouraging insurgency in the state of Assam.

Chapter Five: Counter Insurgency in Assam Since 1985 (Government Policies and Response)

This chapter attempts to study various governmental policies, which are followed in dealing with insurgency movements in the state of Assam. The chapter has been divided into two sections to accomplish above-stated task. The first section highlights the basic concept and meaning of counter insurgency. The second section describes major counter insurgency operations, which were carried out against the insurgent outfits and various non-military actions taken by the state and central governments. The chapter has followed a descriptive approach.

Chapter Six: Impact

In this chapter, the attempt has been made to understand the impact of insurgency and counter-insurgency on the state of Assam, Northeast region and Indian Territory. It would be rather inconsistent to study the impact of insurgency movement and counter-insurgency operation separately because it consists of social, economic, political and military aspects. Therefore, the descriptive and analytical approach has been followed in this chapter while studying the impact of insurgency. For this purpose, the chapter has been divided into (1) Social Implication: (a) psychological aspect, (b) displacements, (c) implication with community; (2) Economic Implication; (3) Political Implication; (4) Military Implication; (5) Strategic Implication; (6) Implication of Environment.

Chapter Seven: Conclusion

The concluding chapter contains findings followed by recommendations, which might help to curb the violence from the region in general and state of Assam in particular.

References

1. Robert Jackson and George Sorensen, Introduction of International Relations (New York, 1999), p. 68.

2. Rajesh M Basurur, ed., South Asian Security in New Millennium: Views from South Asia (Colombo, 2001), p. 1.

3. The very existence of a nation state largely depends on its capacity to protect its national security.

4. Suresh R. "India's security Policy in the Post –Cold War Period" in Mohanan B. Pillai, ed., India's National Security: Concerns and Strateies, (New Delhi, 2013), p. 36.

5. Sanjay Kumar, India's National Security: Past, Present and Future, (New Delhi, 2013), p. xi

6. *Ibid.*, p. xiv.

7. Peter Hough, Understanding Global Security (London, 2004), p. 3.

8. John Baylis and Steve Smit, The Globalisation of World Politics (New York, 2001), p. 255.

9. Barry Buzan, People State and Fear (Sussex:Wheatshet Boos, 1983), p. 247.

10. *Ibid.*

11. *Ibid.* pp. 252-53.

12. Kumar, n. 5., p. xv.

13. *Ibid.*

14. The core values are divided from the vision and ideology that nation defines/chooses for itself. Geopolitics and other factors also define the vital interest of states; often these values and interest are in competition and conflict with those of another state as indeed is the case between India and Pakistan. For example, India set about establishing its nation state on the idea that every human being is equal. Hence, democracy, adult franchise, secularism, social justice etc. are the main components of the constitution. Pakistan, on the other hand, set about creating a state on the basis of religion and discrimination where women would have different rights and non-Muslims would be denied equal status. See, "Jasjit Singh, Vision for Peace in 2020" available online at http://planningcommission.gov.in/reports/genreo/bkpap2020/22_be2020.doc accessed on 26/10/09.

15. It is generally agreed that integration becomes true and successful when a humanist system or social order implies complete equality mutual coherence and reciprocity among all individuals and ethnic groups. But when the frame of order is based on the dominance of an exploitative class or race on another, it becomes an imposition.

16. See Human Development Report 1993 and 1994.

17. Shirish Kadwai, "Internal Security, the State and Civil Society: A Human Security Perspective", in Shrikant Paranjpe, ed., India's Internal Security: Issues and Perspectives (Delhi, 2009), p.101.

18. *Ibid.*, p. 97.

19. *Ibid.*, p. 97.

20. Alkire, Sabina, "A Conceptual Framework for Human Security - CRISE Working Paper 2, University of Oxford, 2003, available online at www.crise.ox.ac.uk/pubs/workingpaper2.pdf accessed on 26.10.09

21. Basically insurgency is threat to India's unity and integrity. The term insurgency however, clubbed with term movement because insurgency in India's North East Region is not recognised as belligerency.

2

A Profile of Northeast Region

There are eight states in the Northeast region of India.[1] These are Arunachal Pradesh, Assam, Manipur, Meghalaya, Mizoram, Nagaland, Tripura and Sikkim.[2] (*See map 2.1 on next page)* The idea of 'Northeast' came into existence from the history and geography of the region. It did not come from its location on the Indian map. The geography, history, racial composition and demography are the distinctive features of this region. Considering these features, an attempt has been made to understand the Northeast Region of India. The chapter is divided into two sections. The first section contains a profile of Northeast region. This section discusses about the present socio-economic, racial and geographical status of the Northeast region. The second section highlights the past political and socio-cultural development, which has shaped the present Northeast region. This Chapter has followed descriptive and analytical approach.

2.1 Landscape

Section I

2.1.1 Geography and Geo-strategic Significance

The Northeast region is located between 21.57° to 29.30° north latitude and 88° to 97.3° east longitude.[3] The eight states together cover a total geographical area of 2,62,185 sq.km.[4]

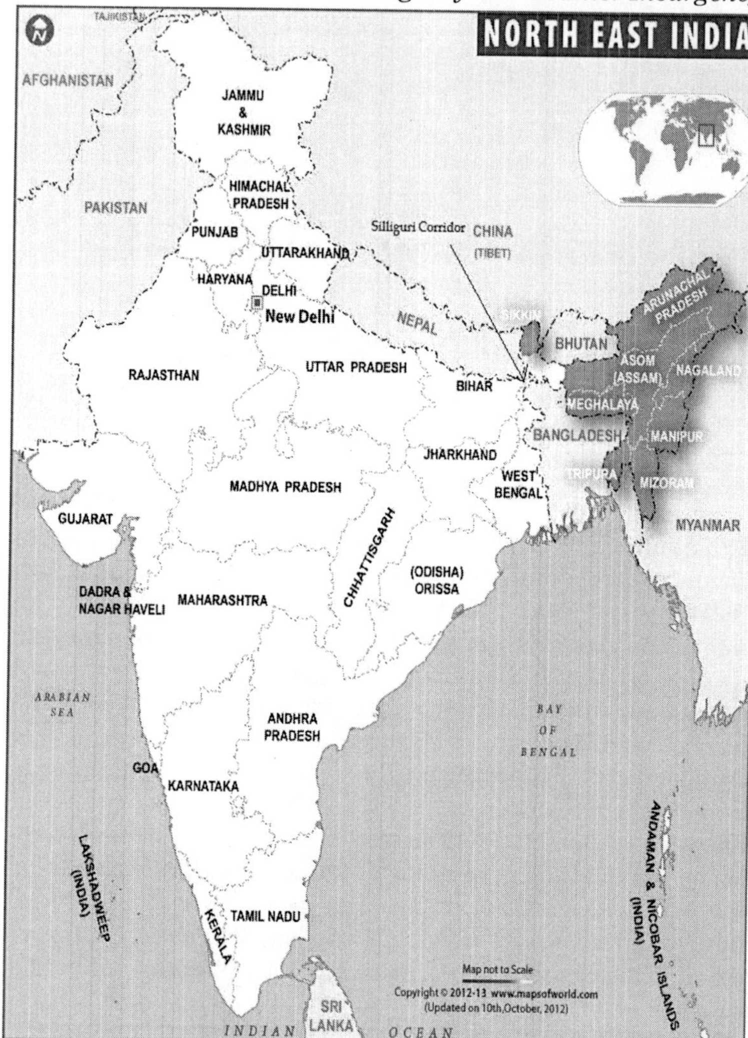

Source: Maps of India, available online at http://www.mapsofworld.com/map- download/save_map.php?id=http://www.mapsofworld.com/india/maps/north-east-india- map.jpg, accessed on 11.02.15

Map 2.1
showing location, States of Northeast Region and Siliguri corridor.

(*See map 2.1)* It occupies 7.9 per cent of the total land of the country.[5] The state of Sikkim is the smallest, which covers comparatively small area of 7,096 sq.km., whereas Arunachal Pradesh covers about 83,743 sq.km. The region connects to the main land of India by a narrow passage of foothill land in North Bengal, which is 33 km in width on the eastern side and 20 km on the western side. This passage, popularly known as Siliguri corridor or Chicken's neck, is occasionally disrupted due to heavy rains and floods.[6] (*See map 2.1)*

The Brahmaputra-Barak river and its branches cover the whole Northeast region. Assam valley (Brahmaputra), Purbanchal and Meghalaya Mikir (Bodo) regions are three different parts of Northeast region.[7] Assam valley covers an area of 58,274 sq.km., which is 720 km. long and 80 km. wide.[8] Eastern Himalayas, Patkai Naga Hills and Garo, Khasi and Mikir Hills split the valley. The valley consists of the districts of Assam that are important from an administrative point of view, such as, Lakhimpur, Sibsagar, Nowgong, Darrang, Dibrugrah, Kamrup and Goalpara.[9] Purvanchal region covers an area of 94, 800 sq.km. It consists of the states like Nagaland, Manipur, Tripura, Mizo Hills, Cachar Hills and Arunachal Pradesh. This region is surrounded by Bangladesh at south-west, Myanmar at southeast and by China at north-west.[10] Meghalaya Mikir, the third part of the Northeast region, spreads from Dhansiri at the east to Singmari to the west, which is 400 km. long and 40 km. wide. It covers an area of 35,291 sq.km. It comprises the state of Meghalaya and a portion of Karbi Anglong and North Cachar Hill districts of Assam.[11] From the physiographic point of view, Northeast region is divided into three major groups. The first group includes Northeastern frontier mountainous range; second is south-eastern hill ranges and the third part consists of Assam plateau, Assam valley and Cachar plains.[12]

The Northeast region is rich in natural resources, such as tropical forest,[13] potentials of Brahmaputra and its tributaries, tea, coal, timber, silk and jute.[14] The region has a capacity of producing 63,257 MW hydro power. It contributes 42.54 per cent of the total hydro power of the country.[15] Arunachal Pradesh alone contributes 34 per cent of the total hydro power of the country. It has a potential of producing 50,328 MW hydro power.[16] There are large and medium rivers in this region, which constitute 37 per cent of river water of the country. It also has huge deposits of limestone and dolomite and a few other minerals.[17] Besides this, the region produces 50 per cent of tea production and 20 per cent of oil production of the country.[18] Moreover, the region has more than one-third of the country's total biodiversity.[19] The region is also rich in terms of genetic and ecosystem diversity.[20] Varieties of medicinal plants with high international value are found in this region.

The region shares 98 per cent of its total borders with international borders. It shares merely two per cent of its borders with India.[21] The Northeast region has a connectivity of its borders with the countries like Bangladesh, Bhutan, China, and Myanmar along with Nepal, which is located near the Siliguri corridor (*See Map 2.2*). Thus, the region is considered as the epic center of South Asia with strategic hold by these nations. The region is also considered as the beginning of Southeast Asia. The Southeast Asia consists of ten independent countries, viz. Myanmar, Vietnam, Laos, Thailand, Cambodia, Brunei, Malaysia, Indonesia, Philippines, and Singapore.[22] (*See Map 2.3*). Along with Shillong and Guwahati as the central cities, the key cities like Kolkata, Lhasa, Kunming, Mandalay, Chittagong and the border areas of Vietnam, Laos and Thailand are included in a geographical circle of around 1000 km. (*see Sketch 2.1*) Thus, considering traditional market across the border, which determines the development interest of the region, its strategic significance for India has increased.[23] The nearness to international borders has become a cause for concern, especially in the light of the wars that India had with China and Pakistan since 1962. Moreover, racial groups of this region have a similarity with their counterparts in neighbouring countries. Therefore, considering geostrategic location of Northeast region of India, particularly in terms of India's

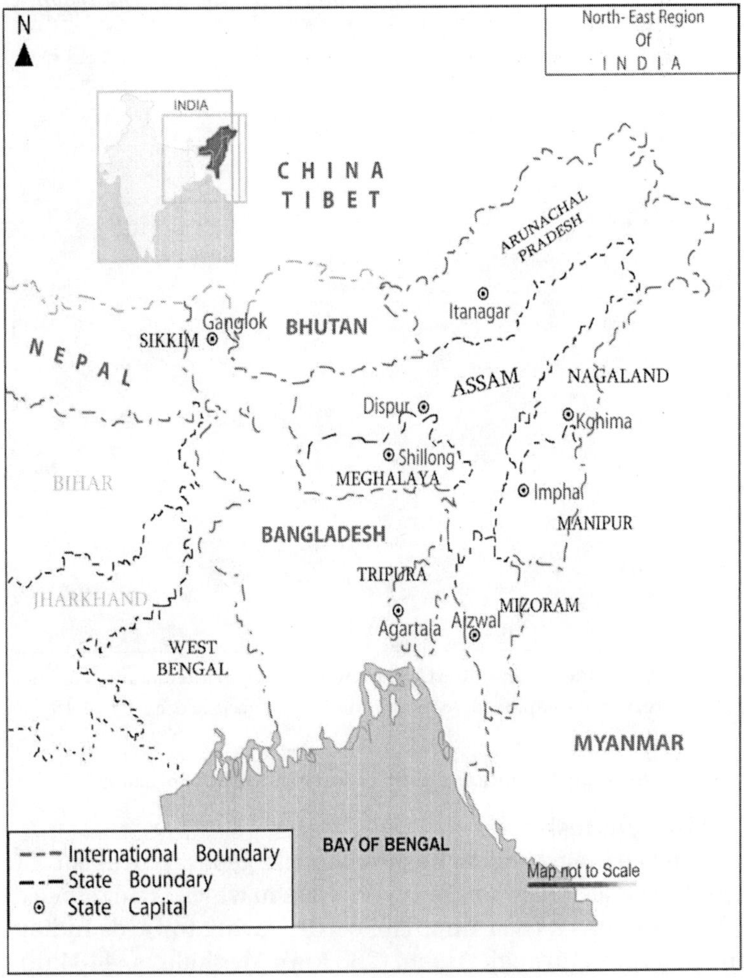

Socurce: Maps of India available online at http://themotorcycletrail. files. wordpress. com/2011/08/maps-of-india-north-east.jpg accessed on 05.07.12

Map 2.2
Showing eight states of the Northeast region and its international borders

national security, it is relevant to have a glance on the international borders which the Northeast region shares with the neighbouring countries.

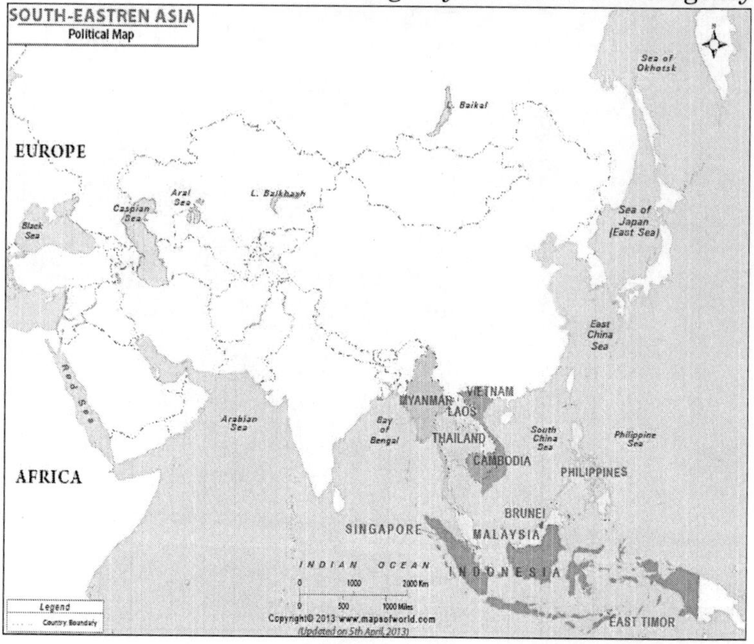

Source: Available online at http://www.mapsofworld.com/asia/regions/south-eastern-asia-map.html Available online at accessed on 02.01.15

Map 2.3

Showing 10 independent countries of South Asia

2.1.2 Bangladesh

The Northeast region has the longest geographical border with Bangladesh. The border covers plateau which is surrounded by hills and has a river line. The border facing towards Indian continent goes through Assam (263 km), Meghalaya (443 km), Mizoram (318 km), Tripura (856 km), and West Bengal (2216.7 km). The density of population is very high, therefore, the cultivation is carried out up to the last inch of the border.[24] People living on both sides of this entire border belt have similar racial identity and they possess similar cultural characteristics. They also reveal same physical characteristics.

The river line border, mostly in Dhubri district of Assam and southern West Bengal, presents peculiar problems.

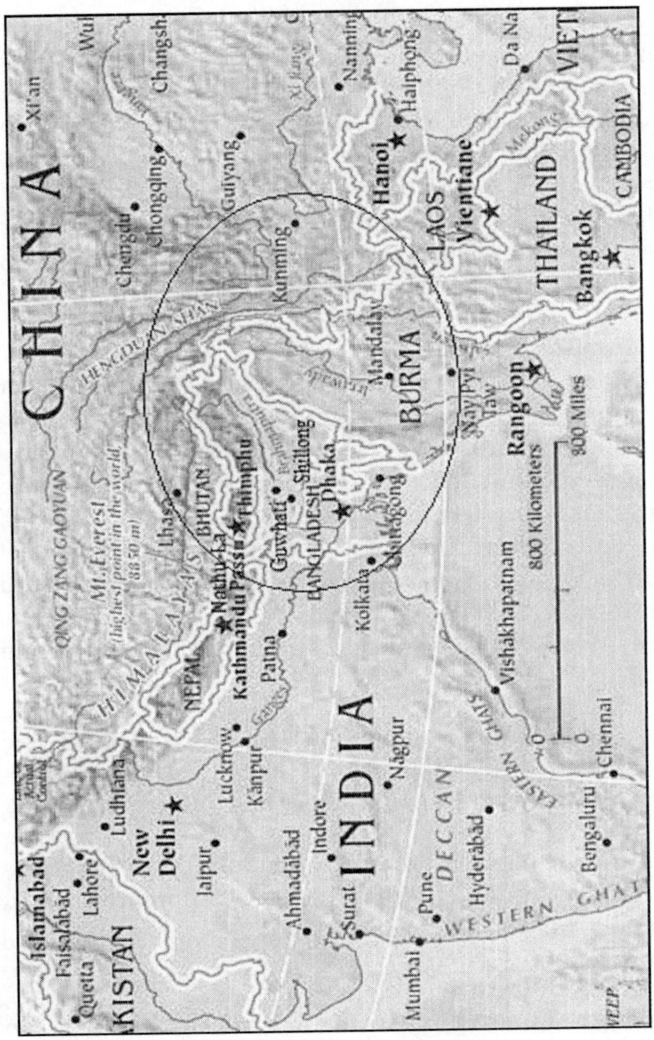

Sketch 2.1

Showing important cities covers in 1000 km. of geographical circle.

It is difficult to locate Permanent Border Outposts (BPOs) in the area due to the heavy floods of Brahmaputra and other rivers. Thus, in rainy season the populated areas suffer badly, which makes the patrolling in such areas difficult.[25]

It is obvious that if the Siliguri corridor would be blocked in the future due to unavoidable circumstances; India would lose its connectivity with the Northeast region. In such condition, connectivity can be established with the Northeast region only through the territory of Bangladesh. The significance of this alternative way was realised during the 1962 Sino-Indian war, when China threatened to cut off India's line of communication in the Seven Sisters, particularly in North East Frontier Agency (NEFA), which is now called as Arunachal Pradesh.

2.1.3 Myanmar[26]

India has a long geographical border and maritime border with Myanmar in the Bay of Bengal.[27] It shares 1643 km long land border[28] in the Northeast region. The states of the Northeast region that share their borders from north to south are Arunachal Pradesh (520 km), Manipur (398 km), Mizoram (510 km), and Nagaland (215 km).[29] Similarly, the borders of Kachin State, Sagaing division, and Chin State of Myanmar touch their borders in Northeast region.[30] From geo-strategic viewpoint, Myanmar is significant for India for the following reasons :

1. Myanmar shares its border with China and Bangladesh;
2. China's growing strategic influence over Myanmar;[31]
3. China's investigation and electronic intelligence systems on the Coco Island, located just 18 kilometers from Andaman and Nicobar Islands of India.[32]

2.1.4 China and Bhutan

The length of Indo-China border is 3,488 km. It has spread from Kashmir at the north-west along the Himalayan ranges upto tri-junction of India, Myanmar and China. This border is categorised into western, central and eastern sector.[33] At the eastern sector, the states of Arunachal Pradesh and Sikkim share a border of 1325 km.[34] In Arunachal Pradesh, it is 1073 km. long. It has spread from the Bhutan-India-China tri-junction at the west to the India-China-Myanmar tri-junction at the east.[35] China does not acknowledge the McMahon Line as an international boundary and claims that the Arunachal Pradesh is its own territory. China want the watershed to be suitably modified. Thus, Tawang, Longu, Kangri Karpo Pass and Walong could be recognised as the part of the international boundary. For India, McMahon Line is an international boundary as negotiated in Shimla conference of 1913-14.[36] Thus, the Indo-China border has still remained disputed. The border is un-demarcated and has inhospitable land. This makes it extremely difficult to guard the borders. Consequently, it has led to numerous incidences of violations of the line. For instance, the difference of boundary perception has led to many clashes between India and China. It has also resulted into a war in 1962. This had serious consequences for Bhutan as it shares 699 km border with Northeast region of India.[37] This international border ranges from east to west i.e. from Sikkim, Assam and Arunachal Pradesh to West Bengal. This border is open for Indians and Bhutanese up to certain kilometers of both the nations' territory.[38] There are three following reasons for Bhutan's geo-strategic significance from Indian point of view :

(1) A long-standing political disputes and border conflict with China;

(2) China's continuous engagement in construction of military logistic infrastructure within India-China border areas.[39] For example, China has substantially constructed the military logistics infrastructure in Tibet by actively building new roads, supply lines and airfields very close to the Line of Actual Control[40] (LAC) in Arunachal Pradesh;

(3) China's claim on the western sector of Bhutan near Chumbi valley to widen its military base. India concerns it most because it is merely 500 km away from Siliguri corridor,

which is the only access point to reach India's Northeast region.[41]

2.2 Economy and Development of the Northeast Region

Central Government of India has established North East Council (NEC) in 1971 and Ministry of Development of North Eastern Region (DoNER) in 2001 to accomplish sustainable development and to boost up economy of the region. Moreover, the states of Northeast have special category status, which is protected under a policy of positive discrimination, as many of these states are not economically developed.[42] In spite of these provisions made for the Northeast states, these states are suffering from low per capita income, low capital formation, inadequate exploitation of natural resources, low progress in industrial sector, lack of private and foreign direct investment and high unemployment rate among the relatively high literate people.[43] Agriculture is still the primary sector of Northeast economy. Farmers of the hilly and plain areas still carry out an age-old farm practices, such as, slash and burn (jhum), shifting cultivation and single crop farming, which results in low level of agricultural production.[44] Besides this, mining in Meghalaya and Arunachal Pradesh and forestry and logging industries in Nagaland stand significant.[45] Industries in the Northeast region are mostly engaged in manufacturing of food and wood-based products. There some metallic industries, mining sectors and primary tea, oil, gas industries in the region. Coal and limestone mining is prevalent in Meghalaya. Most of the leading industries such as tea, petrochemicals, paper, cement, jute, and spinning mills are located in Assam. Other large and medium scale industries located in the region include sugar, fertilizers, plywood, and veneer products. Handicrafts play an important role in the small-scale sector.[46] Moreover, the service sector in the Northeast region is being flourished well due to sound application of public administration. As a result, most of the budget provisions are made for the salaries and establishment expenses.[47]

2.3 Infrastructure

According to the 12th Finance Commission Report 2005-10, which quotes the latest UNDP report, says that Northeast region in terms of infrastructure index have been ranked lowest in the country.[48] For instance, the railway network is confined to Assam with 2436.34 km. The states like Sikkim and Meghalaya have not been connected through rail route and the states which have been connected by narrow gauge line at the edge of the states are Mizoram, Manipur, Tripura and Arunachal Pradesh. Even though the state of Nagaland is connected by broad gauge rail line at the edge of the state of Dimapur town, it is not easy for the majority of the people of the state to reach Dimapur.[49] Besides, there is a lack of well-developed network of national highways in the region. The number of banks and its branches is insufficient, which is not in the proportion of population living in the region and the area of the region.[50] The Northeast states have small capital cities and a few regional district hubs, which confine its growth. In case of agricultural development, there is an absence of small market towns, where farmers can deliver and sell their produce easily at competitive price.[51] Thus, the above fact indicates that the pace of development of commercial, industrial, agricultural and financial activities in the states of Northeast region is slow as compared to other states of Indian union.

2.4 Population of Northeast Region

According to 2011 census, the Northeast region has a total population of 4.54 crore. The population ratio varies among its eight states. The state of Sikkim has the lowest population of 6.10 lakhs whereas Assam's population is 3.12 crore. The density of population in Arunachal Pradesh is 17 in Arunachal Pradesh whereas it is 398 in Assam. (*see Annexure I*). Since last two decades except the state of Nagaland, other states of this region have shown declining growth rate of population. However, according to 2011 census, the growth rate of the state of Nagaland has declined remarkably. Population growth from 1951-1961 to 2001-2011 has been shown in *Annexure II*.

2.5 Racial Diversity

The Northeast region is racially and linguistically characterised as a diverse region. Each state of this region has its own culture and tradition. It is the homeland of more than 200 ethnic groups.[52] Among these, the Constitution of India has recognised 138 tribal groups as Scheduled Tribes.[53] According to 2001 census, only about one-fourth of the population of the region is tribal.[54] Moreover, according to it, the proportion of scheduled tribes in India is 8.2 per cent of the total population of the country whereas it is 26.93 per cent in Northeast region. The proportion of tribal population varies significantly from state to state. The percentage of scheduled caste population is relatively low as compared to the scheduled tribes in the region.

The racial groups belong to different tribes. They speak different languages and have varied socio-cultural traditions. They have their close cultural ties across the international border such as the ethnic groups inhabiting in the western parts of China, Southwest Tibet, Myanmar and also Southeast Asia.[55] For example, the Meiteis of Manipur valley and the Ahoms of Brahmaputra valley have close cultural and ethnic linkages with the Shans of upper Myanmar and the Thais of Thailand. The Nagas of Manipur and Nagaland have their relations across the border in Myanmar and the Chin Hills in Myanmar. Their origin can be traced from Central China. The Khasis and Jaintias of Meghalaya have similarities in language and culture with Mon-Khmers of Cambodia, Thailand and eastern Myanmar. The population of Northeast region is a mix of tribal and non-tribals. They can be broadly divided into three distinct groups of people; the hill tribes, the plain tribes and the non-tribal population of the plains. The languages spoken in this region are mainly English, Hindi, Assamese, Khasi, Garo, Jaintia, Manipuri, Mizo, Nagamese, Bengali, Nepali, Bhutia (Sikkimese), Bhutia (Tibetan), Lepcha, Limboo and local language.[56]

2.6 Religions in Northeast Region

Various religions such as Hinduism, Islam, Christianity and Buddhism are found in Northeast region. According to 2001 census, the major religion in the region is Hinduism. Its influence is over the Brahmaputra, Barak and Imphal valley and parts of Tripura plains,[57] which cover 35 out of 76 districts of the region. Christianity is the second largest religion in the region. It has been mainly dominant in 31 districts of the region, where people live in the hill areas like Naga, Mizo and Manipur hills. It is also found on Meghalaya plateau and among the tribal population living in Assam valley and hilly areas.[58] Islam is the third largest religion in the region which is mostly found in the six districts of the state of Assam. The influence of Buddhism is confined to two districts of Arunachal Pradesh, one district of Mizoram and one district of Sikkim. Other than these religions, the presence of Sikh and Jain religion is negligible. The population of these religions is very less in the region. Besides this, there is a large number of tribes found in Arunachal and Meghalayan plateau, who practice their own tribal religion.[59] The present racial and religious composition in the region is found due to socio-political developments that had taken place in the past. Some of these developments are discussed in the following section.

Section II

2.7 Migration

During the pre-colonial times, the population flow into Northeast region was mainly originated from the east. According to local mythology, a few thousand years B.C. onwards there were waves of Mongoloid migration. In these waves, a group of Bodo tribes was included. They occupied and established control over the entire area from Uttar Pradesh eastwards by pushing the Austrics and Dravidians into remote areas.[60] Austric people were the earlier inhabitants of the region. They used to speak languages of Mon Khmer groups. The Austrics are the forefathers of today's Khasis and Jaintias of Meghalaya. The group of Bodo tribes had gained control over a large part of the region. In the early thirteenth century, another Mongoloid tribe called the Ahom,[61] which had migrated earlier to Myanmar, invaded Upper Assam.[62] They progressively gained control over upper Assam and came into conflict with the Bodo Kacharis and other princes who had established their kingdom in Central Assam. Consequently, the kings of Kamrupa, presently known as Kamrup, were forced out to Cooch Behar. Ahom established a strong kingdom and ruled over the region for 600 years.[63] They formed their capital at Sibsagar. When the Ahoms were establishing themselves in upper Assam, Kamrupa was driven away by the Muslims who had gained control over Bengal. However, some Muslims settled in lower parts of Assam. Thereafter, some of the Bodo sub-groups in lower Assam established the kingdom of Kamatpur. The kingdom had covered North Bengal, Southern Bhutan, Southern Arunachal and spread all along over the north bank of the river Brahmaputra. Thus, it is evident that the Northeast region was controlled by different rulers due to the frequent migrations of different powers that took place over the time.

After British conquest[64] over the region, the direction of the population flow changed. British encouraged a large scale migration from different parts of British India and Nepal into the Northeast region in order to open up Assam's economy. They brought tribals mainly from Bihar, Orissa, Chottanagpur, Madhya Pradesh and Andhra Pradesh to meet the labour demands in tea gardens, as the local supply of labour was inadequate. The Bengali Muslim peasants from East Bengal migrated to the vast fertile lands in Assam. The Hindu Bengalis migrated in the service sector and Marwari migrated in trade, business and industry. Thus, these four fields where migration was large in number have had long-run impact on the process of nationality formation in Assam. It had intensified the competition for obtaining resources.[65] Further, the successive rulers of Tripura encouraged to migrate the Bengali farmers from neighbouring East Bengal in order to meet the ever increasing tributary demand from British power as well as royal expenses.[66] This migration took place because the indigenous tribes were unable to produce huge surplus. Thus, plain lands had been allotted to the Bengali peasants in order to increase the land revenue. Consequently, native tribes were outnumbered by the immigrants well before the state joined the Indian Union in 1949. The impact of this state-sponsored migration affected native tribal groups in two ways. First, it affected the indigenous tribal groups economically because of the encroachment of their land. Second, it endangered their socio-political existence.[67] Kukis was one of the late migrants into the Northeast region. Their migration and subsequent settlement into the region had also been part of colonial policy.[68]

On the eve of independence of India, partition of the country resulted in quick and large scale migration from East Pakistan (Bangladesh). Moreover, during succeeding decades after independence, population inflow from Indian mainland as well as from Bangladesh changed the demography of the region. This had impacted all the spheres of Northeast Region.

2.8 Partition of the Country

The partition of the country had a huge impact over the Northeast Region. All the means of transportation and communication channels passed through today's Bangladesh during the pre-partition days. However, the partition cut off the river and land access of the region through Bangladesh. Consequently, the region became almost landlocked and the traditional transportation routes like rail, road and river, linking Chittagaon and Kolkata ports, suddenly became unavailable. This condition increased the geographical distance to the mainland of India and also increased the cost of transport. For example, during pre-partition days, ships carrying tea, coal and timber used to reach from Kolkata to Dibrugarh within eight days, whereas at present, a ship from Kolkata to Guwahati takes more than 25 days. It is mainly due to lack of navigation at night and customs formalities at various points.[69] According to another example, at present the distance between Agartala and Kolkata port is 1700 km, however, it was just 375 km during pre-partition days through East Bengal (today's Bangladesh).[70] This has indeed increased the transportation cost. To elaborate further, a truck carrying load of nine tons from Guwahati to Kolkata, covering distance of 1100 kms today costs around Rs 20,000; while a truck going from Chennai to Kolkata covering distance of 1600 kms costs only Rs 16,000.[71]

Partition isolated the Northeast region from the rest of India and cut off the access to traditional markets, specifically the gateway to the East and Southeast Asia.[72] Hence, it not only pulled the region backward by at least a quarter of a century but it also placed barriers on future economic growth.[73] Moreover, the partition and subsequent demarcation of state boundaries put restrictions on free movement of people in the Northeast region in post-independence India.

2.9 Administrative Policies

2.9.1 Colonial Policies

During British rule, they began to form an administration with certain policies in the Northeast region. These policies aimed towards the expansion of the area under control and its administrative rearrangements. For example, before 1874 Assam was governed as a part of Bengal Province. After becoming independent Assam Province it was governed by a Chief Commissioner, who was subordinate to the Lieutenant Governor of Bengal Province. In the year 1905, East Bengal came into existence by merging Assam Province with Bengal Province. However, in 1921 due to strong protest against this amalgamation, Assam province was taken out from East Bengal. Later on, it was directly administered by the Governor-General of Assam Province.

British administered the Northeast region separately and distinctly from other parts of British India throughout their colonial rule. Hence, the administrative system developed for this region was quite different from that in the rest of the country. While administering the region British handed over most of the administration to the local tribal chiefs. Following are some key policies that were followed by the British during their administration over the Northeast region.

1. The "Regulation for the Peace and Good Government of Certain Districts on the Eastern Frontier", 1873 or East Bengal Frontier Regulation, 1873 or Inner Line Regulation, 1873.

2. The Scheduled District Act, 1874.

3. Frontier Tracts Regulation II, 1880;

4. Government of India Act, 1919 and 1935.[74]

British administration in the Northeast region initially made the provision to expand their tea plantation programme on a massive scale. This expansion for tea gardens was achieved through encroachment of tribal land.[75] As a result, the tribals repeatedly raided the tea plantations and constantly created problems to British. British brought Kuki-Chin tribals in large numbers from Chin Hill of Burma to prevent damages to tea plantations caused by the tribals in the region and settled them as a safeguard between the North Cachar Hills and Manipur.

In addition, under the 'East Bengal Frontier Regulation, 1873', British drew an administrative boundary through the declaration of Inner Line Regulation. Due to this boundary, the area under British control was clearly demarcated and divided hills and plains of the region. Consequently, jurisdiction of the plain district ended, along with the foothills of the northern, eastern and south-eastern borders of the Brahmaputra, Surma and Karnaphuli valleys. This regulation prohibited the outsiders to cross this line. As a result, the tribes became free to manage their own affairs beyond such line with an expectation of good conduct.[76] The regulation also made some rules to control the trade and land acquisition beyond inner line.[77] The regulation was followed by 'The Scheduled District Act, 1874'. It was for the purpose to regulate the administration of the tribal areas. Special provision in this act was made for the underdeveloped areas. A large number of districts were declared as 'Scheduled Districts'.[78] The purpose of this notification was to place the plains of Assam in the same legal position like other parts of India.[79] However, in the year 1880, a separate regulation, which is known as the 'Frontier Tracts Regulation II, 1880', was passed for the hilly districts of Assam. The regulation made general laws of the country inapplicable in the hilly areas such as codes of civil and criminal procedures.[80] The provision was followed in the Government of India (GoI) Act, 1919. According to the act, hilly areas were declared as 'Backward' areas and were excluded politically from the scope of the new provincial legislature and the High Court.[81] Later, the term 'Backward' was replaced in the Government of India (GoI) Act, 1935. In this act different hilly areas were declared as excluded and partially excluded areas. The excluded areas covered the North East Frontier, Sadia, Balipura and Lakhimpur, the Naga Hills and Lushai Hills District. The partially excluded areas covered the areas of North Cachar Hills, the Garo Hills, the Karbi Hills, the British portion of the Khasi and Jaintia Hills, other than Shillong Municipality and the cantonment.[82] The excluded areas were under the direct jurisdiction of the British through the executive control of the Governor of Assam. No act of the Federal legislature or of Assam legislature was applicable to these areas. Expenditure incurred in these hilly areas were also not made by the provincial legislature because there were no representatives from these hilly districts.[83] The partially excluded areas were under the control of the Governor of Assam. These districts had five representatives in the Assam Legislative Assembly. These areas were administered by the state government subject to the special powers of the Governor.[84] The core of this kind of governance was that the powers of the provincial legislature were not extended to the excluded and partially excluded areas. Thus, the act created a totally new political status for these areas by excluding them fully from the federal and provincial legislatures as well as the jurisdiction of the High Court.[85]

The British gave following reasons for formulating the policy of segregating the hill tribes from the plain people:

1. To protect the plateau from raids and plunder by the hill tribals;

2. To protect hill tribes from the exploitation by the people of plateau; and

3. To foster a liberal public policy aimed at cultural survival of the hill tribes.[86] However, these policies created a socio-cultural gap between hill tribals and plateau people of the region. As a result, politics from mainstream could not reach in the hill areas and put any influence in the hill areas. Thus, the developments in the hill areas were not significant. Meanwhile, British introduced Christianity in the hill areas of this region. British government helped Christian missionaries to establish political and social contact with hill people to carry out welfare activities. Consequently, considerable conversion to Christianity took place over a period of time.

2.9.2 Post Colonial Period

The first Prime Minister of India stated candidly that the people inhabiting in the region had 'little sensation' of belonging to India.[87] Thus, the Government of India prepared its agenda most carefully and sensitively for this region. The first one and half decade of India's policy towards the Northeast Region was described as "Nehru-Elwin policy". The policy intended for quick administrative expansion associated with the revivalist-protectionist approach towards tribal development. The then government acknowledged the privilege of tribals to retain their way of life and identity. The tribals were brought into the federal frame of the Constitution of India through democratic way. Thus, the Indian government followed the British policy of Inner Line Regulation, which ensured non-interference from the people of the plains. Moreover, special provision was made in the Indian Constitution in the form of 'Sixth Schedule' for the administration of tribal areas. Basically, the objective of the Indian Constitution was to protect the tribal people who were living scattered throughout the country. In this view, the Sixth Schedule was applied to the ethnic groups inhabiting in the hilly region of the Northeast. According to section 20 of the Sixth Schedule, the terms like 'excluded' and 'partially excluded' areas were replaced by 'Part A' and 'Part B' to classify tribal areas. Areas covered in 'Part A' were the United Khasi and Jaintia Hills District, the Garo Hills District, the Lushai Hills

District, the Naga Hills District, the North Cachar Hills District, and the Mikir Hills District. These areas were known as an autonomous districts. The people residing in these areas had limited representation in both state and central legislative assembly. It was governed by the Government of Assam. The areas placed in the 'Part B' were North East Frontier Tract, the Balipara Frontier Tract, the Tirap Frontier Tract, the Abor Hill and Mishmi Hills Districts and the Naga Tribal Area. These areas were administered by the acting Governor of Assam. He acted as an agent of the President of India. Special administrative regions, which were controlled by central government, were created for the former princely states of Tripura and Manipur. The change in policy towards Northeast Region was seen in the early 1960s. The defeat against Chinese aggression in 1962 changed the view of the leaders and Government of India. Since then the changes have been observed in the security and foreign policy of India. This brought back the colonial approach considering the region as a 'frontier' that needs to be protected and defended militarily.

After 1962, the administrative changes were made in the region. During 1962-72, various acts were enacted through which political boundary of Assam was reorganised and administrative changes took place. The Naga Hills were isolated from the Assam Province and upgraded to the status of a full-fledged state in 1963 as Nagaland. However, the formation of Naga Hills into an independent state of Nagaland became a model for other inhabitants of the hill area of the region. They began to demand for statehood or an independent state. Thus, due to the pressure from inhabitants of the hill regions, in 1972, the state of Meghalaya was formed by amalgamating the Khasi, Jaintia and Garo Hills of Assam Province. Manipur and Tripura were granted statehood. In 1987, Mizo Hills of Assam Province and North-Eastern Frontier Agency became Union Territories and were subsequently upgraded to full statehood as Mizoram and Arunachal Pradesh respectively. One of the important points to be noted that the reorganisation of this region was based on ethnic lines rather on language. However, inner line regulation was maintained by the then and successive Indian governments. This restriction was lifted in case of Assam, Manipur (valley), Meghalaya, and Tripura. Indeed, overriding effects of this policy were two-fold. First, the possibility of a process of integration of the communities and tribes within the region that could have been initiated by a common administration, was lost. Second, most of the tribal communities in the region remained isolated from the national flow. As a result, they were isolated from the social and political developments taking place in the main land of India.[88]

2.10 Sum Up

1. Northeast region is vital from geostrategic point of view for India's national security. The region has vast natural resources and huge economic potential. Inhabitants of the region have close ethnic and cultural affinity with their counterparts across the border. The region is encircled by neighbouring countries who share their borders with Northeast region. It is only connected to mainland of India through a narrow corridor. These factors increase the geostrategic significance of Northeast region.

2. The Central and State governments should take initiative for the development of an economy of the region in different sectors, such as, industrial, agricultural, financial, service sector etc. The public sector is the principal sector governed by the public administration, which manages a huge amount of resources found in the Northeast region. Despite rich in natural resources, the region has not been benefitted by converting this resource-wealth into the fruitful development benefits. This is due to the lack of infrastructural development in the region which has kept the region at economic disadvantage.

3. The present ethnic, cultural and linguistic composition of Northeast region is due to the waves of migration that took place in the early and present times in the region. It witnessed to a constant flow of tribes and nationalities belonging to the Tibeto-Burman or the Mon-Khmer in the

region. Moreover, migrations of people in present time and from various directions into the region have significantly contributed towards the growth of racial diversities.

4. British captured the region gradually and controlled over the region by indirect administration. They kept tribal areas distant from their direct administration and let the tribal people to manage their own affairs. Thus, the tribal areas were handled by the inhabitants of the area, who were aware of the tribal needs. At the time of independence, partition of the country disturbed the geopolitical order. It made the region virtually landlocked by disturbing traditional flow of trade from East Bengal (now Bangladesh) and Burma (now Myanmar). It also cut off the communities from their Kings men.

5. Since the independence many political and administrative changes have taken place in the Northeast region.

References

1. Annual Report, Ministry of Home Affairs (Government of India, 2010-11), p. 13.
2. Sikkim becomes the member of North East Council on December 2002 after an amendment of the NEC Act 1971. China recognised Sikkim as an Indian territory in 2004.
3. NEDFi Databank, available online at http://databank.nedfi.com/content/general-information, accessed on 09.06.11
4. *Ibid.*
5. *Ibid.*
6. Joysankar Hazarika, Geo-politics of Northeast India: A Strategic Study (New Delhi, 1996), p. 1.
7. Chandrika Singh, North East India: Politics and Insurgency, (New Delhi, 2004), p.14.
8. V. K. Nayar, Crossing the Frontiers of Conflict in The North East and Jammu and Kashmir:From Real Politik to Ideal Politik, (Delhi, 2005), p. 3.
9. Singh, n.7, p. 14.
10. *Ibid.*

11. Nayar, n. 8, p. 4.
12. Singh, n. 7, p. 15.
13. 54 per cent of the total geographical area is covered by forest. Their proportion varies from state to state in the region. The state of Mizoram covers the highest percentage of forest which is 75.59 per cent whereas it is low in the state of Assam which is 39.15 per cent. Other than Mizoram and Assam the states like Arunachal Pradesh, Manipur, Tripura, Nagaland, and Meghalaya are covered by 61.55, 67.87, 60, 52.02 and 42.34 percentage of forest of the total geographical area of the region respectively. In the hilly regions, the ownership rests with the local communities and, therefore, proportion of reserved forests in those hill states is quite small. North East Resources Databank (NEDFi Databank) available online at http://databank.nedfi.com/content/forest-2, accessed on 05.07.12.
14. Sreeradha Datta, "Northeast Turmoil: Vital Determinants", Strategic Analysis (New Delhi), Vol. XXIII, No. 12, March 2000, p. 2129.
15. Eleventh Five Year Plan, (Planning Commission of India, Government of India, 2008), p. 156.
16. *Ibid.*
17. M. Biswnath Sinha, "Report on Northeast India: The Development Paradigm", available online at http://www.dorabjitatatrust.org/norheast/pdf/ReportNE.pdf p. 5, accessed on 01.07.11.
18. J. R. Mukharjee, An Insider's Experience of Insurgency in India's North – East, (London, 2005), p. 4.
19. Sinha, n. 17, p. 4, Sinha states in his report that the region is one of the 18th hot spots among the other countries in the world. He further figures that the region has 7500 flowering plants, 700 orchids, 58 bamboos, 64 citrus, 28 conifers, 500 mosses, 700 ferns and 728 lichen species.
20 . *Ibid.*
21. Gurudas Das, "Security, Engagement and Development: Development Interest of India's Northeast and the Art of Conduct of India's Relation with the Neighbouring Countries", in C. Joshua Thomas, ed., Engagement and Development: India's Northeast and Neighbouring Countries (New Delhi, 2006), p. 5.
22. Wasbir Hussain, India's Northeast: The Super Highways to Southeast Asia? IPCS Issue Brief, No. 104, June 2009, p. 1.

23. Das n.21, p. 4.
24. Annual Report, Ministry of Home Affairs, (Government of India, 2007-08), p. 29.
25. Anil Kamoj, "Border Management: Bangladesh, Nepal, Bhutan", World Focus (New Delhi), Vol. 27, No. 8, (August 2006), p. 24.
26. Geographical location of Myanmar is very important for India. Because Myanmar is at the tri junction of East Asia, Southeast Asia and South Asia between 10 and 28 degrees North latitude is of critical significance. Myanmar has special place amongst all Southeast Asian nations as it is the land bridge between India and ASEAN.
27. India – Myanmar Relations, available at http://mea.gov.in/Portal/ForeignRelation/myanmar-july- 2012.pdf, accessed on 18.10.12 India's Andaman and Nicobar Islands, some 1,200 kilometers (750 mi) southeast of the mainland, share maritime borders with Myanmar, available online at http://en.wikipedia.org/wiki/Geography_of_India, accessed on 1.2.15
28. Annual Report, Ministry of Home Affairs, (Government of India, 2012-13), p. 34.
29. Management of Indo-Myanmar Border available online at http://mha.nic.in/hindi/sites/upload_files/ mhahindi/files/pdf/BM_MAN-IN-MYAN(E).pdf, accessed on 18.10.12.
30. Udai Bhanu Singh, "Challenges to Border Management in India-Myanmar Relations", n. 25, pp. 31-32.
31. Jason Abbott, "Burma and India: the New Geopolitical Reality" available online at http://www.nl- aid.org/continent/south-asia/burma-and-india-the-new-geopolitical-reality/, accessed on 18.10.12.
32. *Ibid.*
33. Pushpita Das, "Management of India-China Border in Eastern Sector", n. 25, pp. 13-14.
34. Dilip Gogoi, "Northeast India – Gateway to Southeast Asia", South Asia Politics (New Delhi), Vol. 6, No. 7, (November 2007), p. 15.
35. Das, n. 21, pp. 13-14.
36. *Ibid.*
37. Annual Report, n.24, p. 28.
38. Annual Report, Ministry of Home Affairs, (Government of India 2005-06), p. 37.

39. Meeta Deka, "The Stillwell Road and The China Syndrome", in S. K. Agnihotri and B. Datta Ray, ed., Perspective of Security and Development in North East India, (New Delhi, 2005), p. 65.
40. Line of Actual Control is militarily held line which came into existence after 1962 war.
41. Virendra Sahai Verma, Dnaces with Dragons, available online at http://www.thehindu.com/opinion/op- ed/dances-with-dragons/ article3800096.ece, accessed on 18.10.12.
42. Saswati Choudhury, "Towards Sub-regional Cooperation: India's Northeast and Bangladesh", available online at http:// mpra. ub.uni-muenchen. de/34991/1/Sub_regional_ccooperation-NEI_and_Bangladesh.pdf accessed 27.07.12.
43. North East Resources Databank (NEDFi Databank) available online at http://databank.nedfi.com/content/ economy-northeast, accessed on 09.06.2011.
44. North East Resources Databank (NEDFi Databank) available online at http://databank.nedfi.com/content/north- east-india, accessed on 09.06.2011. The pattern of agricultural growth has however, remained uneven across regions and crops. The Northeast region continues to be a net importer of food grains even for its own consumption.
45. NEDFi Databank, n. 43.
46. Draft Final Report, "Northeastern States Trade and Investment Creation Initiative", prepared for the Asian Development Bank, Global Development Solutions, LLC™ (Reston, February 2006), p. 19.
47. Santosh Kumar Das and Ritika Tewari, "India – ASEAN Free Trade Agreement and Development of North East: Prospects and Challenges", Draft Paper for CDS – IIFT - RIS - UNCTAD National Seminar on India – ASEAN Free Trade Agreement & Way Forward 5 – 6th February, 2010 Centre for Development Studies, Trivandrum, India, p. 12.
48. Twelfth Finance Commission (2005-10), Government of India, Chapter 4, pp. 60-61.
49. Komol Singha, "Infrastructure and Regional Disparity: A Case of North Eastern Region of India", Journal of Social and Development Sciences, (October 2011) Vol. 2, No. 4, p. 173, Oct 2011.
50. Draft Final Report, n. 46.

51. *Ibid.*
52. Annual Report, n. 24, p.13.
53. Article 366 (25) of the Constitution of India refers to Scheduled Tribes as those communities, who are scheduled in accordance with Article 342 of the Constitution. This Article says that only those communities who have been declared as such by the President through an initial public notification or through a subsequent amending Act of Parliament will be considered to be Scheduled Tribes. See Statistical Profile of Scheduled Tribes in India, 2010, Ministry of Tribal Affairs, Government of India.
54. Gulshan Sachdeva, "Demystifying Northeast", Dialogue, (New Delhi), Vol. 7, No. 32, p. 75.
55. Concept paper for the Task Force for Recommending A Regional Plan for the Northeastern Region Including Sikkim, available online at http://necouncil.nic.in/writerddata/mainlinkfile/Concept% 20Paperfor%20the% Task%Force%20for%20 Recommending% 20A%20Regional %20Plan%2 0for%20the% 20NER%20 including % 20Sikkim.pdf p. 5 accessed on 01.06.2011
56. NEDFi Databank, n. 3.
57. B. S. Mipun and Debendra K. Nayak, "A Geographical Background of North-East India: A Study in the Dynamics of Identity and Inter-Group Relations", in Kilash Aggarwal, ed., Dynamics of Identity and Intergroup Relations in North-East India, (Shimla, 1999), p. 26.
58. *Ibid.*
59. *Ibid.*
60. Mukherjee, n. 18, p. 5.
61. The Ahom or Tai Ahom rulers of Assam, in ethnic terms, are an offshoot of the Tai people, of Southeast Asia; they are called Shan in Burma, Thai in Thailand, Lao in Laos, Dai and Zhuang in China, and Tay- Thai in Vietnam. The Assamese branch, the Thai Ahoms, came to Assam in the early 13th century, most likely from Mong Mao in China's Yunnan province. See J. N. Pukhan, "The Thai Ahom Power in Assam", in H. K. Barpujari, ed., The Comprehensive History of Assam, (Guwahati, 1992), Vol. 1, pp. 49-50.
62. Mukherjee, n.18, p.7.
63. Renaud Egreteau, "Instability at the Gate: India's Troubled Northeast and its External Implications", available online at http://egreteau.com/images/Documentriespercent20PDF/CSHpercent 200Ppercent20_percentnpercentBO 16.pdf accessed on 28.01.10.

64. Maomaria revolt of 1769 created a political vacuum in the region, which caused Burmese invasion through the Patkai, Lushai and Arakan Hills. The Burmese under the king Bodawapaya (1782-1819) made successive incursion into the area. The Burmese also invaded Manipur. During this invasion, the Burmese ravaged the region, mercilessly slaughtered the population, and also took into slavery very large number of people. Thus the kingdoms from this region, turned to the British for assistance. Hence, in connivance with the tribal's the British forces defeated the Burmese and forced them to withdraw. This resulted into Yandaboo pact - 1826 and accordingly the kingdom lost its independence and suffered annexation to the British. *Ibid*. Gradually they annexed the whole region in the subsequent years. After the end of 19th century as with the rest of India, the entire Northeast region was under British suzerainty.
65. Gurudas Das, "Migration, Ethnicity and Competition for State Resources: An Explanation of the Social Tension in the North-East India, in M. K. Raha and Alok Kumar Ghosh, ed., North-East India: The Human Interface, (New Delhi, 1998), pp. 308-09.
66. *Ibid.*, p. 310.
67. *Ibid.*
68. *Ibid.*
69. Choudhury, n. 42.
70. Jayanta Madhab, "Unbounding the Frontier: Enabling the North East", Dialogue (New Delhi), Vol. 7, No. 3, (n.d.), p. 64.
71. Choudhury, n. 42.
72. Hussain, n. 22, p. 1.
73. *Ibid.*
74. Ved Prakash, Encyclopedia of North East India (New Delhi, 2007), Vol. 1, p. 397.
75. *Ibid.*, p. 395.
76. Vijendra Singh Jafa, "Administrative Policies and Ethnic Disintegration Engineering Conflict in India's North East", available online at http://www.satp.org/satporgtp/publication/faultlines/volume2/Fault2-JafaF.htm accessed on 24.09.10.
77. Prakash, n. 74, p. 396.
78. *Ibid.* p. 397.
79. Hazarika, n. 6, p. 74.
80. Prakash, n. 74, p. 397.

81. Jafa, n. 76.
82. Niru Hazarika, Ethnic Autonomy Question in N.E. India: Search for an Answer, (Guwahati: Delhi, 2005), p. 4.
83. R. N. Prasad, "Sixth Schedule and Working of the District Councils in North-Eastern States", Dialogue (October-December, 2004), Volume 6, No. 2, available online at www.asthabharati.org/Dia_Oct04/ R.N.Pras.htm, accessed on 9.06.11.
84. *Ibid.*
85. Jafa, n. 76.
86. *Ibid.*
87. Harish K. Puri, "Fifty Years of India's Independence and the North-East", Mainstream, (New Delhi, 1998), Vol. XXXVI, No. 11, p. 14.
88. Archana Upadhyay, "Terrorism in the North-East: Linkages and Implications", Economic and Political Weekly (Mumbai), Vol. 41, No. 48, (2-8 December 2006), p. 4993.

3

Insurgency : An Overview

The states of the Northeast region have been widely acknowledged for their weak economy[1], underdevelopment, ethnicity, political immaturity and insurgency. The insurgency factor has come up as a threat to India's national security. In this chapter, an attempt has been made to understand the various 'insurgency movements'[2] of the Northeast region of India. For this purpose, this chapter has been divided into two sections. The first section discusses various definitions of insurgency. Section two describes the origin of insurgency movement and discusses the growth of insurgency in the states of this region. While exploring the origin and growth of insurgency movement, an attempt has been made to highlight those events that have made a significant impact over the Northeast region. It also deals with the reasons behind the prolonged revolt in the region. In this chapter, the historical and analytical approach has been followed.

Section I

3.1 Conceptual Outline of Insurgency

Over the years, various scholars and academicians have given various definitions and interpretations of the term 'insurgency'. For instance, David Kilcullen, who is the chief strategist at the office of the coordinator for counter-terrorism, U. S. Department of State, defines insurgency as “a struggle for control over a contested political space, between a state (or group of states or occupying powers), and one or more popularly based, non-state challengers”.[3] According to him, revolts are emerged in the state where society is divided on the grounds of customs, tribal, clan or community groups, social classes, urban and rural populations, and economic and political institutions. He further states that even though these factors are independent they are interlinked with each other. Thus, every group seeks to maximise their own survivability and advantage, which leads to the rebellion movements. His conception fits while considering Northeast region. The root causes of insurgency in the Northeast region are found in his definition. S. B. Bhattacharya[4], an Indian scholar, feels that insurgency is a meticulous process. He defines insurgency as “a prolonged struggle carried out immaculately step by step in order to achieve specific objectives leading finally to overthrow the existing order.” He further refines the concept by stating that “it is an action process in which one or more organisations pursue strategy of violence to bring change in the society in accordance with some ideology.” For instance, in the state of Nagaland, National Socialist Council of Nagaland (IM and K) both insurgent groups are fighting for greater Nagaland; in the state of Assam, Bodo rebel groups are fighting for Bodoland. Army doctrines and field manual of different nations have also discussed the term ‘Insurgency’. For instance, the United States Counter Insurgency Guide defines the term ‘insurgency’ as “The organised use of subversion and violence to seize, nullify or challenge political control of a region.”[5]

Indian Army doctrine published in 2004 defines insurgency as “an organised armed struggle by a section of the local population against the state, usually with foreign support. Its goals may be seizure of power and replacement of the existing regime or even liberation of a defined area.”[6] In this view, insurgency is a voice of unsatisfied group of people who wishes to fulfill their objectives by their own ways. It could be unconstitutional. While considering insurgency in India’s

Northeast region, S. K. Chaube's definition of insurgency is more applicable. He feels that insurgency is a rebellion which has to be against an order or an authority. According to him an insurgent is the one who is seen so by an authority. He further adds that an authority is one which enjoys legitimate power. Legitimacy, in turn is tied with the prevailing order and that prevailing order is, ultimately, decided by the power – physical, economic, intellectual and the like. He further observes that an insurgent may have a completely different viewpoint on the same issue and he is one who does not accept a prevailing order, for whom an 'insurgency' is an act of resistance or transformation.[7]

Insurgents nowadays are often mistaken with terrorists or guerrillas because mutineers adopt terrorists' or guerrillas' tactics. Although it is very difficult to have a watertight compartment between the definitions of insurgents and terrorists, at this juncture, it would be relevant to have a distinction between the terms 'insurgency' and 'terrorism'. The difference lies in the scope and scale of violence. An act of terrorism rarely results in a political change, insurgency attempts to bring about a change through force of arms. Insurgents are generally natives while terrorists are from both native and foreign soil. But the modes of operations adopted by the insurgents in Jammu and Kashmir and Northeast regions have made it difficult to categorise their operations whether carried out by terrorists or insurgents. In Jammu and Kashmir, Pakistani insurgents are often caught while creating security problems in the area. Even in the Northeast region, non-Indian Maoists are caught by security forces. In such circumstances, it can be said that insurgents are only native but it is difficult to distinguish between the rebellious operations of insurgents and terrorists.

Section II

3.2 Origin of Insurgency in Northeast Region

3.2.1 Nagaland

Insurgency in Northeast region began at different points of time. Initially, it started in Naga Hills which is now an independent state of Nagaland. Angami Zapu Phizo led the Naga movement, who did not want to join the Indian Union. He claimed that Nagaland had never been a part of Indian territory. Thus, on the eve of independence, the idea of insurgency took shape in the Naga Hills and thereafter it spread in the region. The root cause of insurgency in Naga Hills is found in the political history of this region. The British did not interfere in the administration of Naga Hills area. Consequently, Naga Hills remained isolated from the Indian mainstream and people residing in this area never identified themselves as 'Indians'. This encouraged the educated Naga people to think about independence. The literate Naga people formed a club known as 'Naga Club' with an intention to discuss their problems with British. In 1929, they proposed their demand of sovereignty before Simon Commission[8], which was prompted also by a determination to protect their traditional way of life based on customary laws.[9] Subsequently, a crucial development took place in Naga political organisation by formation of Ao and Lotha Council and an emergence of Naga Hill District Tribal Council, which finally merged into Naga National Council (NNC) in 1946.[10] NNC declared the ideas of 1929 of traditional way of life. This was reflected in the memorandum submitted by Naga National Council to the cabinet mission in 1946.[11] In February 1947, NNC submitted a memorandum to the British, wherein a demand was put up for an interim government. This resulted into a nine-point agreement, which recognised the right of Nagas to develop themselves according to their freely expressed wishes. However, due to difference of opinion over the last point in the agreement between central government and Phizo, he raised a revolt against the Indian government on 14 August 1947.[12]

In the year 1953, the insurgency initiated in Nagaland. Angami Zapu Phizo formed a rebel group[13] and several armed groups who openly made revolts against the Indian state.[14] Since then Indian government has been making efforts to put down the insurgency from the state. As a part of these attempts, on 1st December 1963, Indian government granted statehood to the state of Nagaland. However, violent activities continued for absolute independence. In 1964, a peace mission was formed with the help of Naga Baptist Convention. This led to the suspension of operations agreement between the leaders of underground movement and the Indian government.[15] Since then a series of peace talks were held for the next decade. As a result of this, in 1975, an agreement took place between the leaders of underground movement and Governor L. P. Singh. This agreement is known as 'Shillong Agreement'.[16] However, this mission of peace lasted for a short time. A broken group of NNC cadres did not accept the Shillong agreement and formed a new insurgent group on the soil of Myanmar in 1980, which was known as National Socialist Council of Nagaland (NSCN) under the leadership of Thaingaleng Muivah, Isak Chisi Swu and S. S. Khaplang.[17] Since then NSCN emerged as the most radical insurgent group fighting for Naga cause of greater Nagalim.

However, the group was divided into two groups namely, MSCN-IM led by Thaingaleng Muivah, Isak Chisi Swu and NSCN-K led by Khaplang. This resulted into inter-tribal rivalry and clashes between them.[18] Thus, the growth of Naga insurgency can be summarised into four phases. The first phase was from the year 1953 to 1964, when suspension of agreement was arranged. The period between 1964 to 1975 was the second phase, which ended with Shillong agreement. The third phase was during 1975 to 1988, when breakup took place in the group of NSCN. Finally, the fourth phase began from post breakup period i.e. from 1988 onwards. During this period, again there was a split in NSCN (K) and consequently a new insurgent group came into existence in June, 2011 with a name NSCN (KK), which was led by Khole –Kitovi.[19]

Presently, the three groups of NSCN are under the ceasefire with the Government of India. The first came into existence in the year 1997 as NSCN (IM), second in the year 2000 as NSCN (Khaplang) and in 2012, third one came into existence as NSCN (K) splinter group of NSCN – Khole-Khitovi.[20]

3.2.2 Manipur

The roots of insurgency in Manipur are found in the instrument of accession, which was signed by the King of Manipur.[21] However, the King did not join the Indian Union and he introduced Manipur Constitution Act of 1947. Accordingly, elections were held on the basis of adult franchise. However, when the King refused to merge with Indian union, he was arrested and was forced to sign the 'Merger Agreement'. Consequently, the agreement was signed on 21st September 1947. As a result, on 15th October 1949, Manipur was merged with the Indian Union. This incidence sowed the seeds of autonomy in the minds of people of Manipur. A communist leader, Irabot Singh, opposed this agreement and formed a 'Red Guard Army' to fight for an independent Manipur. However, he failed to achieve the goal as he died in the following years but he sowed the seeds of Meitei sub-nationalism.[22]

In 1964, Meitei secessionist insurgency began its operation in the state when United National Liberation Front (UNLF) was formed under the leadership of Samarendra Singh. The group was split in 1968. Oinam Sudhir Kumar led the broken group. He formed Revolutionary Government of Manipur (RGM) to act like parallel government. The UNLF was established after by terminating several movements like Pan-Mongoloid movement and the Manipur Nationalist Party (MNP), which had demanded independence from India in 1953.[23] Socialism appealed many Meiteis; thus, many other secessionist organisations came into existence in the state; for example, People's Revolutionary Party of Kangleipak (PREPAK), People's Revolutionary Army (PLA), Kangleipak Communist Party (KCP). In the year 1990, a broad platform was established by congregating Pan-Mongoloid outfits against the Indian union. This was known as Indo-Burma Revolutionary Front (IBRF). In the same way, Manipur People's Liberation Front (MPLF) was established to bring several Meitei outfits on this single platform. Insurgency in Manipur has three different dimensions, as there are three major communities. These are Meities, Nagas, and Kukis. The first dimension of insurgency is violence carried out by Meitei insurgent groups; second, Naga insurgent outfits created problems in Manipur; and the third dimension is inter-tribal clashes among the Nagas, Kukis and Meiteis in Manipur. Thus, various insurgent groups emerged in Manipur with different objectives. As a result, Manipur continued to witness the outbreak of violence in the Northeast region. According to the Annual Report 2013-14 published by Ministry of Home Affairs, Manipur is an insurgency driven state, which has been affected by insurgent activities of Meitei, Naga, Kuki, Zomi, Hmar and Muslim underground outfits.[24] Currently, underground outfits of the Kuki, Zomi and Hmar are under Suspension of Operation (SoO) Agreement with the Government of India and Manipur.[25]

3.2.3 Mizoram

The disturbance and unrest that existed in Naga Hills and Manipur spread further to Mizo Hills, which led to revolt. Mizo Hills, which was a part of former Assam, sought an autonomy and special financial aid from the Assam government to assist its economic development.[26] However, Assam government paid very less attention to their demand. On the contrary, decision to make Assamese language as an official language of the state of Mizo raised significant concerns about the future of Mizo identity and their culture among the people of Mizo Hills. Moreover, these problems became more complicated as the Mizo Hills suffered by famine 'Mautam' in early 1960s.[27] The Government of Assam did not provide necessary assistance during this famine. It failed to respond to the warnings of the tribal leaders, who needed adequate stocks of rice to be stored in the state.[28] As a result, Mizo National Famine Front (MNFF) emerged, which took an initiative to help the remote villages through several campaigns to survive. Pu Laldenga, an ex-serviceman, led MNFF. Soon after the famine was over, on 22nd October 1961, he turned MNFF into a political party by dropping the word 'Famine'. Thus, Mizo National Front (MNF) came into existence under the leadership of Laldenga that led the movement for secession in 1966, which resulted into violent conflicts.

In Mizoram, insurgency developed through three distinct phases. In the first phase, there was an outbreak of insurgency, which reached to its peak intensity during 1966-71. During the second phase, there was a decline in the intensity after Calcutta Agreement of 1976 and took place the first breakup in MNF as a result of surrender. In the third, phase there were irregular aggressive actions and periodic negotiations after 1977, which finally led to the settlement in 1986.[29] Although, Mizoram has remained free from insurgent violence since the political resolution of the insurgency took effect in the state in 1986, it has been witnessing violence carried out by Bru National Liberation Front (BNLF).

3.2.4 Assam

The unjust attitude of the central government towards Assam has caused an insurgency in Assam. Moreover, an issue related to language has played a significant role in shaping views over the identity concern of the people of the state. The language issue has separated the indigenous and domiciled non-Assamese from the Assamese' mainstream. Along with this problem, an issue of illegal migration from Bangladesh has led to the beginning of a mass movement in the late 1979, which resulted in Assam Agreement in 1985. The success of students' movement in gaining power in the state perhaps encouraged other racial groups to revolt for their demands.

The insurgency began to spread in Assam soon after the Assam agreement of 1985. Various insurgent groups were emerged in the post-agreement period on ethnic and communal lines with their own agenda. For instance, National Democratic Front of Bodoland (NDFB) fought for an independent Bodoland, whereas Islamist Insurgent groups operated their missions in the areas which were dominated by Muslims to safeguard the rights of Muslims. At present all the major insurgent groups from the state are on the negation table with the government of India.

3.2.5 Tripura

The insurgency emerged in Tripura from demographic imbalance. The roots of demographic imbalance can be traced in the history of the region. The British encouraged the peasants of East Pakistan for the cultivation of land to meet the royal expenses of the British government. Moreover, a large number of refugees and immigrants of East Pakistan were settled in Tripura after partition of the country. As a result of increase in the population of immigrants, the tribal population which was in majority became a minority. In the year 1947, the insurgent group led by Seng Kark had opposed the invasion of Bengali refugees for the first time.[30]

In mid 1970s, the formation of insurgent group namely, Tripura National Volunteers (TNV) in collaboration with Mizo National Front (MNF) resulted in the re-emergence of revolt in Tripura. After a decade of violence, an agreement in 1988 ended the insurgency. However, peace could not be long lasted due to the emergence of new insurgent groups namely, All Tripura Tribal Front (ATTF) and National Liberation Front of Tripura (NLFT). Both groups continued their rebellious operations because of their common agenda to drive out Bengali immigrants who were blamed for marginalisation of the indigenous people of Tripura. Even though the intensity of the violence created by these underground groups is low in the state today, there may be the chances that these groups would resume severe violent activities.

3.2.6 Arunachal Pradesh

The insurgency began in the districts of Tirap and Chaglang of Arunachal Pradesh as the insurgency had reached to its peak in the neighbouring states. Tirap and Chaglang districts have a huge Naga population which is dominated by NSCN (K). Thus, various violent incidents took place among various Naga resurgent groups to gain control over these two districts.[31] Moreover, the cadres of ULFA and NDFB have often taken shelter in the region of Arunachal Pradesh and used the state for their transit to neighbouring states and countries as the state shares its borders with Assam and Myanmar. The insurgent outfits have been interfering in the political and economic process of the state, mainly for raising money through extortions.

The NSCN groups have also been making forced recruitment of the cadres.[32]

3.2.7 Meghalaya

The demographic and economic transformation of the state has resulted in the insurgency in Meghalaya. The Bengali and Nepali workers who were settled in the state led to restlessness among the local tribal population.[33] As a result, in late 1980s the insurgency began in Meghalaya. The insurgent groups emerged due to inter-tribal rivalry and common opposition against the outsiders. For instance, Hynniwtrep Achik Liberation Council (HALC) representing all groups in the state was the first tribal organisation, which fought against the outsiders. Later, it was renamed and converted into an insurgent group namely, Hynniwtrep National Liberation Council (HNLC). Besides this, another insurgent group known as the Achik National Volunteer Council (ANVC) emerged in the state. Basically, insurgent activities in Meghalaya are centred around the Garo Hills areas for the last two and half decades.[34] The various insurgent groups like ULFA, NDFB, NSCN (IM) have been using Garo Hills corridor for sneaking in an out Bangladesh, taking advantage of the adverse geographical conditions and the remoteness of the area. The insurgent groups of the neighbouring states have encouraged, trained and nurtured the Garo insurgent groups like ANVC.[35] Presently, ANVC is under the SoO with Government of India.

Every state in the North-east region has been affected by insurgent violence and the number of casualties is huge. For instance, during two decades i.e. 1992-2014 the states like Assam, Manipur, Nagaland and Tripura witnessed widespread conflict (*See Table 3.1 and Annexure III).* According to the report of Ministry of Home Affairs (MHA) 2012-13, in the recent years, the intensity of the violence has come down to a large extent. It is because the major insurgent groups from the Northeast region are under the ceasefire agreement with the Central Government. However, conflict prone situation still exists in the Northeastern society because the groups against the

Table 3.1
Fatalities in insurgency related violence in Northeast region of India since 1992 to 31st March 2014

Heads / *States*	*Civilians Killed*	*Security Forces Killed*	*Insurgents**	*Cumulative Total State-wise (All Categories)*
Arunachal Pradesh	130	35	254	419
Assam	4204	809	2824	7837
Manipur	2295	964	2837	6096
Meghalaya	255	98	230	583
Mizoram	11	22	14	47
Nagaland	908	363	1871	3142
Tripura	2584	464	456	3504
Total	**10387**	**2755**	**8486**	**21628**

Source: (i) South Asia Terrorism Patrol (SATP), http://satp.org (available links are shown in the annexure III)
(ii) Annual Report, (Government of India - Ministry of Home Affairs (MHA), 2003-2004, 2004 – 2005, 2005-2006, 2006-2007, and 2013 - 2014).

ceasefire agreement and the rivalry among different tribes have been responsible for the violence in the region.

Fatalities related to insurgency in the Northeast region are testimonies of this fact, which is alarming. During the years 1992-2014, the Northeastern states of India have recorded 21,628 fatalities. Maximum casualties, within the above mentioned period, have been recorded in Assam, which is followed by Manipur, Tripura and Nagaland. It can be seen from the table that the insurgent groups have been targeting innocent civilians as well as security forces. Such terrible situation has kept local population under constant threat of their life. The insurgents claimed that most of the civilians killed by them were not the original inhabitants of the area of their operation. However, the fact remains that the innocent civilians are being killed and the threat of violence is being used to create psychological fear in the minds of the local inhabitants.

Various insurgent groups from Northeast region have different objectives. They differ in their operational methods and organisational structures. However, they share some common features. These are as follows:

1. Projection of people's representatives;

2. Separatist or secessionist;

3. Clear or vague agenda to attain sovereignty.[36]

It has been observed that the demands of insurgents' groups lead to conflict against the government and among the insurgent groups. For instance, NSCN (IM) has been fighting for greater Nagaland. The greater Nagaland includes five out of the six districts of Manipur and some other parts of the states of Assam, Arunachal Pradesh and bordering areas of Myanmar. This has resulted into the conflict not only between the government and NSCN (IM) but also between the groups of NSCN (IM) and NSCN (K) in the parts of Arunachal Pradesh. This demand has also resulted into the conflict between Nagas and Kukis inhabiting in Manipur. Moreover, insurgent groups from Assam like Dima Halim Dagoah (DHD), which were supported by NSCN (IM) in the initial years, found their demands overlapping with that of NSCN. The objective of DHD is to create a separate state of 'Dimaraji' for the Dimasa ('sons of the great river') tribe, comprising of Dimasa-dominated areas of the North Cachar Hills and Karbi Parts of Dimapur district in Nagaland.

The revolts have not only been sustained over the years, but also have multiplied in the Northeast region. Whenever an insurgent group has signed an agreement with the Government of India in a particular state, the gap has been immediately filled up by other insurgent groups on the grounds of familiar allegation of betrayal, negligence and alienation of the region. Thus, in spite of agreement of peace signed by various insurgent groups, insurgencies have never been eliminated in the Northeast region. For instance, after Phizo, Muivah formed NSCN in Nagaland. Soon NSCN fell down and Khaplang challenged Muivah.[37] Similarly, in Tripura after the agreement with TNV, the insurgent groups namely, ATTF and NLFT emerged. In Mizoram, after the 1986 agreement, there were no recorded instances of revolt. However, smaller ethnic groups like Brus and the Hmars have begun armed struggle in the last two decades for their own share in the state.[38] Thus, throughout the last six decades, various insurgent groups have emerged in the Northeast region with an intention to prove their own identity and claim their control over the region. These rebellious groups are acting with common or different agendas. They have posed a threat to native inhabitants of the Northeast region and the Government of India. In such situation, it has become a challenging task to bring to end insurgent activities for the Indian government as well as Northeastern society struggling for peace.

3.3 Factors responsible for the sustained growth of insurgency

In the initial period, every insurgency movement began their campaign in separate constituency to deal with the prolonged grievances of the inhabitants against administration.[39] This stance of the outfits helped them to strengthen their base amongst their respective societies in the initial period. It is important to note that insurgency movements in Northeast region were set up in the backdrop of World War II. The revolutionary Naga leader Angami Zhapu Pizo, who founded the NNC as the forbearer of the Naga insurgency, had trained with the British forces fighting against the Japanese on the warfront in Burma, along with Mizo and Manipuri groups. Such war experience, military training in jungle warfare and guerilla tactics helped in sustaining initial insurgency movements in Northeast region.[40] Moreover, other certain factors are responsible for the growth of insurgency in the region. These factors are discussed as below :

3.3.1. Drug Trafficking and Small Arms

Easy availability of small arms is one of the major factors that have sustained the insurgency in the Northeast region. It has been reported that weapons such as AK-47 and AK-56 rifles, anti-tank grenades, rocket launchers, pistols, Sub-Machine Guns (SMGs), rockets, semi-automatic spot rifles; tommy guns, hand grenades are easily found in the Northeast region. Apart from the weapons produced in ordnance factory, the Northeast region has also witnessed a dissemination of the arms produced in the region. Moreover, many of the insurgent groups have modern arms and equipment than the state police.[41]

These weapons have helped the insurgent groups of the Northeast region in their criminal activities and to engage in fight with the Indian state.[42] The spread of arms is closely related to drug abuse[43] and narco-trafficking in the region because of profit factor. Arms are usually used in exchange of drugs.

Indian intelligence agencies have confirmed that Bangladesh Intelligence and ISI are continuing their policy of arming the insurgent groups in the Northeast region. It has been observed that Bangladesh Intelligence is acting as an agent for the insurgents and money gained through drugs is being passed to Bangkok for the purchase of weapons in Thailand. Weapons

Table 3.2
Rise of ULFA inventory between 1986 and 1996

Weapons	*1986*	*1996*
G Series	None	250+
AK-47/56	1	60
Semi-Automatics	2-4	130
LMG	None	20
Sten/Carbine	None	116
American Carbine	None	62
Pistols	9-10	336
Handmade Weapons	10-20	6
Grenades	None	1,143+
Ammunition	Unknown	70,000

Source : Kartha, Tara, "Tools of Terror : Light Weapons and India's Security", (New Delhi, 1999, Knowledge World and IDSA), p. 269.

Table 3.3

State-wise Surrendered and Seized Figures of Weapons from 2002-2004

Year / *State*	*2002*	*2003*	*2004*	*All State Wise Cumulative Total*
Arunachal Pradesh	30	34	16	80
Assam	252	795	309	1356
Manipur	84	32	66	182
Meghalaya	51	57	42	150
Mizoram	00	00	14	14
Nagaland	133	79	31	243
Tripura	66	198	139	403
Total	**616**	**1195**	**617**	**2428**

Source : Ministry of Home Affairs, Annual Report Government of India, (2003-2004 and 2004-2005).

are transported by sea to Teknaf and other areas near Cox-bazar. Then these weapons are moved through Chittagaon Hill Tracts (CHT) along the Indo-Myanmar border and delivered into the North Cachar Hills. Moreover, it is also observed that, a well established set up (Atlee Command) has been created under the absolute control of NSCN (IM) for training and co-ordination of movements of arms for the insurgents of the Northeast region.[44]

During 1993-1998, a total number of weapons seized is 928. United Liberation Front of Assam (ULFA) from Assam had a huge share of 729 weapons alone.[45] The rapid increase in the possession of small arm weapons by ULFA during 1986-1996 is shown in Table 3.2.

And expectedly, between 2002 and 2004 these figures including surrendered arms rose up to 2428, in which state of Assam alone shares 1356 small arms. The state-wise seized and surrendered arms are shown in the Table 3.3.

However, the number of weapons shown in the Table 3.3 does not give the actual number of weapons available with insurgents; however, it indicates the nature of weapons used by the insurgents. From the above table, it becomes clear that the insurgent groups still have a good stock of weapons which are believed to be stored secretly.

3.3.2 Porous Borders and Role of External Powers

Porous borders and the role of external powers is another factor which have helped to sustain insurgency in the Northeast region. Due to the leaky nature of the border, smugglers and infiltrators easily cross over to India. For instance, the border of Bangladesh which is shared with India in Northeast region consists of plains, river land, hills, jungles with hardly any natural obstacles; moreover, the border is thickly populated which facilitates border crossing.[46] This border at some places has not been demarcated on the ground. As a result, a border cuts through the middle of several villages. In some cases, while one section of a house is in the territory of one country, the other lies in another's land. For example, in West Bengal and Tripura, there are more than 100 villages located right on the zero line, and in many such villages, there are houses where the front door is in Indian territory while the rear door opens into Bangladesh.[47] The insurgent groups have been routinely exploiting these loose borders by maintaining training and logistics centers across the borders. Several sections of these borders are under almost complete control of insurgent groups, who maintain their own border check-points to extort money for their rebellious activities. It has also been observed that many times insurgents enter into the Northeastern states, attack largely at will, and then go back to their relative safe places across the international border.

According to the Border Security Forces (BSF), prior to the present Awami League government, various insurgent groups from the Northeast region had set up camps in different parts of Bangladesh, specially Sylhet district and Chittagong Hill Tracts sharing borders with the states of Tripura, Mizoram and Meghalaya. However, Bangladesh government has denied its involvement in such rebellious activities that are being carried out by various insurgent groups on Bangladesh land. However, Awami League government under the leadership of Sheikh Hasina has taken firm action against insurgents from Northeast region and prosecuted two former army generals,[48] of Bangladesh, namely, Major General Rezakul Haider Chowdhury and Brigadier General Abdur Rahim for anti-India activities from their soil. This is clear evidence to the fact that Bangladesh has provided all kinds of support to the insurgents of Northeast region. It has also been observed that Pakistan's Inter Services Intelligence (ISI) has developed safe locations in Bangladesh and close links with the intelligence organisations of Bangladesh which have provided weapons, training, shelter to the insurgent groups of Northeast region. For instance, Bangladesh provided safe hideouts for training camps in the north and south Bangladesh sharing common border with that of the Northeast region. United Liberation Front of Assam (ULFA) has initiated the highest number of training camps within this area, which covers Sherpur district in the north sharing borders with the west Garo Hills in Meghalaya, and with Cox's Bazaar in the south near Myanmar. Similarly, the camps of NLFT and ATTF have covered the area in three Bangladesh districts of Rangamati, Moulavi Bazaar and Khagrachari in conjunction with the Bangladesh-Tripura border and also at Dhanmandi in Dhaka. Moreover, Borok National Council of Tripura and Bru National Liberation Front have also their camps in Rangamati district. The NDFB, DHD have their camps in Maulavi Bazaar. Hynniwtrep National Liberation Council (HNLC), People's Liberation Army (PLA), Kanglei Yawol Lub Kanba Lub (KYKL), United National Liberation Front (UNLF), 'People's Revolutionary Party of Kangleipak'

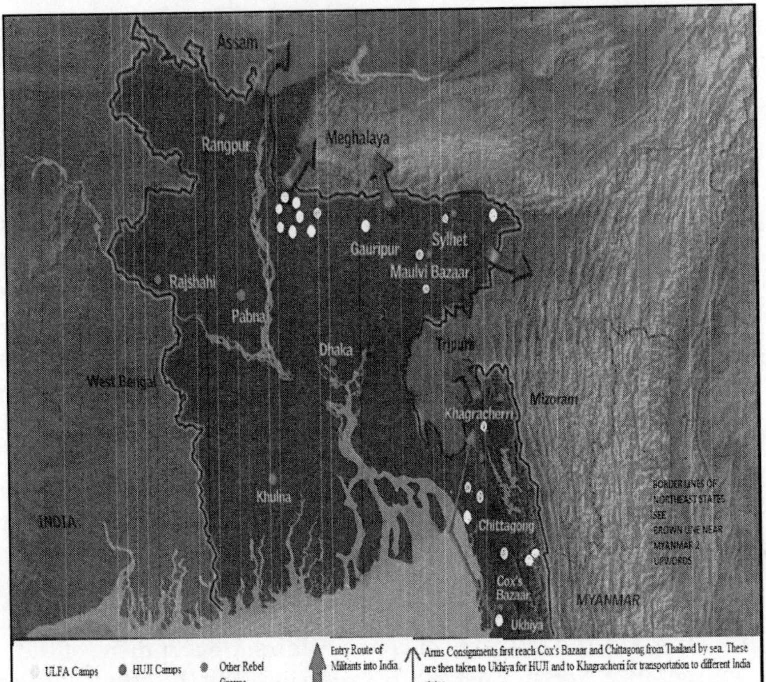

Source : Times of India (Mumbai), 27 May 2007.

Sketch 3.1 Showing the Training Camps and Entry Routes of the Insurgents Group.

(PREPAK), Kamatpur Liberation Organisation (KLO), MULTA and Islamic United Reformation Protest of India (IURPI) are reportedly located in Madrassas in Kurigram district.[49] All the insurgent groups of the Northeast region receive all kind of support from Bangladesh. Similarly, China has also been involved in the armed conflict in the region through providing aid and assistance to the insurgent groups in the form of money, arms and training. Insurgent groups from Nagaland, Mizoram and Manipur have received support from China. From the early 1960s and throughout 1970, China was involved through providing material and moral support to insurgents of the Northeast region.

3.3.3 Criminalisation of Politics

Criminalisation of politics is another factor, which is responsible for the sustained insurgency in the Northeast region. It is believed that there is a complex collusive arrangement among various political parties, administrators and officials, on one hand, and different insurgent groups, on the other.[50] There are instances of insurgent groups involved in regional politics. There has been an association between particular political parties and insurgent groups in the region with an exception of the states like Arunachal Pradesh, Meghalaya and Mizoram.[51] Many times, insurgent groups exercise violence to support certain political organisations or politicians. In return they enjoy protection for the crimes brought about by them. They use this political influence to bribe and threaten government officers who do not fulfill their demands. They claim a share from the financial aid that comes from the centre. Such corrupt behaviour of the insurgent outfits has sidelined the vital constructive potential of the region.[52]

In 2003, the Ministry of Home Affairs, Government of India had set up a North- East Study group to study the situation and come up with a futuristic vision for the entire Northeast region. The members of this group were senior government officers and others. Study conducted by this group has revealed that corruption, insurgency, and contractor raj are the major reasons for the worse situation of Northeast region. The chairman of this study group S. K. Agnihotri, who had been Chief Secretary of Arunachal Pradesh, told newspaper reporter that, "A parallel system of governance run by a colluding mass insurgents, ministers, MLA's bureaucrats and cops is responsible for the political instability."[53] Moreover, journalist–author Sudeep Chakravarti has explained the share of different bureaucrats in the funds given for a development project by government and actual amount of funds used for the said project as follows: 10 per cent to the local MLA, 10 to 40 per cent to the local underground organisation, 10 per cent to the minister in-charge of the concerned ministry, 10 per cent to the person who actually allots the contract, between 7.5 per cent and 10 per cent to the layer of concerned bureaucracy depending on his need and greed, 10 per cent to the appointed collectors of the Chief Minister. The remaining amount, which is between 10 to 40 per cent, goes to the undertaken project, unless a total fraud is exposed. The project is shown on paper and the funds disappear along the apportioned lines.[54] Insurgency has become big business in the Northeast region. Many of the smaller insurgent outfits are virtually indistinguishable from criminal gangs. They operate only to make money through extortions and kidnappings. These groups have no certain political ideology. The governance and law and order have become corrupt as the politicians, members of the bureaucracy, the police and even local judiciary are involved in the circle of corruption and bribery. Thus, both guardians of law and order and governance have become convicts in the 'insurgency for convenience'.[55]

3.4 Sum up

1. The roots of the insurgency have already existed in the society; however, adjacent causes have mounted up the insurgency movement in the Northeast region.

2. The insurgent groups from the region are characteristically different from each other due to their different objectives, operational environment and methods of operation.

However, one thing is common, which is the violence exercised by them.

3. Initially, insurgency began in the state of Nagaland and then it spread like epidemic all over the region. However, the origin of such conflict varies within different states of the Northeast region. No two situations are alike. For example, the origin of insurgency in the state of Nagaland is quite different from that in the state of Assam. It has sustained over the years due to the factors like small arms circulation, drug-trafficking, leaky borders and support from external powers.

4. There are various insurgent outfits, which are not active in the region. However, they re-emerge occasionally and get involved in criminal activities, such as, extortion and racketeering. They commit such unlawful activities because these groups have no ideology or clear agenda. It is also found that many times the insurgent groups, which are active in the region, have diluted their original agenda and involved in criminal activities.

5. Insurgency succeeds when interference from opposed country is possible, particularly when there is a common border shared between both countries. Furthermore, geographic isolation of the area, suitability of terrain such as hills and forests, support of local population, etc. are such conditions that help in promoting insurgency.

References

1. As all the eight states of this region has been dependant on central fund of resources, as they don't have independent economy.

2. Basically insurgency is threat to India's unity and integrity. The term insurgency however, clubbed with term movement because insurgency in India's North East Region is not recognised as belligerency.

3. David Kilcullen "Three Pillars of Counter Insurgency" Speech delivered at the U.S. government counter insurgency conference,

Washington D. C. p. 2, available online at www.au.af.mil/au/awc/awcgate/uscoin/3pillars_of_coounterinsurgency.pdf accessed on 06.09.12.

4. Bhattacharya, Tribal Insurgency in Tripura, (New Delhi, 1989), p. 11.

5. United States, Counter Insurgency Guide, (Bureau of Political-Military Affairs, United States, January 2009), p. 2, (January 2009), available online at www.state.gov/documents/organisation/119629.pdf accessed on 26.08.12.

6. Indian Army Doctrine, Part 1, 2004, pp. 16-17. available online at http://ids.nic.in/Indian%20Army%20Doctrine/indianarmy doctrine_1.doc, accessed on 01.09.12.

7. S. K. Chaube, "Insurgency in Northeast India: A Heretical View", in B. Pakem, ed., Insurgency in North East India (New Delhi, 1997), p. 29.

8. K. V. Krishnarao, Prepare or Perish: A Study of National Security, (New Delhi), p. 260.

9. Charles Chasie and Sanjoy Hazarika, "The States Strikes Back: India and the Naga Insurgency", Policy Studies paper 52, (Washington, 2009), p. 3.

10. *Ibid.*, pp. 3-4.

11. The points of the memorandum are: 1. The Naga stands for solidarity of all Naga tribes; 2. The council strongly protest against the grouping of Assam with Bengal; 3. The Naga Hills should be constitutionally included in an autonomous Assam, in a free India, with local autonomy and safeguards for the interest of the Nagas; 4. The Naga tribes should have separate electorate. - Krishnarao, n.8, p. 260.

12. *Ibid.*, pp. 260-61.

13. It is known as Naga federal government.

14. E. A. Vas, The Search for Security: Controlling Conflict and Terrorism, (Dehradun, 1989) p. 65.

15. *Ibid.*, pp. 65-66.

16. Krishnarao, n. 8, p. 264.

17. Ajai Sahani, "Survey of Conflicts and Resolution in India's Northeast" available online at http://www.satp.org/satporgtp/publication/faultlines/volume12/Article3.htm accessed on 24.09.10

18. *Ibid.*

19. Annual Report, Ministry of Home Affairs, (Government of India, 2013-14), p. 18.

20. Gautam Das, Insurgencies in North-East India: Moving Towards Resolutions, (New Delhi, 2013), p.103

21. S.P. Sinha, "Insurgency in North-East India: An Appraisal", *Askrosh,* (New Delhi, 2000), Vol. 1, No. 7, p. 46.

22. *Ibid.*

23. Das, n. 20, p. 118.

24. Annual Report, n. 19, p. 17.

25. *Ibid.*

26. Walter C. Ladwig (B), Managing Separatist Insurgencies: Insights From North East India, A paper prepared for International Studies Association Annual Conference 16-18 February 2009, New York, p. 10, available online at http://users.ox.ac.uk/~mert1769/Managing_Separatists.pdf accessed on 06.09.12.

27. The famine caused due to the flowering of bamboo which led to increase in the population of rat who devoured the rice and cereal harvest.

28. Subir Bhaumik, Insurgent Crossfire: North-East India, (New Delhi, 1996), p. 142.

29. Subir Bhumik, "Insurgencies in India's Northeast: Conflict, Co-option and Change", Working Paper, East West Centre,

Washington,p. 14, available online at http://scholarspace.manoa. hawaii.edu/bitstream/handle/10125/3540/EWCWwp010. pdf? sequence= 1 accessed on 06.09.12.

30. Sinha, n.21, pp. 47-48.

31. Dhruv Katoch, "Viable Strategy to Fight Insurgency in Northeast", National Defence College Thesis available online at http:// ndc.nic.in/pdf/44-katoch.pdf accessed on 19.01.10.

32. Annual Report, n. 19, p. 15.

33. Renaud Egreteau, "Instability at the Gate: India's Troubled Northeast and its External Implications", available online at http://egreteau.com/images/Documentriespercent20PDF/CSH percent 200 Ppercent20_percentnpercentBO16. pdf accessed on 28.01.10.

34. Annual Report, n.19, p. 18.

35. *Ibid.*

36. M. S. Prabhakara, "Degrees of Separatism", Frontline (Madrass), (22 September 2006), p. 42.

37. Nagaland Post, 4 May 2010.

38. *Ibid.*

39. Wasbir Hussain, "Northeast: From Insurgency to Terrorism?", in D. Suba Chandran and P.R. Chari, ed., Armed Conflict in South Asia 2011: Promise and Threat of Transfomation (New Delhi, 2012), p. 176.

40. Mirza Zulfikar Rahaman, "Northeast India: Turn Towards Sustainable Peace?" *Ibid.*, p. 84.

41. Mandy Turnur and Binalakshmi Nepram, "The Impact of Armed Violence in Northeast India: A Mini Case Study for the Armed Violence and Poverty Initiative", Centre for International Studies, University of Bradford, November 2004.

42. *Ibid.*

43. The World Drug Report 1997 says that the rapid disintegration of traditional social structure has been a contributing factor to new pattern of drug abuse in the countries in transition; and feeling of marginalisation, of non-identification with the cultural environment are attributed to reason for drug abuse.

44. V .K. Nayar, Crossing the Frontiers of Conflict in the North East and Jammu and Kashmir: From Real Politik to Ideal Politik, (New Deli, 2005), p. 298.

45. See Kartha, Tara, "Tools of Terror: Light Weapons and India's Security", Strategic Analysis (New Delhi, 1999).

46. Anil Kamoj, "Border Management: Bangladesh, Nepal, Bhutan", World Focus (New Delhi), Vol. 27, No. 8, (August 2006), p. 24.

47. *Ibid.*

48. In the Chittagong arms seizure case (2 April 2004) the accused persons revealed that senior political leaders along with civil and military intelligence chiefs of the then Khaleda Zia government were involved in the botched arms shipment. Thus, two army generals were prosecuted for facilitating the landing of Chinese arms meant for insurgents in India's Northeast region and trying for smuggle these into India.

49. Times of India (Mumbai) 27 May 2007.

50. Kotach, n.31.

51. Bethany Lacina, "Does Counter Insurgency Theory Apply in Northeast India?", (Indian Review), Vol. 6, No. 3, July-September, 2007, p. 174.

52. *Ibid.*

53. Das, n. 20, p. 3.

54. *Ibid.*, pp. 3-4.

55. *Ibid.*, p. 4.

4

Insurgency in Assam Since 1985

In this chapter, an attempt has been made to explore and analyse certain important factors, which are responsible for the disorder and prolonged violent eruption in the state of Assam. For this purpose, the chapter has been divided into four sections. The first section gives a brief summary of the state of Assam. The geographical, demographical, linguistic and ethnic aspects of the state have been covered in this section. In section two, various factors responsible for the insurgency movement in the state and its rising hierarchies have been explained. The falling situation after the Assam agreement has been discussed in the third section. This section also gives a brief profile of major insurgent groups operating in the state. The fourth section explains the role of neighbouring countries in encouraging insurgency in the state.

Section I

4.1 Assam : An Overview

4.1.1 Geography

Assam is geographically located between the latitudes 24° N to 28° N and longitudes 90° E to 96° E.[1] According to census of India 2001, Assam covers an area of 78,438 sq.kms.,[2] which is 2.4 per cent of total geographical area of the country.[3] Geo-strategic importance of the state lies in the fact that it shares

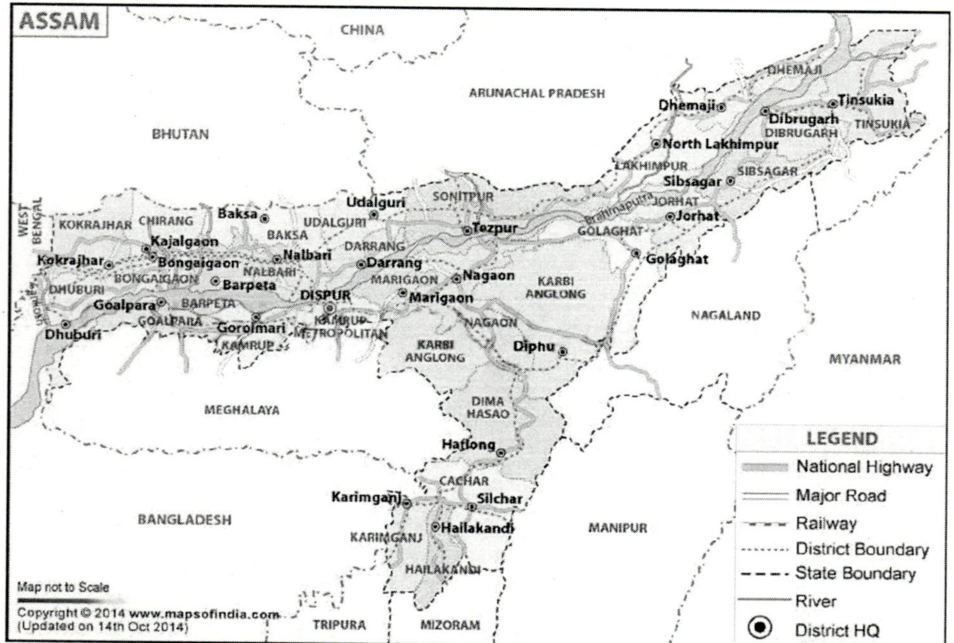

Source: Maps of India, available online at, http://www.mapsofindia.com/maps/assam/, accessed on 11.2.15.

Map: 4.1 showing the road and rail links passes through Assam to other states of the Region.

its border with seven states viz. Arunachal Pradesh in the east and north, Manipur and Nagaland in the east and south, West Bengal in the west, Meghalaya in the west and south and Mizoram and Tripura in the south.[4] Assam is the only state in the Indian Union that shares its border with seven states. The state also shares its border with two neighbouring countries viz. Bangladesh in the west and Bhutan in the north.[5] Moreover, Assam is the gateway to other states of Northeast region as it establishes a link between these states and Indian Territory through Siliguri corridor. As the state shares its border with the other states of the region all the roads and railway tracks pass through the state of Assam. (*See map 4.1*) Therefore, the state performs a role of a facilitator for the exploitation of huge stock of hydel found in Arunachal Pradesh and minerals found in other states of the Northeast region to meet the requirement of raw material for the produce of finished products.[6]

The state is enriched by natural resources. It is gifted with abundant supply of water through rivers, huge stocks of hydrocarbon i.e. oil and gas, large quantities of low ash coal resources, limestone and dolomite deposits, forest resources especially bamboo as well as a few other unexplored minerals.

4.1.2 Population of Assam

According to census of India 2011, the total population of Assam is 3,12,05,578 whereas it was 2,66,55,5287 in 2001. The decadal population growth rate of the state during 2001-2011 is 17.07 per cent.[8] It is comparatively less than the growth rate of the state during 1991-2001, which was 18.92 per cent during 1991-2001.[9] Similarly, as per the census of India 2001, the density of population was 340, which has gone up to 398 in the year 2011 as said by the census report of India.[10]

4.1.3 Linguistic and Ethnic Composition

The inhabitants of the state of Assam belong to different ethnic groups, follow different religions and speak different languages. Few tribal groups are also living in the state. They have their own religion and language. Assamese, Bodo,

Karbi are the official languages of the state.[11] Generally, languages such as Assamese, Mising, Karbi, Manipuri, Garo and Rabha are considered as indigenous languages of Assam. On the contrary, languages like Bengali, Hindi, Nepali, Oriya or Santhali are considered as non-indigenous languages. However, it is difficult to categorise such languages. For example, Bengali may be considered as an immigrant language in Brahmaputra Valley, while it would be difficult to say that it is an immigrant language in Cachar district where most of the people speak Bengali.[12] A considerable number of people speaking Bengali and other languages and dialect also live in Assam. Assamese population is concentrated in the Upper Assam, while Bengalis form the majority in the three southern districts of Assam, namely, Cachar, Karimganj and Hailakandi. The substantial Muslim population is found both in Assamese in Upper Assam and in Bengalis in South Assam. The Karbis and Dimasas live in the hilly districts of Karbi Anglong and North Cachar hills. They have their own dialects and cultures, because of which they do not resemble fully with Assamese people. Similarly, the plain tribes like Boros, Rabhas, Koch Rajbamshis, etc, maintain their separate identity apart from Assamese. On the contrary, few plain tribes like Deuris, Tiwas Sonowal, Kacharis, Mech Cacharis, etc, have been assimilated into Assamese nationality.[13] There is also a population working in tea gardens of Assam, who speak the languages such as Hindi, Santhali, Mundari, Oriya and Tamil. They have been working for several decades in Assam and have developed their own distinct character and identity.[14]

Section II

4.2 Genesis of Insurgency

There have been many factors responsible for the constant disorder in state of Assam since past till the date. In this context, it is relevant to mention some of the key factors which are accountable for such mess in the state of Assam.

4.2.1 Emergence of Assamese' Nationalism

National awareness of Assamese emerged during the British rule when British introduced Bengali as an official language of the state in 1837. At this time, many Bengali people were in the administration. They not only dominated the economy of Assam but also began to speak about the social and cultural life of Assam and labeled Assamese language as a dialect of Bengali.[15] As a result, newly emerged Assamese middle class began to oppose an imposition of Bengali language on Assamese. Consequently, after the years of agitation, in the year 1873 Bengali was replaced by Assamese as an official language of the state. However, in 1874 Sylhet district was incorporated in the state of Assam, where the population was mainly Bengali. This made the Assamese more worried that they would be in minority in their own homeland.[16] Thus, with the end of 19th century, Assamese national awareness began to take shape.

In the year 1946, at the time of Assam Congress election, Congress leaders made an appeal that "unless the province of Assam be organised on the basis of language and Assamese culture, the survival of Assamese nationality and culture would become impossible."[17] As a result, on 4th May 1948, the revenue department issued a circular to bring the linguistic homogeneity in the state. This circular stated that "accept Assamese as mother tongue and we give you land."[18] The huge number of Muslim migrants who had come to Assam since the days of Saddullas declared Assamese as their mother tongue in the census of 1951 to retain their lands in their occupation.[19] This resulted into the growth of Assamese speaking population from 31 per cent in 1931 to 56.7 per cent in 1951.[20] In such circumstances, the Assamese leaders thought they would be able to rule over minorities of undivided Assam viz. Bengalis, Bodos, Khasis, Mizos, Chakmas and Nagas.[21] The Government of Assam declared Assamese as the only official language of the state in 1960 with an intention to make Assam a homeland of Assamese like other states in India. This resulted into a widespread controversy amongst the tribals and linguistic minorities. Further, the language movements in non-Assamese area and riots in Brahmaputra valley took place. This further resulted into the reorganisation of Assam. After the reorganisation in 1972, the All Assam Student Union (AASU) demanded to take up Assamese as a medium of instruction in Guwahati and Dibrugarh Universities. This demand created irritation in the district of Cachar where there was a majority of Bengali speaking population. The Assam government decided to approve the resolution of Assembly and promised to form a separate university for Cachar district. This decision created widespread violence against Bengali population of the state. Finally, the Assam government decided not to abide with the assembly resolution and declared that Assamese language would be compulsorily taught in all the non-Assamese schools of the state. This resulted into a protest not only from the Bengali speaking population of the state but also from the Bodos and other tribes in the state.[22]

4.2.2 Awareness of Isolation

At the time of independence and after independence, an awareness of isolation began to rise among the Assamese. This can be traced from the several incidences which took place during this time. For example, at the time of independence, the state of undivided Assam was placed under group 'C' under the 'Grouping Plan'. However, due the efforts of the Assam Provincial Congress Committee led by Gopinath Bordoloi, today Assam is a part of India. With Mahatma Gandhiji's support, he acted against the Congress central leadership and ensured that the Grouping Plan would be scrapped.[23] In the year 1962 during Sino-Indian war, the then Prime Minister Pandit Nehru addressed to the Assamese vis-à-vis Chinese advance[24] which had a negative impact on the Assamese mind.

On the other hand, the people of Assam believe that the centre is exploiting the natural resources of their own land but at the same time it is making discrimination in respect of their share in the development of the country. This was observed by them when central government decided to establish the public sector refinery at Barauni in Bihar. Another example of discrimination and exploitation by the centre is the public sector oil industry. Discovery of oil in several areas of upper Assam in the late 1960s pushed up the crude oil production figure to an average of 3.5 million tons per year. From 1970 onwards, the figure touched five million tons per year.[25] However, the royalty paid by the centre to Assam was not satisfactory. The state government and people of Assam demanded to raise the royalty. However, central government refused the state government's demand for the revision of royalty on crude oil. As a result, the feeling spread among the people of the state that the centre was merely exploiting the resources of the region without considering Assam's ever deteriorating economic situation.[26]

4.2.3 Illegal Migration

Assamese became aware that along with economic exploitation by the centre, they had to face forthcoming danger of being a minority in their own state. The vast growth in Muslim population had overburdened the state. Moreover, Bengali Muslims who had initially identified themselves as Assamese speaking population began to register themselves as Bengali speaking people especially between 1971 and 1991.[27] During the by elections of Mangaldoi Parliamentary Constituency in April 1979, the intensity of the problem of language became more evident. The Mangaldoi Parliamentary Constituency had a heavy concentration of Muslim voters of Bengali ancestry. At that time immigration on a large scale took place from Bangladesh to Assam. The number of these voters in Mangaldoi constituency had gone up phenomenally in the two years even though the previous election had given alarm. It was observed that 45,000 voters or one-sixth of the total number of voters were not the citizens of India. Thereafter, the thousands of complaints were made during the revision of electoral rolls. These complaints challenged the citizenship of such voters on the list. In such circumstances, a large number of Indian citizens - Muslim of Bengali origin, Bengali Hindus and some ethnic Assamese Muslims- were harassed in order to find out forged voters. Thus, after annoying the local people, the search for bogus voters had to be stopped. Further, in order to stop an illegal migration of Bangladeshis and their participation in the election, in 1979, All Assam Student Union (AASU) and All Assam Gan

Sangram Parishad[28] (AAGSP) made a massive protest. Moreover, the Plain Tribal Council of Assam (PTCA), and several tribal organisations joined with AASU-AAGSP.

4.2.4 Bodo[29] Movement

The Bodos are the earlier settlers of the plains of the state. This tribe is a largest tribe amongst the earliest settlers in the state. This tribe is mainly concentrated on the north bank of the Brahmaputra river and they have also scattered in other parts of the state. Socio-economic condition of this tribe was miserable in the initial years after the independence. They were deprived of their constitutional right of protection. Bodos were considered as another form of Assamese sub-nationality. In addition to this, they were isolated from the land due the encroachment of their land by illegal migrants. Further, the situation became more severe when they were deprived of government jobs on the ground that the knowledge of the Assamese language is essential. The newly emerged middle class amongst them tried to draw the attention of the government to their issues but they remained unattended. Consequently, they initiated a movement on the ground of negligence of Bodo language, economic deprivation, inattentiveness of ethnic Assamese and cultural discrimination.[30] The Plain Tribal Council of Assam (PTCA) was formed on 27th February 1967 at Kokrajhar Rongjasali. PTCA made its first demand for the autonomous region within the state with a name Udayanchal. The very purpose of this demand was to uplift the Bodo tribes of the plains. The All Bodo Student Union (ABSU) which was formed prior to PTCA on 15th February 1967 supported the demand of PTCA. Later, with the passage of time PTCA made a demand for a separate state (UT).[31]

In the years of 1972 and 1973, the demand of Bodo people for a separate state was on a peak. However, in the year 1974-75, the well-known Roman script movement for Bodo language was immediately misunderstood in the following year, as the movement for separate state. Ever since the formation of PTCA, ABSU had been actively supporting PTCA for a separate state.

However, ABSU stopped supporting when PTCA abandoned the cause of separate state in 1977. During the next decade, significant developments took place in the movement, such as, formation of PTCA-P (Progressive) and their subsequent demand for Mishing Bodoland. Meanwhile ABSU tried for the merger of PTCA and PTCA-P but it did not succeed. Latter PTCA-P was dissolved and a new political front United Tribal National Liberation Front (UTNLF) was formed. Subsequently, it was renamed as United Bodo National Liberation Front (UBNLF).

4.2.5 Karbi and Dimasa Movement

Karbi Anlong and North Cachar Hills are two districts of Assam where insurgency took place for the demand for statehood. It is an outcome of the political aspirations of the hill people and cultural discrimination by Assamese. However, the demand for statehood had its roots in the formation of United Mikir (later renamed Karbi Anlong) and North Cachar Hills district (UMNC) in 1951. Although they got Autonomous District Council (ADC) on 23rd June 1952 under Sixth Schedule, their demand for autonomy persisted.

The leaders of the hills became aware that the ADC did not have adequate powers to develop within the hills. Moreover, 'Official Language Bill of 1960' gave a boost to the demand of autonomy in two hill districts. Consequently, the demand for statehood was made in April 1970 when the state of Meghalaya was created as an associate state. However, these districts did not insist for the statehood like Meghalaya because Central Government assured them that if they would remain in Assam then they would be given equal facilities like other districts for developing their own areas.[32] Accordingly, to keep them away from the separatist movements in other hill districts, in addition to the twenty-nine departments transferred under the Sixth Schedule, on 1st June 1970, Central Government transferred thirty development departments/subjects to the ADC of UMNC Hills district.[33] The expectation of the youth and leaders of the hill areas increased due to the government's assurance and also because of transfer of certain more district council of these hill areas. However, they were disappointed when the Academic Council of two universities of the state decided to make Assamese as the sole medium of instruction in college education. Besides organising protest meetings, in 1973, the Mikir and North Cachar Hills leaders' conference submitted a memorandum to the Prime Minister, wherein they explained how they were persuaded to remain in Assam, how the central grants under Article 275 were misused and how the Assamese leadership was determined to impose Assamese language and culture upon them. The leaders urged to the Prime Minister to create a separate state comprising the Mikir Hills, North Cachar Hills and neighbouring tribal areas in Assam. Similar memoranda were submitted to the Prime Minister in the years 1980, 1982, and 1987.

Meanwhile, Assam movement, which was initiated in 1979 ended with Assam Agreement that took place in 1985. The participants of this agreement were the Union Home Secretary, the Assam Chief Secretary and representatives of the AASU and AAGSP.

Section III

4.3 Insurgency in Assam since 1985

4.3.1 Emergence of Insurgency

The United Liberation Front of Assam (ULFA), an insurgent group, was formed in 1979 and marked the beginning of insurgency in Assam. The main aim of ULFA was to "liberate Assam through armed struggle from the exploitative attitude of the Central Government towards Assam and establish a sovereign independent Assam." The group remained dormant during the Assam movement; however, it supported Assam movement. The Assam movement was against the illegal migrants. ULFA also raised the similar issue, which gained popularity and acceptability of the common population.[34] During the state assembly election in 1985, leaders of Assam movement formed a political party called Assam Gan Parishad (AGP) to contest the election. They won the elections and came into the power. However, within two years AGP government failed to fulfil the desires of the people. During the same period, ULFA gained support and sympathy from the people for their cause. In 1988, the popularity and public influence of the ULFA amongst the Assamese raised remarkably.[35] They involved in the activities like social reforms. Such as, they put a ban on the consumption of alcohol, which helped them to gain popularity among the women. It is said that, in the late 1980s, the ULFA ran a parallel government in Assam.

AGP government, after coming into power, imposed a new language policy, which made it obligatory to learn Assamese for government services. All Assam Tribal Students' Union (AATSU) along with the non-Assamese firmly opposed this decision taken by government. The problem became more severe when Upendra (Upen) Nath Brahma, after signing an agreement, made a demand for the implementation of the clause 10 stated that "the existing law would be strictly enforced to prevent illegal occupation of tribal belts and blocks and those occupying tribal land would be evicted."[36] However, the leadership took rigid stand on this and other issues, which left no alternatives for Brahma but to cut off connection with AGP government.[37] Allegations had been made that the Congress (I) government at the centre used the Bodo leadership to embarrass the AGP government. Rajiv Gandhi is said to have warned the Chief Minister that unless the government solve the Bodo problem, there would be no alternative for the Union government than to dismiss AGP government and impose President's rule in Assam.[38] Assam Chief Minister Mahanta complained in a press conference that the Research and Analysis Wing (RAW) played an important role by sending arms and explosives to Bodo insurgents to destabilise the AGP government.[39] It is believed that the AGP government failed to fulfil the aspirations of the Assamese. Also, the government could not satisfy Bodos, Karbis and other minorities of the state.

The local Assamese population lost faith in AGP government as it failed to meet the expectations of the people. AGP government was dismissed a month before their term was completed. President rule was implemented till the next election. In June 1991, elections to the assembly were held and Congress (I) government under Hiteshwar Saikia came into power.

During the tenure of AGP government, the young Bodo leaders began to mobilise a large number of Bodos in support of a demand for a separate state.[40] ABSU presented a memorandum to the Chief Minister Prafulla Kumar Mahanta on 1 January 1987 and also to the Governor of Assam and Meghalaya B. N. Singh on 10th January 1987, containing a 92 point charter of demands.[41] Later, they suspended 89 demands of the 92 point charter and decided to fight only for three political demands. They are as follows :

1. Creation of a separate state of Bodoland;

2. Creation of two District Council on the Southern bank of the river Brahmaputra i.e. Neelanchul and Lalung;

3. Inclusion of Boro-Kocharis of Karbi-Anglong into the Sixth Schedule of the Indian Constitution.

The proposed separate state of Bodoland was spread over an area of 25,478 Sq.Kms. with a total population of 77,72,440. The proposed state was supposed to cover ten districts of Assam i.e. Dhubri, Kokhrajhar, Bongaigaon, Barpeta, Nalbari, Kamarup, Darrang, Sonitpur, Lakhimpur and Dhemaji.[42] Along with democratic protests, the movement turned into a radical one with the establishment of the Bodo Security Force (BdSF) and armed wing of ABSU, the Bodo Volunteer Force (BVF) under Prem Singh Brahma as a military chief. They simultaneously began a wide-ranging insurgency campaign marked from the very beginning by struggles between the two Bodo groups.[43] Due to the hostility between these two Bodo groups the movement continued for a long. It is also believed that the reason behind this is that the Rajiv Gandhi government at the centre supported the Bodo movement. The opponent parties later accused the Congress for building up BdSF through

Central Intelligence Agencies as a counter to both ULFA and the AGP. The forum for restoration of civil liberties, in a letter to the Prime Minister, said so as follows :

1. RAW was involved in Bodo agitation, and supplied weapons to them. They were targeting only Assamese and Assam Police, not others.

2. Seema Shastra Bal was giving training to the ABSU extremists.

3. Special Frontier Force was directly involved in conducting bomb attacks in different parts of Northern Assam... 'SFF was a secret agency of the Cabinet Secretariat and its most recruits were Tibetans and Khampas. They were inducted into Assam to help Bodo extremists and they resembled them... Assam police seized large quantities of explosives whose sophisticated variety showed that the source of supply could only be the government'.[44]

With the passage of time the dialogue began between Government of India and ABSU.[45] On 1st May 1990, Upen Brahma - President of ABSU - died. It was a big shock to ABSU. He was succeeded by Sanchuma Khungur (S.K) Bwismauthiary. However, with the return of Congress (I) government under Saikia in the state, he invited Bodo leaders for fresh discussions.[46] During the talks, Bodo leaders made a demand for 4443 villages in nine districts. During some more meetings, another 209 villages with some Bodo population and 1035 villages with no Bodo population as per official records were added in a demand. Later on 20th February 1993, the Bodo Agreement was signed by Chief Minister of Assam Saikia, additional chief secretary of Assam government, ABSU President S. K. Bwiswmauth on the behalf of Bodos and Bodo People Action Committee's (BAPCs) Chairman in the presence of Rajesh Pilot, Union Minister of State for Home.[47] This agreement paved the way for formation of Bodo Autonomous Council (BAC), which covered the area of nearly 2300 sq.kms. in the lower districts of Kokrajhar,

Bongaigaon, Barpeta, Nalbari, Darrang, Mangaldai and Sonitpur. Subsequently, BVF surrendered and the new president of ABSU - Garla Botha Basumatiry - dissolved the BPAC and BVF.[48] S. K. Bwismutiary became the first Chief Executive Member (CEM) and P. S. Bramha as an Executive Member (EM) of BAC. Later, S. K. Bwismutiary quit as CEM over the issue of boundary demarcation of BAC and inclusion of more 515 villages in it. Consequently, P.S. Brahma was appointed as a CEM of BAC without conducting regular election. On 10th December 1993, Assam government issued a notification to settle the boundary demarcation issue. According to this notification, the area spread upto 5,186 sq.kms., which included 2750 villages, but excluded a wide belt of 10 kms. by the side of the Bhutan border and Manas reserved forest. Even though the prime objective for signing the agreement was to bring peace in the area, situation became worse after the signing the agreement. Neither the Bodos nor the non-Bodo tribes were satisfied with this agreement.[49] The BdSF, which was renamed as National Democratic Front of Bodoland (NDFB), did not accept this agreement and sustained their armed rebellion. In 1996, BVF, which was officially dissolved by the accord, re-emerged with a new name 'Bodo Liberation Tiger Front' (BLTF/BLT) under the leadership of Prem Singh Brahma.[50] Consequently, the BLT and the NDFB were engaged in a destructive struggle to gain influence even though they had common interests. While the NDFB was firm on its demand for an independent Bodoland, the BLT was satisfied with its claim for an autonomous Bodoland state within the Indian Union. BLT merely wanted the BAC's rights and jurisdiction to be redefined.[51]

However, with the passage of time, the BLT along with NDFB made a demand of liberation of Bodoland. The insurgents raised the slogan "Liberated Bodoland" is for Bodos only. Since 1994 they followed an action plan to change the ethnic composition of villages within the BAC areas by driving out non-Bodo settlers, including Hindu and Muslim Bengalis from former East Pakistan and Adivasi groups like Santhals, Oraons, Mundas and Rajbansis.[52] The insurgent groups knew that the Bodos in the

BAC dominated areas were not in majority and hence non-Bodos were driven out in order to dominate the region. By slaughtering people, burning houses and grabbing land, Bodo insurgents forced thousands of non-Bodos to run away from their villages and take shelter in the camps set up by the government. It is relevant to mention that Bodo insurgents not only attacked non-Bodos in Bodo-dominated areas but they also attacked non-Bodos who had taken shelter in government camps. For example, in Banbhari relief camp unarmed inmates were killed cruelly. Moreover, in May-June 1996, a Bodo-Santhal riot also resulted in number of killings and dislocation of Santhals. The depth and intensity of this killing was similar to the Nellie slaughter. This, in turn, resulted in significant displacement of the Bodo population from areas where they were a minority.

Apart from the racial wash out, on 27th December 1996 BLT blew up RCC Bridge at Rakholduli in Bongaigaon district and cut off road link between the region and the rest of the country. After this incidence, Bodo insurgents once again took over the movement. As a result, the centre took an initiative to control the situation as requested by the state government. This resulted into a fresh dialogue in New Delhi on 18th September 1997 among the centre, the state and the major Bodo groups. The ABSU and other groups refused to accept the terms of the joint working group, which was set up during the meeting.[53] In the early June 1999 when the NDFB and BLT leaders met on 30th May 1999 and decided to maintain peace by bringing to an end the clashes between their groups. The BLT remained active in the districts of Kokrajhar, Bongaigaon, Nalbari, Barpeta, Goalpara, Kamrup, Darrang and Dhemaji until cease-fire agreement was signed with Indian government on 29th March 2000. Subsequently, the BLTF was involved in political negotiations with governments both the State and the Central.[54] Eventually, the BAC was dissolved on 20th April 2000 and a 'monitoring committee' of Members of Legislative Assembly (MLAs) had been installed.[55] It is believed that the BLTF had dissolved itself and its leaders had agreed to resolve the issue within the framework of the Indian Constitution. Therefore, on 10th February 2003, Hagrama

Basumatary, chairman of BLT signed a tripartite agreement with the Central Government (R. C. A. Jain, Secretary, Border Management, MHA) and State Government (P. K. Dutta, Chief Secretary) to end up a decade long insurgency. The Memorandum of Settlement (MoS) was signed in the presence of Deputy Prime Minister L. K. Advani, Chief Minister Tarun Gogoi, and the two MoS in the MHA were also signed in the presence of I. D. Swami and Harin Pathak.[56] Accordingly, the constitutional amendment had been made to include Bodoland Territorial Council (BTC) in the Sixth Schedule. The Sixth Schedule mentions special provisions for only the hill areas in the state of Assam, Meghalaya, Manipur and Mizoram. The Government of Assam issued the notification to authorise the constitution of BTC after nine months. The notification was delayed, especially because of controversial issue of demarcation of the council's territory. The final hurdle was cleared on 31st October 2003 when government agreed to include 25 more villages in the BTC territory, taking the total number of villages to 3108.[57] *(See map 4.2),* An outcome of MoS is as below:

1. The University;
2. Inclusion of Bodo language in the Eighth Schedule;
3. Besides Kokrajhar, three new districts of Udalguri, Baska, and Chirang;
4. More autonomy to the proposed Bodoland Territorial Area District (BTAD) under the sixth schedule;[58]
5. Annual allocation of Rs 100 crore.[59]

Hagrama Mahilary, the former Commander-in-Chief, BLTF, sworn in as the Chief Executive Member (CEM) of the Bodoland Territorial Council in the first week of December 2003. In the second week of December 2003, 2600 cadres of the Bodo Liberation Tiger Force (BLTF) surrendered at Kokrajhar. The former members of the non-operational BLTF pledged to uphold the constitution and sovereignty and integrity of India.

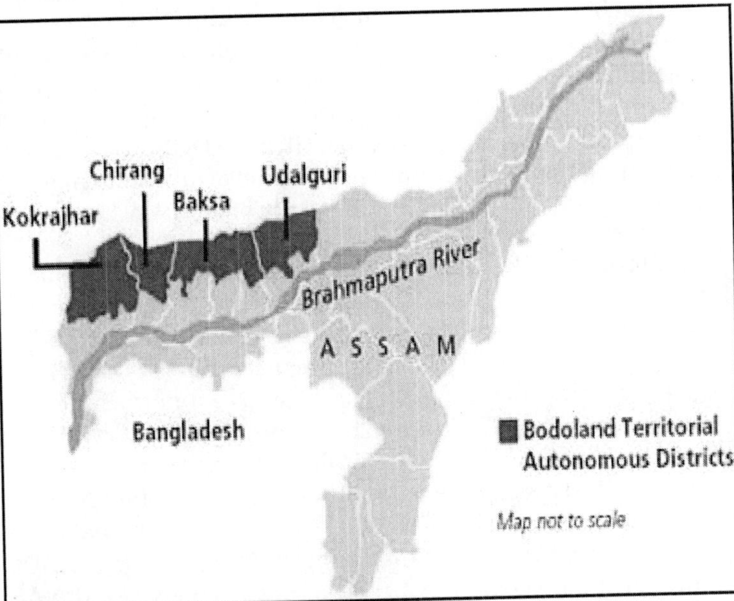

Source: available online https://cvinodscribes.files.wordpress.com/2012/11/assam- bodoland.jpg, accessed on 11.2.15

Map 4.2: Showing Bodoland Territorial Autonomous Council.

NDFB opposed the BTC and declared to continue to fight for a sovereign Bodo state.[60] In 2005, the leaders of NDFB expressed their readiness to give up their demand of a 'Sovereign Bodoland' and to settle their grievances within the framework of the Constitution of India. Their demand now is for a separate Bodoland state, which was being supported by Hangrama Mahilary, Chief of the BTC, according to whom the BTC could be scrapped if the NDFB would have agreed for a separate state. In 2007, Mahilary had also said publicly that the Bodos must get a separate state within the next two decades.[61] However, in 2008, 2012 and 2014 the violence exploded twice within BTC between the Bodos and Muslims. The violence erupted in 2012 because All Bodo Minority Student Union demanded more representation in BTC.

Simultaneously, when Bodo representatives has been engaged in struggling for the Bodoland, another ethnic group viz. Karbis and Dimasa from Assam asking their share in the state. On 17th May 1986,[62] the Autonomous State Demand Committee (ASDC) was formed under the CPI (ML) leadership due to the demand for a separate state was put up by Karbis. The Autonomous Demand Committee (ADC) headed a strong mass movement demanding the creation of an autonomous state under Article 244 (A) of the Constitution.

Moreover, the movement became more loud in the post-reorganisation of Assam when Karbi Student Association (KSA) joined with the ASDC. Besides the constitutional path, the formation of Dimasa National Security Force (DNSF) in the early nineties took a violent path to give a new dimension to the movement. DNSF wanted to restore the lost glory of Dimasa kingdom, which was the capital at Dimapur in old times. In early 1991, the students of North Cachar Hills set up All Dimasa Student Organisation (ADSO). They wanted Dimaland and reportedly set up by Assam Congress to oppose the ASDC".[63] Though the movement was active in both districts, the ASDC was more active and influential in Karbi Anglong district. But more importantly, the demand, though similar, has different consequences for two districts. As a result, on 1st April 1995, a Memorandum of Understanding (MoU) was signed between Chief Minister Saikia and the leaders of ASDC (from both districts), KSA, Dimasa Student Union and North Cachar Hills Student Federation at New Delhi. Accordingly, the ASDC agreed to accept enhanced powers more than those given in the Sixth Schedule. Moreover, ASDC gave up its insistence on the creation of sub-state, associate State, or autonomous state under Article 244-A of the constitution.[64] These two ADCs were not only granted vast powers but they were also upgraded as "Autonomous Councils". However, this step could not satisfy the ADC and it revived its demand.[65]

According to ASDC, the inadequacies of the ADCs and the Assamese machinations and manipulations were related to the absence of the job opportunities and lack of economic development. So they made a demand for a sub-state in spite of the opposition by the smaller tribes and minorities. Karbis and

Dimasas demanded two states for both districts. Their demand for statehood gathered strength as expressed by the United Peoples' Democratic Solidarity (UPDS) of the Karbis and the Dima Halam Daogah (DHD) of Dimasa respectively.[66] The proposed Karbi state included areas of present Karbi Anglong and North Cachar Hills, adjacent Karbi-dominated areas of Nagaon, Morigaon and Kamrup districts of Assam and Ri-Bhoi district of Meghalaya. The DHD envisioned Dimarji as a state that would comprise the Dimasa inhabited areas of Karbi Anglong and North Cachar, Nowgaon districts and parts of Dimapur district of Nagaland.[67] This implied that the Karbi community continued to remain in the North Cachar hills. Similarly, some Dimasa communities were included in Karbi Anglong district. In the years 2002 and 2003, UPDS and DHD had entered in a ceasefire agreement with the Indian government. After the ceasefire agreement between UPDS and the centre in 2003, there was split in UPDS and a group of UPDS began to oppose the peace talks. The anti-talk group renamed itself as the 'Karbi Longri National Liberation Front' (KLNLF). On the other hand, other ethnic groups like Hamars in North Cachar hills district and Kuki in Karbi Anglong district were not satisfied with the developments that took place in these two hill districts. They formed a group to safeguard their interest. Hence, after the ceasefire agreement, conflict continued between the DHD and Hamar Peoples' Conference (HPC) in North Cachar hills district and UPDS and KRA in Karbi Anglong district.

4.3.2 Islamic Militancy

After 1985, the nature of insurgency in Assam was changed due to the emergence of religious fundamentalist attitude in the state. There were seventeen Muslim fundamentalist groups active in state. These groups are as follows :

1. Muslim United Liberation Front of Assam (MULFA);

2. Muslim United Liberation Tigers of Assam (MULTA);

3. Islamic Liberation Army of Assam (ILAA);

4. United Muslim Liberation Front of Assam (UMFLA);
5. People's Liberation Front (PLF);
6. Muslim Volunteer Force (MVF);
7. Adam Sena (AS);
8. Muslim Security Force (MSF);
9. Muslim Security Council of Assam (MSCA);
10. United Liberation Militia of Assam (ULMA);
11. Islamic Security Force of India (ISFI);
12. Islamic Sevak Sangh (ISS);
13. Student Islamic Organisation (SIO);
14. Student's Islamic Movement of India (SIMI);
15. United Reformation Protest of Assam (URPA);
16. Harkat-ul-Jihad-al-Islami of Bangladesh (HuJI);
17. Harkat-ul-Mujahiddeen of Pakistan (HuM) etc.

Almost all these organisations came into existence as a result of a fear that the administration was not aware of the problems of the Muslim community. The incidents that are generally quoted in this context are :

1. The deletion of the names of thousands of Muslims from the voters list;
2. The attacks on Muslims by the Bodos in 1994, 1995 and 1996 in order to discourage them from occupying the Char areas;
3. Violence in Muslim dominated areas during the elections.[68]

These insurgent organisations did not declare their aims and objectives like the ethnic insurgent outfits such as the ULFA and the NDFB. However, a few have stated their goals about the establishment of separate Islamic homelands.[69] Some of the demands of these organisations were valid to a certain extent. For example, the demands of MULTA in Assam included -

1. Thirty per cent reservation in education and employment for Muslims;

2. Establishment of Muslim Court in Assam;

3. Reservation of seats in Legislative Assembly for the Muslims of the Barak Valley.[70]

However, ostensibly, these Muslim organisations claim to safeguard the interest of the Muslims in Assam, their long-term aim is to destabilise Assam, Northeast region and then India. In this context, it is relevant to mention that the objectives of these organisations, as analysed by the intelligence, are two pronged as below :

1. To spread the fundamentalism in Muslim Community for Pan-Islamisation of the region.

2. To stimulate serious political and religious riots in the area, compelling the government to send the SF, especially Indian Army, to control the situation.[71]

The very purpose of Muslim organisations is to create anti-army and anti-India sentiment among the people by compelling army to suppress the riots and thus giving further scope for creating disorder and unfriendliness in Assam. Moreover, their intention is also to weaken India's anti-terrorism capability in Jammu and Kashmir and to give a greater opportunity to Pak-trained foreign immigrants to carry out their activities to separate the valley from India.[72] Various reports state that jihadi organisations such as Pakistani-based L-e-T and Bangladesh based Harkat-ul-Jehad-al-Islami (HuJI) and Jamma'atul

Mujahideen (JuM) have made significant inroads in the state. In addition to this, the commander of the Army's 107 Mountain Brigade, Brig. Kanwaljit Singh has given the alert that the LeT, HuJI and JuM have began to operate in certain minority areas of lower Assam,[73] particularly where suspected migrants from Bangladesh have an ample presence. Reports of intelligence agencies indicate that almost all these MFO's, operating in Assam, are working for a common cause. They have approached several Muslim countries and organisations like OIC, with an active involvement and also asked help from the ISI to achieve their aims. Among the fundamentalist organisations Harkat-ul- Mujahideen (HuM) and Harkat-ul-Jehad (HuJ) are the most passionate in their ideology and functioning. These organisations are the most dangerous and cruel, which have been directly raised as they are, by the ISI.[74]

4.4 Profile of Insurgent Groups

Various insurgent groups and organisations have emerged and are active in Assam due to the fear of imposition of cultural and geographical imperialism and domination as well as increasing levels of economic and political competition. This has resulted in frequent violence in the state among many ethnic groups. Partly, these factors are also responsible for the rise of different insurgent outfits in the state. The insurgent outfits began to grow in state on the ground of ethnicity, religious and cultural split. The cultures of violence propagated by the ULFA and the Bodo outfits have set up a pattern for a number of copycat insurgents groups in the Northeast region. As many as 34 insurgent groups have been operating in the state. Amongst all the groups, the United Liberation Front of Assam (ULFA), the National Democratic Front of Bodoland (NDFB), United People's Democratic Solidarity (UPDS), Dima Halim Daoga (DHD), Muslim United Liberation Tigers of Assam (MULTA) and Muslim United Liberation Front of Assam (MLUFA) are the major insurgent groups. The ULFA operates mainly in the upper Assam whereas NDFB operates in the Bodo-areas of North and North West river of Brahmaputra. The UPDS/DHD dominates the Karbi-Anglong and North Cachar hill districts.

Islamic fundamentalist groups are active in the Muslim-dominated area of Assam.[75] Brief profiles of major insurgent groups have been given below :

4.4.1 United Liberation Front of Assam (ULFA)

ULFA was formed on April 7, 1979 in a meeting at Rang Ghar, the famous Amphi-theatre of the Ahom royalty, at Sibsagar. ULFA remained inactive till 1986, except recruitment of cadres during late 1983 to early 1984. The ULFA leadership thoroughly mobilised recruits from different parts of Assam and continued sending fresh batches of trainees to the NSCN camp.[76] The outfit was active in the late 1980's and early 1990's. They operated freely till the security forces initiated-counter-insurgency operations in Assam. Continued operations against ULFA by the Security Forces (SFs) since December 1990 have restricted the arms of this organisation. K. Hrishikeshan, in his article[77] "Assam Agony: The ULFA and Obstacles to Conflict Resolution", writes -"AGP government was sympathetic to the ULFA; the latter had a free run in the state. The outfit utilised this period for massive fund collection and recruitment. It can, thus be seen that while the Congress party's greed for power at any cost thrust an untimely election on the Assamese and thus helped the ULFA to enhance its popularity at a crucial formative stage, the support given to this outfit by the first AGP government helped it improve its fortunes and consolidate its position. Political parties in Assam, irrespective of their ideologies and public statements, have thus contributed significantly to the birth and subsequent dramatic growth of ULFA."

ULFA has given selective and conditional support to different political parties and candidates. It has restricted the activities of the target party during election campaigns to weaken its poll prospects. Thus, the outfit manages to increase the comparative advantage of its favoured political party candidates.[78] In return, the succeeding governments have offered their support to ULFA for their own interest. The outfit created a terror in the mind of the people of the state and also outside of the state as they frequently carried out the troublesome activities like cutting off communications in the state, hitting various economic targets, kidnapping prominent businessmen for payoff. ULFA began to kill civilians and government officials to create psycho fear among the people and government officials in the state.[79]

In 1986, ULFA established contacts for the first time with the United National Socialist Council of Nagaland (NSCN) and the Kachin Independent Army (KIA) of Myanmar for organising training camps and mobilising arms. When KIA camps were raided,[80] the outfit came under pressure to shift its base. Subsequently, the outfit shifted its training camps to Bangladesh. Since 1989, its training camps have been functioning from the Bangladeshi soil. Documents seized from the outfit and interrogations of some arrested cadres of ULFA indicate that the Defence Forces Intelligence (DFI) of Bangladesh had given training to cadres of outfit in Sylhet district of Bangladesh.[81] However, after 1995, Bangladesh government attacked the training camps of ULFA in Bangladesh. As a result, the outfit shifted its several camps to the forest areas of Southern Bhutan.[82] However, in December 2003, Royal Bhutanese Army's (RBA) military operation 'All Clear' extricated the training camps of ULFA. Recently, Bangladesh government has taken a strong action against the outfit, which has enforced this organisation to shift their bases. At present, the outfit has set up a base which has been established by ULFA's military chief Paresh Baruah, in China's Yunnan province.[83]

Over the years, ULFA has killed a large of number of innocent people. Some of the major assassinations done by the outfit include that of Surendra Paul in May 1990, the brother of businessman Lord Swaraj Paul. In 1991, a Russian engineer was kidnapped along with others, who were killed. In 1997, Sanjay Ghosh, a social activist and a relative of high-ranking Indian diplomat was kidnapped and killed.[84] In the same year, an unsuccessful assassination attempt was made to kill AGP Chief Minister Prafulla Kumar Mahanta. In 2000, Nagen Sharma, a senior officer, was assassinated by the outfit.

On 23rd October 2000, ULFA attacked Hindi-speaking Non-Assamese people in Tinsukia and Dibrugarh districts.[85] In another incident on 27th October 2000, nine people were slaughtered in Nalbari district.[86] On 16th November 2000, ten people of non-Assamese origin were killed in Sibsagar district at the time when a parliamentary team of the Bhartiya Janata Party (BJP) was on tour to monitor the law and order situation in the state.[87] On 7th December 2000, near Sadiya ULFA cadres killed 28 Hindi-speaking petty traders and farm workers who had come from Bihar.[88] In 2003, the AASU protested against the recruitment of Biharis in the Northeast Frontier Railways, which further led to violence against the Biharis. When the AASU protested recruitment of the candidates from Bihar in the North Frontier Railway, ULFA went one step ahead to attack and drive out the domiciled Biharis in Upper Assam.[89] In the same year, the ULFA killed many innocent Biharis in Assam. They executed this slaughter as a revenge of molestation and raping of Assami girls when they were travelling in a train in Bihar. This incident created anti-Bihari sentiment in Assam. Moreover, ULFA continued to make infrequent attack on government security forces, particularly, coinciding with the important dates of calendar for nearly two and half decades. The outfit attacked symbols of government authorities like railway stations, rail tracks, oil pipelines, police stations on and around such important dates.[90] The ULFA intentionally made these attacks to create terror in the state instead of following strategy of attacking the selected targets in the state. In the Dhemaji bomb attack on Independence Day, nineteen people were killed, while most of them were school children.[91] According to security agencies, ULFA executed these terrorism on account of extreme despair to raise the total of deaths in attacks carried out by its cadres.[92] The outfit killed more than one hundred persons in Tinsukia, Dibrugarh, Dhimaji, Shibsagar, Golaghat, Kokrajhar districts in the series of attack in the month of January 2007.[93] AASU advisor Dr Samujjal Bhattacharya says, "The outfit is attacking and driving away the Bihari and other Hindi-speaking people so that their space can be taken by Bangladeshi infiltrators".[94] They also threatened government officials and ruling party leaders by making attacks on them in response to the counter-insurgency operations being carried out by the security forces in the State.

4.4.2 National Democratic Front of Bodoland (NDFB)

The NDFB was originally established as the Bodo Security Force (BdSF) under the leadership of Ransaigra Nabla alias Ranjan Daimary. Later on 3rd October 1986, the outfit changed its name to National Democratic Front of Bodoland (NDFB). However, in spite of the support given to the Bodo people by NDFB, it bitterly opposed another Bodo insurgent outfit the Bodo Liberation Tiger (BLT). NDFB killed several BLT leaders and the members of civil society organisations having sympathy with the BLT. In the month of December 2003, Royal Bhutanese Army destroyed twelve camps of the NDFB located in Bhutan. This attack seriously impacted on the capability of the outfit to carry on its insurgent activities. After the ceasefire with the government, NDFB cadres were supposed to stay in three selected camps but only a few are currently staying in the camp.[95] Prior to declaration of ceasefire with security forces, the outfit also had its camps in Myanmar and Bangladesh. Moreover, there are several temporary camps at different locations in Arunachal Pradesh and in the Garo Hills region of Meghalaya.[96]

Since its establishment, the NDFB has remained engaged in violent activities. It was also indulged in a conflict with rival outfit BLT. The severe struggles between these outfits have caused a heavy loss of human life. In the year 1994 and onwards, NDFB has taken up ethnic cleansing programme in BAC area to wipe out non-Bodos. Their initial target were Muslims, however, Hindu settlers of East Bengal origin also became victims.

The NDFB was also involved in Bodo-Santhal riots. On 13th June 1998, Surojit Mitra who was professionally lawyer was shot dead by the outfit.[97] In early 2000, the NDFB attacked non-Bodos settlements, especially Adivasis,[98] with an intention of radical cleansing of the settlers. On 14th July & 17th October 2007, the outfit had killed nine Non-Bodos in a relief camp at the forest village near Kokrajhar and twenty one were shot dead in Kokrajhar district.[99] After the NDFB entered into the ceasefire agreement with the government, the anti-talk group under the leadership of Ranjan Daimary had carried out nine serial explosions. In these blasts, about a hundred people and more than five hundred people were injured.

4.4.3 Dima Halim Daogah (DHD)

Dima Halong Daogah (DHD) is a by-product of the former Dimasa National Security Force (DNSF). Dimasa tribe is mainly found in Dimasa-dominated areas of the North Cachar Hills and Karbi Anglong districts of Assam and in some parts of Dimapur district of Nagaland. All the cadres of DNSF had surrendered in 1995, except its self styled Commander-in-Chief Jewel Garlossa, who subsequently initiated the DHD. On the ceasefire issue, some scholars opine that Jewel Garlossa left the outfit; however, some scholars say that he was exiled on the charges of anti-DHD activity. On 24th June 2004, Pranab Nunisa, the former Commander-in-Chief of the outfit and the head of the outfit's armed wing the Dima National Army, took over the command of DHD.[100] Nunisa, in a press statement, said that Garlossa has already formed a separate outfit on 31st March 2003, named 'Black Widows', which also has a private army. The outfit mostly operates in Cachar, NC Hills, Karbi Anglong and Nagaon districts of Assam. It also has a strong presence in the Dimasa-dominated Dhansiri area of Karbi Anglong districts.[101]

The frequent armed attacks carried out by the DHD include sudden attacks on police forces, other tribes and businessmen with automatic weapons, which resulted in a large number of fatalities. The outfit has been fighting against other insurgent groups such as UPDS to establish their supremacy in the region.[102] Moreover, outfit has also reportedly engaged in the conflict with Hamars Peoples' Conference after entered into the ceasefire agreement.

4.4.4 United People's Democratic Solidarity (UPDS)

The United People's Democratic Solidarity (UPDS) was formed in the month of March 1999, with the merger of two insurgents groups - the Karbi National Volunteers (KNV) and Karbi People's Front (KPF) - of Karbi Anglong district in Assam. Due to the differences in the outfit, there are two groups: Pro-talk and Anti-talk. In May 2004, the outfit (Anti-talk) renamed itself as the Karbi Longri North Cachar Hills Liberation Front (KLNLF), and its armed wing as Karbi Long NC Hills Peoples' Resistance Force (KNPR).[103]

By joining hands with ULFA, the outfit planned to target the areas of non-Assamese Hindi speaking people. This isolated area is referred to as 'Hindi Belts'.[104] Hence, the main activities of the outfits are against the non-Karbi settlers including Biharis, Bengalis and Nepalese. The outfit has attempted to take advantage of the anger of the Karbi tribal population against the economic influence enjoyed by the Biharis and other outsiders. The outfit has also launched operations targeting the Kuki population residing primarily in Diphu sub-division.

4.4.5 Financial Sources of the above mentioned Insurgent Outfits

The main source of income of these outfits is from extortion, mainly from businessmen, politicians, government employees, industrialists and tea companies.[105] In the case of ULFA, at the initial stages of its growth, an extortion served a dual purpose i.e. collection of a huge amount of funds and, ironically, earning the goodwill of the people. This was achieved by targeting only those individuals and groups who were known to have accumulated wealth by corrupt and illegal means. In the initial period, the ULFA, through this kind of extortion, could collect huge amounts and it also obtained an image like Robin Hood. However, during the following times, the hunger of funds of the outfit went on increasing. As a result, ULFA cadres began to effect bank robberies and other criminal activities for this purpose. Even innocent and honest people were targeted. Moreover, the outfit is actively involved in drug trafficking to generate their funds. All these anti-social and criminal activities of the outfit have resulted in losing its image as a group of revolutionaries who could do nothing wrong in the eyes of a large section of the population in the state.

On the other hand, from the very beginning, the NDFB followed the way of extortion to acquire funds for purchase of arms and ammunition for the outfit. The NDFB has regularly extorted the tea companies in Assam, especially in the districts of Darrang and Sonitpur. According to seized 'Summarised Financial Reports' of the outfit, individuals and corporate firms have been listed along with government departments as donors.[106] According to sources, it is evident from the reports that the majority of the donors were forced to pay to NDFB. Vijendra Singh Jafa, the then Chief Secretary of Assam, said, "We have in our possession audited accounts of the outlawed NDFB, which shows that the group (William Son Magor) has been paying money to the outfit".[107] Seized 'Summarised Financial Report' of tea companies also reveals a link between the NDFB and various government departments who have unknowingly channelled huge funds to the outfit. The outfit had received over Rs 96 lakhs from just a single source – the Shrirampur Octori check post located at Assam West border. This particular check post, identified as the most crucial leakage point for the funds, has officials in the departments of sales tax, forest and motor vehicle departments designated on a regular basis. Consequently, funds from all these three departments have flowed into the outfit treasury. The report shows that from 1st August 1994 to 28th February 1996, the NDFB had received Rs. 96.31 lakhs from these three departments through this check post.[108] Moreover, besides corporate firms, and government departments, the NDFB has extorted the non-Bodo families in various parts of Bongaigaon and Kokhrajhar districts. Civilians and business establishments are given regular notices for payment of tax and donations to the outfit. The army, operating in the districts of Kokrajhar and Bongaigaon of lower Assam, has claimed that the NDFB is involved in illegal cutting of trees. They also collect taxes from timber contractors involved in illegal business at the rate of Rs 20,000 per Truck. Small timber merchants also pay at the rate of Rs 50 to Rs 100 per handcart of timber. Those who failed to pay were attacked by the outfit. In July 2000, the Chief Minister of Assam alleged that the NDFB along with the ULFA were channelling funds through the

"Bhutanese diplomatic pouch" to their leaders based in Southeast Asian Capitals.

DHD, even after entering into the cease-fire agreement with the government, has continued its illegal activities to generate funds.[109] The DHD also raises funds from illegal timber trade. This group has also received financial assistance from rich people of Dimasas settled in various places of Assam.[110] The anti-talk group of UPDS generates a considerable amount for revenue by targeting the ginger producing Kukis in the Singhason Hills area. The outfit also extorts non-Karbi traders to collect funds.

4.4.6 Nexus Summary

For better results, various insurgent outfits in the state have joined hands together against the state. In fact, these insurgent outfits in the state have formed three types of linkages. These are -

1. Between any two outfits cutting across the commanding area;
2. Amongst outfits operating within the commanding area;
3. Broad fronts consisting of insurgent outfits operating in different areas.

As a result, alliances among outfits often involve arms supply, financial support and logistical assistance. These outfits have at one time or other have/had reached close understanding among them *(See Table 4.4)*.

It is clear from Table 4.4 that the NSCN-IM was the only outfit in the region that provided early assistance to the insurgent outfits in the state. Moreover, a noteworthy trend has been developed among these outfits i.e. though they have different agenda, they have accompanied in greater cooperation and coordination. For example, ULFA, who initially acted against illegal migrants, has joined hands with MULTA to carry out joint operations in the areas dominated by immigrants who are

Table 4.1 : Nexus among Outfits

ULFA	Kachin Independent Army (KIA), National Democratic Front of Bodoland (NDFB), National Socialist Council of Nagaland (IM) (ULFA shared a fraternal relationship with the NSCN (IM) till 2001. However due to the over emphasis of the Naga outfit on inclusion of areas within Assam in its proposed Nagalim such ties have been disrupted. All Tripura Tiger Force (ATTF), Muslim United Liberation Front of Assam (MULFA), Karbi Longri North Cachar Hills (KLNLF), Kamatpur Liberation Organisation (KLO) Harkat – ul –Jihad – al – Islami of Bangladesh (HuJI) and Harkat – ul – Mujahiddeen (HuM) of Pakistan.
NDFB	ULFA, NSCN (IM) and (K), Kamatpur Liberation Organization (KLO), Achik National Volunteers Council (ANVC)
DHD	NSCN (IM), NDFB
UPDS	United National Liberation Front (UNLF), Peoples Liberation Army (PLA), NSCN (IM), NDFB, ULFA

mostly Indian citizens. In fact, the supply of arms and weapons is being made to ULFA from MULTA and MULFA through Bangladesh.[111]

4.4.7 Muslim Fundamentalist Organisations (MFOs)

Most of the Muslim Fundamentalist Organisations were formed in 1990s and in the early 2000.[112] Most of these MFOs have established foreign linkages with organisations such as the HuM. The MULTA has a strong link with ISI of Pakistan. The MULTA has also close connections with Sunni radical group, Sipahi-i-Sahab Pakistan (SSP).[113] Moreover, almost all the MFOs have defined their objectives and goals, only the MULTA and the HuM have actually carried out religious propaganda and they have been assisting one another to achieve their goals.[114] The establishment of the Bangladesh Islamic Manch (BIM)[115] in Bangladesh, which has the MULTA as an important member, could be a forerunner to unite all of the MFOs in the region. Such unification has already taken place with MULTA representing the MFOs in a statement along with the lines of BIM.[116]

4.4.8 Muslim United Liberation Tigers of Assam (MULTA)

The main aim of the MULTA is to protect the interest of the Muslims in Assam, especially the illegal migrant Muslims from Bangladesh who continue to be its main support, and to set up their own region for Muslims in Assam. The outfit is struggling to create a separate homeland for Muslims in the districts of Nagaon, Dhubri, Kamrap, Karimganj and Hailakandi in Assam.[117]

The MULTA was established in the month of August 1996. It seeks to mobilise the Muslim youth to fight for the rights and powers of Muslims in Assam. The agenda of the outfit is to establish a university for Islamic studies; ensure reservation of thirty per cent of jobs in central and state government services; check the deletion of names of Muslims from the voter lists; provide full protection to the lives and properties of Muslims;

and ensure the allotment of adequate funds for the maintenance of Madrassas and Mosques.[118] At the religious level, the MULTA wants to establish a chain of Islamic courts in Assam to dispense justice in accordance with doctrine of Shariat.

On the other hand, according to Indian intelligence report, a group of thirteen outfit cadres were trained by the ISI in Bangalmora in North Lakhimpur district of Assam. Moreover, during the late 1999 and the early 2000, a joint group of MULTA and MULFA consisting 160 cadres underwent three months' training at Chatak and Jayantipur in Bangladesh under the supervision of an ISI Major Nizamuddin Shah and Captain Iqbal Ali.[119] The report has also indicated that al–Qaeda is giving training to the cadres of MULTA and MULFA in Bangladesh.[120] In addition to this, outfit cadres travel to Bangladesh and Pakistan for the purpose of training. For example, a news report had stated that a team of twenty eight men of the outfit, led by its Second Lieutenant Abdul Jalil, had entered Assam after completing a three months arms training course.[121]

4.4.9 Muslim United Liberation Front of Assam (MULFA)/Muslim Liberation Army (MLA)

The major objective of the MULFA is to establish a separate Muslim State. Besides this, it demands thirty per cent reservation for Muslims in government services and educational institutions and protection and preservation of Muslim Personal Law. Muslim United Liberation Front of Assam (MULFA) was formed in the year 1994.[122] In 2000, a few outfit cadres were received training in Bangladesh. In April 2000, some of them were selected for a six-month guerrilla course under a Taliban instruction camp in Peshawar.[123] In January 2002, a few outfit cadres had gone to Lamuchari Rohingya training camp under Naikhingchari PS, district in Bandarban for arms training, according to an agreement between the Rohingya insurgents and the MULFA.[124] The main activities of these outfits are extortions, murders, abductions and illegal arms manufacture and trade of arms. These outfits, according to clear instructions from ISI, also have plans to create communal disturbances in the state. However, the outfits, in comparison with the ULFA or the NDFB, are quiet militant organisations. Their intention is not to take on the Indian security forces, but to expand their bases as quietly as possible without attracting attention.[125]

4.4.10 Financial Source

Extortion and illegal sale of weapons are the sources of finance of these outfits. Moreover, MULTA, MULFA and most of the MFOs are provided the funds by trusts and fronts which are the channels for money from the ISI, al-Qaeda and other such international networks with coordinators in Saudi Arabia, Iraq, Iran, Sudan, Yemen, Indonesia, Malaysia and Singapore.[126]

Section IV

4.5 Foreign Support

Although, the country like Pakistan which do not share the border with the Northeast region and particularly Assam, the Pakistan's Inter Service Intelligence (ISI) is a prominent agency aiding and assisting to insurgent outfits of the Northeast region and particularly Assam. The involvement of Pakistan in Northeast region of India goes back to the early 1960s. In 1968, the former Prime Minister of Pakistan, Late Z. A. Bhutto, wrote about the geo-political aims of Pakistan in his book, "*The Myth of Independence*" wherein he writes "that it would be wrong to think that Kashmir is the only dispute that divides India and Pakistan, though undoubtedly the most significant one, at least is nearly as important as the Kashmir dispute is that of Assam and some districts of India adjacent to East Pakistan. To these East Pakistan have very good claims, which should not have to remain quiescent."[127] However, the loss of earlier East Pakistan was a big shock to the military establishment of Pakistan. It resulted into a loss of foothold in India's Northeast region, where Pakistan want to motivate and arm insurgent outfits in the Northeast region with the help of China and Myanmar. While initially, till the Awami League under Bangabandhu, Sheikh Mujibur Rehman was in power, there was no scope to re-establish this foothold. However, after his assassination, ISI of Pakistan got an opportunity to make a foothold in Bangladesh when Bangladesh National Party's Major General Ziaur Rehman came in power.[128] On 7th August 1999, the Assam police claimed to have arrested four hardcore ISI functionaries in Guwahati.[129] It was disclosed by them that ISI had plans to train 10,000 people in Assam for jihad to liberate Assam and establish an Islamic country comprising the territory of the state and certain other parts of India.[130]

There are numbers of evidences available to prove this fact. According to the Indian Army operating in Assam, the ULFA was involved in the passing of information to the ISI. The ULFA was allegedly pressured by the ISI to make anti-Indian statements, primarily supporting the liberation of Kashmir.[131] It has also been reported that the genocide was perpetrated by the ULFA during the last months of the year 2000 when they began to systematically target Hindi-speaking Assamese, which was planned by the ISI. Intelligence reports have suggested that the members of Bangladesh-based Jamaat-e-Islami's Student Islamic Chhatra Shibir, operated along with the ULFA to carry out the acts of terror.[132] The reports of the Ministry of Home Affairs are testimonials to this fact. In February 2000, the Ministry of Home Affairs (MHA), in a booklet 'Bleeding Assam' accused Pakistan and ISI of giving training to the North-east insurgents in guerrilla warfare and rocket launching.[133] Unfortunately, in the state, outfits like ULFA and NDFB are substantially influenced by external anti-India elements like the ISI and the HuJI. According to various reports, the ULFA – ISI nexus began in the early 1990s. The NDFB also followed the same way like ULFA. In due course of time, this alliance grew rapidly. For the ISI and the HuJI combined, the ULFA and NDFB are trusted allies to promote random violence in the region and the state. The ISI, an active network in Bangladesh, has been supplying sophisticated weaponry, tactical advice and imparting guerrilla training to the insurgents from the state. Also, the ISI network in the state has continued recruiting cadres from among the local Muslim youth, who were sent to the camps in Pakistan for arm and religious training. In 2001, the Assam police arrested 34 of Harkat- ul-Mujahiddeen (HuM) recruiting cadres.[134] Moreover, some of the madrassas (Seminaries) in Assam have come under the influence of ISI.[135] Another aspect of the ISI related to madrassas in Assam is that ULFA insurgents are often given shelter in such seminaries. Thus, ISI is taking disadvantage of the official hesitation and public sensitivity when security forces raid on these religious places.[136]

Thus, the successive reports of Union Home Ministry indicate that there is increase in the influence of Islamic fundamentalists and insurgent groups in Assam, which receive support from Pakistan and Bangladesh. The ISI has developed the strong connection with ULFA and its main leaders. They were given an intensive training in Pakistani military camp in Peshawar near the Afghan border.[137] This training included insurgent tactics, explosives and bombing strategies, intelligence, disinformation and propaganda. The ISI, Pakistani soldiers and Mujahideen in the Afghanistan–Pakistan border areas formed and trained a volcano unit of the Assamese outfit, which is specialised in explosives.[138]

The top leader of ULFA was reportedly taken to camp on the Pakistan-Afghanistan border, where he not only received assurance of military help in the form of arms and logistical support but also an assurance of co-operation and logistical support of all international organisations having loyalty to Bin Laden, including International Jehad Council, the Tehrik–ul-Jehad, Harkat–ul–Jehadi–e–Islami (HuJI), apart from the Al-Qaeda. Pakistan has facilitated the visits of Paresh Baruah and other ULFA leaders to Singapore, Thailand and other countries. Similarly, Pakistan has also created a channel for the transfer of funds and arms. Several Madarassas (seminaries) and mosques, which are sponsored by the ISI in the Sylhet and Cox's Bazaar areas, are being used to store and transfer arms procured by the ULFA from Thailand and Myanmar. The ISI has enabled ULFA to buy arms in Cambodia. The hard currency required for payment of such purchase routed through Nepal. Besides this tactical support, some children of top ULFA leaders were reportedly studying in the USA and Canada under ISI protection. Reports indicate that the ULFA's mouthpiece, ULFA's website and newsletter Swadhinta also known as 'Freedom' receive editorial support from ISI agents in Pakistan.[139] The arrest of Anup Chetia in Bangladesh in 1997 as well as the surrender of the prominent ULFA cadre, "Captain" Lohit Deuri (2000) had disclosed the hidden participation of the ISI. Deuri has publicly admitted that ULFA had received funds from various ISI agents and had reached an agreement with Chinese army officials through the ISI for arm supplies.[140] It is relevant to mention that like Pakistan's ISI, ULFA was in close contact with China especially in the 1990s. In 1993, some ULFA cadres had reportedly went over to China by way of Bhutan to negotiate the purchase of light weapons, which might have been delivered by a Chinese traveller of the Bangladesh coast (Cox Bazaar) in early 1995.

Similarly, the delivery of arms, under a contract negotiated in 1997, took place two years later in one of the ULFA camps in Bhutan.[141] In spite of this limited role, Chinese strategist asked Beijing to support ULFA to make Assam independent from India.[142]

It has also been reported that at one point of time, the Pakistani High Commission in Bangladesh's capital Dhaka has emerged as the 'nerve centre' of ISI activities,[143] especially with regards to networking and coordinating with trusted agents and linkmen for the objective of building terror network. In doing so, the Commission had been assisting and sponsoring terror camps in Bangladesh where Northeast insurgents obtain extensive guerrilla training. During the seventh Indo-Bangladesh Home Secretary level talks held in Dhaka in August 2006, the Union Home Secretary V. K. Duggal pointed towards the existence of 172 camps belonging to the Indian insurgent outfits active in the Northeast region. He further pointed out that Bangladesh-based fundamentalist outfits like HuJI, which is sponsored by the ISI, supported these insurgents with funds from the Gulf countries like Saudi Arabia.[144] Besides assisting major insurgent outfits like ULFA, the ISI's has contacts with several home grown Islamic fundamentalist outfits like the MULTA.[145] The ISI has also been attempting to organise a grand alliance namely, All Muslim United Liberation Forum of Assam (AMULFA) by unifying several small Islamic fundamentalist organisations under one banner. In fact, MULTA and MULFA have already began to operate under AMULFA.[146] The ISI ensures the loyalty of Islamic terrorist organisations and intends to create large-scale disorder and terror in this region, particularly in the state of Assam.

It is relevant to mention that the statement of the then state Chief Minister Prafulla Kumar Mahanta, made in the Assam Legislative Assembly in Dispur on 6th April, 2000 about ISI activities in Assam includes :

1. Promoting random violence in the state by providing active support to the local militant outfits.
2. Creating new militant outfits along the ethnic and communal lines by initiating ethnic and religious groups.
3. Supply of explosives and sophisticated arms to various militant groups.
4. Causing damage to oil pipelines and other installations, communication lines, railways and roads.
5. Promoting fundamentalism and militancy among local Muslim youth by initiating them in the name of Jehad.
6. Promoting communal tension between Hindu and Muslim citizens through false and inflammatory propaganda related to religious beliefs.[147]

In the above context, it would be pertinent to state that Pakistan's involvement in the region appears to be purely strategic. Moreover, Pakistan's ISI operations in the state have been conducted in order to compel the Indian military to move to the state of Assam from their primary role in Kashmir. Thus, the development in this context has clearly shown that a systematic plan of destabilisation and terrorism in the state seems to be ongoing as well. Besides Pakistan and Bangladesh, other neighbouring countries like Bhutan and Nepal have also played a significant supplementary role of providing safe havens as well as transit facilities to insurgents' outfits of the state.[148] According to the report, the insurgent outfit like ULFA has developed linkages with several officers and personnel of Royal Bhutan Army (RBA) and Bhutan police force. Among other things, they have ensured a steady supply of rations, logistical support as well as aid and contacts for money laundering. The insurgent outfit like NDFB is also supported by RBA. As per report, several Bhutanese officials have visited the training camps located in Bhutan and they have openly aided and supported the NDFB cadres. NDFB along with ULFA has been channelling its funds through the Bhutanese diplomatic channel of their leaders based in Southeast Asian capitals. Thus, it is evident that Pakistan's ISI, with the assistance from several international Islamic organisations from the countries like Saudi Arabia, Iran, Iraq, is providing arms, weapons, military training and financial aid to the insurgent outfits, such as, ULFA and NDFB with an intention to create disorder and terror in the State of Assam.

4.6 Sum up

1. Geographical location of Assam is between the latitudes 24° N to 28° N and longitudes 90° E to 96° E. According to Census of India, 2001, the state of Assam covers an area of 78,438 sq.kms. According to 2011 census, its population is 3.12 crores. The decadal population growth rate of the state during 2001-2011 is 17.07 per cent. It is comparatively less than the growth rate of the state during 1991-2001, which was 18.92 per cent. Assamese, Bodo and Karbi are the official languages of the state.

2. Insurgency in the state of Assam was the result of combination of various factors such as language politics, sense of economic exploitation, political distortion and illegal migration. The issue of illegal migration led to a movement, which is popularly known as 'Assam movement', which

ended with the Assam Agreement in 1985. The success of Assam's student leaders in sustaining a prolonged campaign and then capturing political power inspired other student movements in the state. Thus, the situation became worst than before.

3. Various factors are responsible for the outbreak of insurgency in the state of Assam, such as, language politics, awareness of economic exploitation, political distortion and illegal migration. Insurgencies in Assam began after the Assam Accord, which was signed in 1985. Initially, insurgency movements were carried out on ethnic lines; however, later insurgent outfits began to operate on communal lines. Thus, Assam witnesses insurgency on ethnic and communal lines. There are some hazardous insurgent groups in Assam, such as, ULFA, BdSF – NDFB, BVF - BLTF, DHD, UPDS, MULFA and MULTA. ULFA, which was formed in 1979, emerged as a prominent insurgent outfit in the state after the agreement. They almost ran a parallel government in the state. Other insurgent outfits are prominent in their respective areas such as Bodo Insurgent outfits in Bodo dominated area, DHD in North Cachar Hills and Karbi Anglong districts, UPDS in Karbi Anglong districts and Muslim Fundamentalist Organisations (MFOs) MULFA and MULTA are prominent in Muslim dominated areas. They form contacts with other insurgent outfits within and outside the state and the region. Extortion, kidnapping, money laundering etc. are the major sources of funding of these outfits.

4. Even though, except Pakistan, the neighbouring countries like Bangladesh, Nepal, Bhutan, Myanmar etc. have apparently stopped helping the insurgents in the state; at one point of time they had played a very significant supplementary role in providing assistance to the insurgent outfits. They provided shelter, training, money, arms, ammunition etc. to the insurgent outfits. Pakistan's Inter Services Intelligence (ISI) is the prominent agency, which

plays a central role in sustaining and exploding the insurgency in the state. In February 2000, the Ministry of Home Affairs (MHA), in a booklet "Bleeding Assam" accused Pakistan's ISI of giving training to the Northeast insurgent outfits. Besides Pakistan and Bangladesh, the role of neighbouring countries like Bhutan and Nepal has remained supplementary. These two nations have provided safe shelter as well as transit facilities to the insurgent outfits of the state.

5. Thus, it can be concluded that the insurgent groups like ULFA, NDFB and many other major native insurgent outfits along with Muslim insurgent groups like MULTA in the state and Northeast region have been attempting to destabilise the law and order and the economy of the state as well as other states of the Northeast region. However, in spite of their insurgent activities during the course of time, they have not reached to their goal to free Assam and other states from Indian continent. In such circumstances, Pakistan's Inter Services Intelligence (ISI) agency has come forward to play a central role in assisting these insurgent outfits in the state to achieve their objective by providing all military assistance and financial aid from every possible way with a very purpose of separating the state from India.

References

1. Directorate of Economics and Statistics, Government of Assam, Profile of the State, available online at http://www.eco stat assam.nic.in/ accessed on 01.08.11.

2. NEDFi Data Bank, available online at http://databank.nedfi.com/content/generalinformation accessed on 09.06.11.

3. Directorate of Economics and Statistics, Economic Survey of Assam, (Government of Assam-2005-06), p. 5.

4. *Ibid.*

5. *Ibid.*

6. Rangan Dutta, "Development of Assam: A Strategic Perspective", in Anuradha Dutta and Ratna Bhuyan, ed., Genesis of Conflict and Peace: Understanding Northeast India, (2007), p. 129.

7. A-2, Decadal variation in population since 1901, Assam, available online at http://www.censusindia. gov.in/2011census/PCA/A-2_Data_Tables/18%20A-2%20ASSAM.pdf accessed on 21.08.14
8. *Ibid.*
9. *Ibid.*
10. NEDFi Data Bank, available online at http://databank.nedfi.com/content/general-information-0 accessed on 04.01.15.
11. Official website of Assam government, http://www. assam govt.nic.in/glance.asp accessed on 11.05.10.
12. Language Movement - A Crisis of Identity, available online at, http://shodhganga.inflibnet.ac.in:8080/jspui/bitstream/10603/13531/8/08_chapter%204.pdf, p.114, accessed on 29.04.15.
13. B. C. Bhuyan, Political Development of the North-East, part-1 (Delhi, 1989), pp. 50-55.
14. R. K. Kar, "Plantation Workers and Hetero Ethnicity: An Appraisal of Tea Labour in Assam", in B. C. Bhuyan, ed., Political Development of the North East, part II (New Delhi, 1989), pp. 80-95.
15. Apurba Baruah, "Roots of Conflict" in Imdad Hussain, ed., The Guwahati Declaration and Road to Peace in Assam, (New Delhi, 2005), pp. 39-40.
16. *Ibid.* p. 41.
17. Udayan Misra, "Identity Transformation and the Assamese Community: Illusion and the Reality" in Kailash Aggarwal, ed. Dynamics of Identity and Intergroup Relations in North-East India, (Shimla, 1999), pp.103-4.
18. Dinesh Kotwal, "Insurgency in Assam: The Demographic Dimensions", Strategic Analysis, (New Delhi), Vol. XXV, No. 2, (May 2001), p. 318.
19. *Ibid.*
20. *Ibid.*

21. Balbir Punj "A Bend in the Brahmaputra" Asian Age (Mumbai), 14.03.06.

22. See Udayan Misra, The Transformation of Assamese Identity: A Historical Survey, (Shillong, 2001).

23. Dipankar Sengupta and Sudhir Kumar Singh, ed., Insurgency in North-East India: the Role of Bangladesh (New Delhi, 2004), pp. 2-3.

24. *Ibid.*

25. Dilip Gogoi, "Quest for Swadhin Asom: Explaining Insurgency and Role of State in Assam", n. 23, p. 45.

26. *Ibid.*

27. *Ibid.*, n. 23, p. 4.

28. To make agitation more broad based and gain support of regional parties, cultural and volunteer organisations and tribal All Assam Student Union formed All Assam Gan Sangram Parishad at Dibrugarh in August 1979.

29. The Bodos are often known as Kacharis, particularly among the non-Bodos. But they themselves prefer the term 'Bodo' is a genus of large number of ethnic communities like the Boros, Boro-Kacharis, Sonowal- Kacharis, Thangal Kacharis, Deuries, Rabhas, Tiwaas, Mising, Mechs, Dimasas, Hajais, Karbis, and the Barmans (of Cachar). But presently the term generally embraces the Bodos, the Boro-Boro Kacharis and Mechs.

30. Sanjib Baruah, India Against Itself: Assam and the Politics of Nationality (New Delhi, 1999), pp. 188-92.

31. All Bodo Student Union, Why Separate State: Demand and Justification, (Kokrajhar (Assam), n.d.), edition 2, p. 3.

32. Memorandum submitted to the Prime Minister on behalf of the Mikir and North Cachar hills leaders' conference on 9th June 1973.

33. The subjects that still remained outside the jurisdiction of the ADC were law and order, supplies, excise, elections, census and district Rural Development Agency.

34. Sanghita Das, North Eastern Insurgency: Problem of Assessment, (New Delhi, 2012), p. 31.

35. Sunil Nath, "Assam the Secessionist Insurgency and the Freedom of Minds", available online http://www.satp.orgtp/publication/faultlines/volume13/Article2.htm accessed on 24.09.10.

36. H. K. Barpujari, Northeast India: Problems, Policies and Prospects: Since Independence, (New Delhi, 1998), p. 78.

37. *Ibid.*

38. *Ibid.*

39. *Ibid.*

40. Baruah, n. 30, p. 187. Since 1987 'Udayanchal' being called as 'Bodoland', which has to be set on the North Bank of the Brahmaputra.

41. ABSU, n. 31, p. 26.

42. *Ibid.*, p. 29.

43. Renaud Egreteau, "Instability at the Gate: India's Troubled Northeast and its External Implications", available online http://egreteau.com/images/Documentries%20PDF/CSH%200P%20_%n%BO16.pdf accessed on 28.01.10.

44. Ved Prakash, Encyclopedia of North East India (New Delhi, 2007), Vol. II, p. 697.

45. The first round of talks between the government of India and ABSU was held on 28 August 1989.

46. This was because earlier talks resulted in the three member experts committee under Dr Bhupinder Singh, IAS. This committee was set up on 25th February 1991 when Assam was under Presidents' rule. It submitted its report on 30 March 1992, and recommended the creation of two Autonomous councils. But, the Bodo leaders rejected the report.

47. It is essential to mention here that the former Union Minister of State for Home (Internal Security) Rajesh Pilot virtually forced former Assam Chief Minister Hiteswar Saikia to sign the accord, despite Saikia's reservations on boundary demarcation and other

issues. Saikia was keen that the BAC boundary be demarcated clearly before the accord was sign with ABSU and the BAPC.

48. Prakash, n. 44, p. 700.

49. This is because some areas under the BAC had more than fifty per cent non-Bodo population- composed of Asamiya, Hindus, Asamiya Muslims, Santhals and Nepalis. And BAC was formed without a clear cut boundary therefore the implementation of the accord became very difficult.

50. Egreteau, n. 43.

51. *Ibid.*

52. Prakash, n. 44, p. 717.

53. The Bodo leadership was in favour of such a working group but did not want that the committee's terms of reference to be confined to submitting recommendations for functional, administrative and financial autonomy for development of Bodoland. The Bodo leaders presented their proposal regarding the committee's terms of reference and made it clear that the panel should be authorised to look at the problem from a border perspective and not just on the matter of financial, administrative and functional autonomy.

54 . Ajai Sahni, "Survey of Conflicts and Resolution in India's Northeast", available online at http://www. satp. org/ satporgtp/ publication/faultlines/volume12/Article3.htm, accessed on 19.09.10.

55. M. S. Praphakara, "The Bodo Question", Frontline (Madras), Vol. 19, No. 15, 20 July 2002.

56. Praksh, n. 44, p. 725.

57. *Ibid.*, pp. 729-30.

58. 39 departments had been transformed to it within a month of its constitution.

59. Prakash, n.44, pp. 725-26.

60. Anil Kumar Sing, "Insurgency in India: Internal and External Dimensions", Akrosh (New Delhi), Vol. 7, No. 25, (October 2004), p. 59.

61. M. Amarjeet Singh "Resolving the Bodo Militancy", available online at http://www.idsa.in/idsastrate giccomments/Resolving Bodo Militacny_ MASingh_ 201008_ M.AmarjeetSingh, accessed on 30.10.10.

62. Anil Kamoj, "Complexities of the Twin Hill District of Assam", Dialogue (New Delhi), Vol. 7, No. 3, p. 109.

63. Prakash, n.44, p. 575.

64. *Ibid*., p. 577.

65. *Ibid*., p. 578.

66. Editorial, "Elusive Identities", Economic Political Weekly (17 December 2005), p. 5351.

67. *Ibid*.

68. Jaideep Saikia, Terror Sans Frontiers: Militancy in Northeast India, (New Delhi, 2004), pp. 126-27.

69. *Ibid*.

70. *Ibid*.

71. Prakash, n. 44, p. 601.

72. *Ibid*.

73. M. Amarjeet Singh, "Growing Fundamentalism in the Northeast", available at www.idsa.in/idsastrategiccomments/Growing Fundamental isminthrNortheast_MASing_190207, accessed on 23.01.10.

74. Prakash, n. 44, p. 601.

75. Sahni, n. 54.

76. Nath, n. 35.

77. K. Hrishikeshan, "Assam Agony: The ULFA and Obstacles to Conflict Resolution, available online at www.satp.org/satporgtp/publication/faultlines/volume12/Article2.htm accessed on 24.09.10.

78. For details see- "ULFA leaves bloody trail in Dibrugarh", Indian Express, May 5, 2001; "Congress Used Insurgents to win Polls:" Mahanta, Indian Express, 16 May 2001; EC Caught in Cong-AGP Crossfire", HT; 8 May 2001, for party position in 1985, 1991, and 1996 election, see: - http://www.expressindia.com/election/assam/asm-map.htm

79. Sahni, n. 54.

80. It was Burma (Myanmar) who was engaged in counter insurgency operations against its own insurgent outfits, numbering over half a dozen.

81. United Liberation Front of Assam, available online at www.satp.org/satporgtp/countries/india/states/assam/terrorist_outfits/ulfa.htm accessed on 17.11.10.

82. Most and other establishment of the outfit were in Sandrup Jongkhar, a district in Southern Bhutan that borders Assam's Nalbari district.

83. Militant Groups Profile, ULFA, available online at http://www.cdpsindia.org/assam_mgp.asp accessed on 11.11.10.

84. The outfit has published a clarification about the case of Sanjay Ghosh. In the clarification it has said: The ULFA has been observing for almost two years the covert activities and subtle propaganda of Mr Sanjay Ghosh operating from his base at the Majuli river islands against the liberation struggle of the people of Assam. When the matter was first reported to the higher authorities, a two-man special inquiry team headed by the zonal commander was instituted on 4 November 1996 to conduct a thorough investigation on his activities. On the basis of the report submitted by the inquiry team, Mr Ghosh was arrested on 4 July 1997, in connection with the following charges against him: that Mr Ghosh maintained close contact with Lt. Gen. S. K. Sawhney, commander of IV crops of the Indian army…and Inspector General of Police, Bipul Kalita. There is conformed report that the two major operations conducted by the Indian army in the Majuli islands to arrest outfit leaders was on the basis of information given by Mr Ghosh. Either this is a cause of being an informer or

an agent planted by the Indian intelligence agencies using the NGO as cover....

85. The Hindustan Times (New Delhi), 24 October 2000.
86. Time Line 2000, available online at www.axom.faithweb.com/timeline/, accessed on 17.11.10.
87. *Ibid.*
88. *Ibid.*
89. Indian Express, (Mumbai) 14 January 2007.
90. When ISI wanted ULFA to disrupt communications and economic targets like oil refineries and gas fields and create chaos to pave the way for a general uprising against the government", both Paresh Baruah and Sunil Nath, two of ULFA's top leaders, expressed strong opposition to any major attacks on government property, as that would alienate us from the people...this was early stage. Ved Prakash, n.46, Vol. 1, p. 169.
91. Udayon Misra, "ULFA: Beginning of the End", Economic and Political Weekly, (26 December 2009), Vol. XLIV, No. 52, p. 14.
92. Wasbir Hussain, "Assam: ULFA's Success or a Counter-Insurgency Faluer?", available online www. satp.org.satporgp/sair/Archives/3_5html #ASSESS MENT2 accessed on 17.11.10
93. Free Press Journal (Mumbai), 10 January 2007.
94. Indian Express, n. 89.
95. National Democratic Front of Bodoland – Terrorist Group of Assam, available online www.satp.orgtp/countries/india/states/assam/terroris_outfits/ndfb.htm accessed on 17.11.10
96. *Ibid.*
97. Surojit Mitra, a lawyer who had been able to get the bail for insurgents with an unerring regularity, had become an over ground link with the outfit. He arranged a 45 minute telephonic talks between the outfit and Fernandes. Outfit shot him for crowing about his achievement publically. For more detail see India Today 26 July 1998.

98. The preferred nomenclature, for those who were once known as tea garden labour and ex-tea garden labour.

99. Prakash, n. 44, p. 713.

100. Dima Halim Daogah, Terrorist Group of Assam, available online http://www.satp.org/satporgtp/ countries/india/states/assam/ terrorist_outfit/dhd.htm, accessed on 18.11.10

101 *Ibid.*

102. Sushanta Talukadar, Violence in the Hills, Front Line (Madras), Vol.22, No. 23,(5-18 November 2005), p. 40.

103. The Sentinel, (Culcatta) 16 May 2004.

104. Prakash, n. 44, p. 580.

105. With rampant corruption in all spheres, particularly in business, politics and administration, the mere threat of violence, with a few murders to convince the unwilling, was enough to make the corrupt elements and profiteers cough up the demanded amounts. A simple threat over the phone, the display of weapons by outfit cadres, friendly advice, an occasional roughing up, was enough to help local traders part with millions of rupees. See, Sanjoy Hazarika, Strangers of the Mist: Tales of War and Peace from India's Northeast (New Delhi), pp. 185-86.

106. See Venkitesh Ramkrishnan, "Dealing with Delhi", Frontline (Madras), Vol. 14, No. 20, (4-17 October 1997).

107. See Kalyan Chaudhari, "Tea Terror", Front Line (Madras), 17 October 1997.

108. See Asit Paul, "Starting Disclosures in Bodo Ultras Financial Report", Herald News Service (New Delhi 7 September 1997).

109. *Ibid.*

110. Dima Halim Daogah, available online at Indian army.nic. in/ Site/FromTemplete/ frmTemp SimpleWithTwo Para.aspx? Mnld=x 25YGCOGKvK=&Pare ntID= KDe+m3KVGiw= accessed on 17.11.10.

111. North East Sun, 1-14 April 2001.

112. Except two student organisations, Student Islamic Organisation (SIO) and the Student Islamic Movement of India (SIMI), those were formed in 1985 and 1971 respectively.

113. The MULTA leaders signed an agreement with SSP leaders at a meeting of Jamait – ul – Uloom Ali Madrassa in Chittagong in February 2001. Thus, the SSP decided to back the MULTA in its militant activities in Assam.

114. Sakia, n. 68, p. 127.

115. Indian intelligence reports disclose that in the beginning of May 2002, nine Islamist fundamentalist groups met at a camp near the Bangladesh town of Ukhia (South of Cox's Bazaar) and formed the Bangladesh Islamic Manch (BIM). The new umbrella organisation in a bid to expand the Islamic Solidarity in the region has included non-Bangladeshi MFOs such as the Rohingya Solidarity organisation and the Arakan Rohingya Islamic Front from Myanmar. The Indian intelligence sees the BIM as a replica of the United Jihad Council in Pakistan. While the United Jihad Council coordinates the struggle for Kashmir forced merger with Pakistan, the BIM, in its inaugural declaration, says it will work for the "willful merger" of areas of Assam and Arakans, which have large Muslim populations of Bangladeshi origin. Saikia, n. 68, p.165 and BIM – "Formation and Alignments", report prepared by the Special Bureaus Bangladesh Desk June 2002.

116. Saikia, *Ibid.*, p. 127.

117. *Ibid.* p. 163.

118. Saikia, n. 68, p. 165.

119. *Ibid.*, p. 165.

120. *Ibid.*

121. The Sentinel, 22 May 2003.

122. Saikia, n. 68, p. 168.

123. *Ibid.*

124. *Ibid.*

125. *Ibid.*, p. 140

126. *Ibid.*

127. Pahi Saikia, "Beyond the Roots: Undocumented Bangladeshi Migrants in Assam and the Question of Ethnic Assamese Identity", n. 23, pp. 73-74.

128. Anil Bhatt, "ISI's Eastward Operations: Old Links in North-East India and New Ones in South –East Asia", n. 23, p. 236.

129. Pahi Saikia, n. 23, p. 74.

130. *Ibid.*

131. The Pakistani misadventure in Kargil brought out into open the ULFA – ISI nexus.

132. Saikia, n.68, p. 80.

133. P. G. Rajamohan, "Fundamentalism and the ISI in the North Insurgency", available online at http://www.ipcs.org/article/terrorism/fundamentalism-and-the-isi-in-northeast-insurgency-1090.html, accessed on 25.01.11.

134. The then Chief Minister of Assam, Prafulla Kumar Mahanta, quoted in "Exposing the ISI – ULFA Nexus," Northeast Sun, Vol. 5, No. 18, April 15-30, 2001, p. 10.

135. *Ibid.*

136. *Ibid.*

137. Hazarika, n. 105, pp. 171-75.

138. Regarding the training of several ULFA cadres in Pakistan in 2003 in the use of Programmable Time Devices. See Assam Tribune, 31 January 2005 and The Sentinel (Guwahati) 20 September 2001.

139. ULFA, n. 81.

140. The Sentinel, 14 August 2001.

141. *Ibid.*

142. Militant Groups Profile, ULFA, n. 83.

143. Krishna Gopal, "Islamic Fundamentalism in Bangladesh and its role in North east Insurgency", n.23, p. 195.

144. "ISI Activities in Assam" available online at www.satp.org/satporgtp/countries/india/states/assam/documents/papers/isi_activities.htm accessed on 19.09.2010.

145. *Ibid.*

146. Rajamohan, n.133.

147. North East Sun, (New Delhi), 15-31 May 2000.

148. Northeast Sun, (New Delhi) 1-14 December 1998.

5

Counter Insurgency in Assam Since 1985 (Government Policies and Response)

The present chapter attempts to study various government policies, which are followed in dealing with insurgency movements in the state of Assam. The present chapter has been divided into two sections to accomplish above-stated task. The first section highlights the basic concept and meaning of counter-insurgency. The second section describes major counter-insurgency operations, which were carried out against the insurgent outfits and various non-military actions taken by the State and Central Government. The chapter has followed a descriptive approach.

Section I

5.1 General Concept of Counter Insurgency (CI)

The US Joint Publication defines Counter Insurgency (CI) as "Those military, paramilitary, political, economic, psychological and civic actions taken by the government to defeat insurgency, also called CION ."[1] Indian army's doctrine for sub-conventional operations defines counter-insurgency as "The use of all measures taken to combat insurgency, including operations by the military, central para-military forces, economic development, political reforms and management aimed at winning hearts and minds of people."[2] From the above definitions, it can be summarised that counter-insurgency refers to the efforts taken by the government either military or non-military to control or restrain the insurgency. However, the measures taken to control or restrain the insurgency depend upon the type and shape of the insurgency. For example, forces were used to restrain the secessionist movements in Punjab; whereas, in Jammu and Kashmir, both military and non- military measures were taken to curb the insurgency on its land. Generally, the nature of CI is not fixed but changeable and it evolves in response to the changes in the form of insurgency. Thus, there is no any single CI measure that could be applied to all kinds of insurgencies or a particular type of insurgency throughout its life cycle. The deployment of army as a part of CI measure against the insurgents is generally known as 'Counter Insurgency Operation' (CION). Other than deployment of army against insurgents, CION includes various protective measures, such as, sealing of borders, protecting lines of communication, safeguarding all military and civil installations.

In the Indian context, CI approach consists of four key components viz; establishment of command of the state through the deployment of security forces, accommodation (OR endorsement) of at least some of the demands of the insurgents, socio-economic development in the affected areas and re-establishment of the democratic process.[3] CI measures adopted in the state of Assam have largely been limited to military operations at the initial stage. During the following period, some significant steps were taken, such as, peace initiatives, execution of surrender and rehabilitation policy, reimbursement of security-related expenditure, increasing the reserve battalions and modernisation of police force, construction of border roads and fencing of borders, management of international borders, and diplomatic, strategic and economic initiatives.

Section II

5.2 Military Initiatives

In the late 1980s, the United Liberation Front of Assam (ULFA) was at its peak during the government of Assam Gan Parishad (AGP). In the end of 1990s, the situation in the state became more distressed. It was observed that the All Assam Student Union (AASU), All Assam Gan Sangram Parishad (AAGSP) and ULFA maintained a close link amongst them. When an ULFA suspect was arrested, AASU declared a *bandh* while the AGP leadership could secure his release from custody.[4] Despite, the disordered situation in the state, the then government of V. P. Singh at the centre was unable to act against ULFA as they had alliance with AGP. Later, the Doom Dooma[5] incident prompted a strong action against ULFA. This was followed by dismissal of AGP government on 27th November 1990. On the same day, ULFA was banned and the state of Assam was declared as a disturbed area. On the next day, counter-insurgency operation (CION) began in the state.

5.2.1 Counter Insurgency Operations (CION) Operation Bajarang

The Government of India initiated an offensive operation called 'Operation Bajarang' as the first CION against the ULFA. In this operation, in addition to the local police and Indian army, the services of the Central Reserve Police Force (CRPF), the Border Security Force (BSF) and the Assam Rifles (AR) were involved. As many as thirty thousand army personnel of the second and twenty-first divisions were involved in this operation.[6] At first, the Indian army attacked Lakhipathar camp, which was the Head Quarter (HQ) of the ULFA. In this attack, they searched for the abandoned camps. The situation was similar in other camps also. It is believed that the insurgents probably had the information about an army attack more than a week earlier. Thus, the outfits' high-ranking leaders left their respective camps. It was reported that Arbinda Rajkhowa, the chairman of the group along with some of the cadres shifted to nearby training camp at Saraipung and then to Meghalaya on the way to Bangladesh.[7] In this operation, many outfit cadres including some middle level leaders were arrested. However, forces could not arrest chief leaders of the outfit as they successfully escaped. Operation Bajarang turned out to be a great dampener for the army because of the lack of resistance in the encounters.[8] This operation achieved limited objectives but it was marked for two things. First, it exposed ULFA's inability to fight against an organised force and face its violent face. This was observed particularly in Lakhipathar, at the HQ of ULFA. The army captured this HQ in a single-day operation.[9] However, the army failed to eradicate the outfit due to lack of intelligence, which found to be the main barrier in this operation. Besides, the method followed of this operation alienated the people especially from the rural areas, which resulted into a lack of co-operation from these people.[10] This counter-insurgency operation had continued until 20th April 1991. The operation was suspended due to the assembly elections, which gave an opportunity to the ULFA to regroup and emerge as a more dangerous outfit. Meanwhile, ULFA kidnapped and killed the ONGC engineers T. S. Raju and B. P. Shrivastava. This incident created dreadful fear and the situation became more serious. As a result, the army was called back on 14th September 1991 and the next counter-insurgency operation called as 'Operation Rhino' began.[11]

5.2.2 Operation Rhino

Almost forty thousand army personnel from second, fourth, twenty-first and twenty- seventh divisions had been deployed in Operation Rhino.[12] The army was given adequate information about Assamese culture and it was acquainted with other relevant local aspects with an intention to avoid the mistakes made in operation Bajarang. This operation achieved more success than the earlier operation Bajarang as it was based on firm intelligence. During the operation, the army seized five crore rupees cash and thirty-two gold bars, some of it from the Narco trader.[13] In this operation, some of the top and middle level leaders were arrested. Some of the members of the outfit were also arrested without employing the technique of barricade and search operation.[14] This operation succeeded in destroying the outfit largely but could not destroy the outfit. This resulted into declaration of unilateral ceasefire by the ULFA on 17th December 1991.[15] However, operation Rhino continued until January 1992. The peace talks between the government and ULFA stopped army operations temporarily. Simultaneously, the then Chief Minister of Assam Mr Hiteshwar Saikia successfully split the ULFA and encouraged the leaders and cadres of the outfit to surrender. However, some ULFA leaders were against the arms surrender and negotiation. Therefore, the army operation resumed in April 1992 in six districts of the state and continued for one year. Later, the operation was suspended in April 1993. However, on 7th May 1996, just before the elections, two electoral candidates were killed allegedly by the ULFA, which resulted into the re-launch of operation Rhino.[16]

5.2.3 Formation of Unified Command Structure

The then Assam government requested the Union Ministry of Home Affairs (MHA) to deploy the army in Kokrajhar and the adjoining Bodo-dominated districts because of the violence broke out on 15 May 1996 in Bodo Territorial Council (BTC).[17] This resulted into the set-up of unified command wherein the army, state police and para-military forces in Assam were brought under one command as 'Unified Command Structure'.[18] The objective of creating such unified command structure was not only to deal with the situation in the Bodo-dominated areas, but also to counter the insurgent outfits, primarily the ULFA, in the entire state.[19] The unified command structure was formed with an intention to build a strong coalition amongst security forces to act powerfully against the insurgent outfits. It was an outcome of efforts which taken to overcome on loose coalition amongst security forces to act against the insurgents outfits. The earlier loose coalition was formed in 1991, which consisted of military, paramilitary, and police forces.[20] It was formed because various security agencies were involved in CION and it was observed as a major obstruction to CION. The formation of loose coalition resulted into the first attempt to coordinate a multipronged attack on insurgents. However, this plan did not overcome the basic problems of multi-force cooperation.[21] Thus, in response to the request of Assam government, the Ministry of Home Affairs (MHA) at centre, by issuing an order dated 4th January 1997, took a crucial decision to bring the army; state police and the paramilitary forces under a single chain of command.[22] The then Union Home Secretary K. Padmanabaih signed the MHA order. He said :

"For operational purposes, a Unified Headquarters would be set up under chairmanship of GOC IV Corps with operational control over all forces, including central paramilitary and state police employed on counter-insurgency duties, for coordinating the entire operations..."

Later, on 24th January 1997, the then Governor of Assam issued a notification regarding the constitution of the Unified Headquarters, which placed three forces under it.[23] Accordingly, a three-tier structure was formed which consisted of the Strategy Group, the Operational Group and the District-level Coordination Committee.[24] The strategy group comprised a committee, which was headed by the state chief secretary. The other members of the strategy group included the General Officer Commanding (GOC) IV corps, the Additional Chief Secretary and the State Director General of Police (DGP). According to the notification, "the committee (comprising the strategy group) would work out the broad strategies, ensure policy coordination and meet as often as necessary, but at least once in two months."[25] The operational group of the Unified Headquarters comprised the following personnel : GOC IV Corps (Chairman), Additional Chief Secretary, Assam, State Director General of Police, Brigadier (General Staff) of IV Corps, Inspector General of the Border Security Force (BSF), Inspector General of the Central Reserve Police Force (CRPF), Inspector General/Additional Director General of Assam Police (Operations), Inspector General of Police (Special Branch), the seniormost local official of the Subsidiary Intelligence Bureau (SIB), and a representative of the Research and Analysis Wing (RAW).[26] The Deputy Commissioner (DC) headed the district-level coordination committee. The other members included the District Superintendent of Police (DSP) and representatives of the army, central paramilitary forces and intelligence agencies.

The aim of operational group was to achieve the following four broad objectives:

1. To synergise counter-insurgency operations conducted by the Army, Central Paramilitary Organisations (CPO) and the State Armed Police, including deployment/re-deployment.

2. To take a decision regarding the modification of the areas of operation between the army and the CPOs in relation to the projected action plan.

3. To monitor the proceedings of the district-level coordination committees.

4. Crisis management.[27]

This decision, however, became controversial for democratically elected state government. An elite group of the society protested publicly against Unified Command Structure within three weeks after its formation. They argued that, when an elected government would come in power, the Unified Command structure would lead to destruction of the democratic system in the state.[28] However, the then state government launched heavy counter-insurgency operation under a Unified Headquarters. Hare Krishna Deka, former DGP of Assam, stated that the Unified Command achieved immediate success in its operations against the ULFA. He further observed that despite desperate attacks on the security forces, the outfit's activities were limited and its middle-level leaders were frustrated.[29] From 1st January 1998 to 31st December 2000, during counter-insurgency operation, 375 ULFA insurgents were killed, 2,948 were arrested and 2,385 surrendered to the authorities of the forces. Furthermore, 468 arms, 5,810 rounds of ammunition and Rs 17, 29,315 in cash were confiscated from the ULFA cadres.[30] During the same period, 184 cadres of the NDFB were killed in encounters, 615 cadres were arrested and 214 cadres were surrendered.

In the mid 1990s, a new dimension was added to the CI programmes. The then government at the centre began to give emphasis on aggressive regional diplomacy to give more prominence to its CI programmes.[31] Since 1995, Indian government initiated diplomatic efforts for convincing all the neighbouring countries to act against the Northeast insurgents. The first co-ordinated operation against Northeast insurgents took place in March-April when Burmese army helped Indian army during 'Operation Golden Bird.'[32] Since then other minor Indo-Burmese military operations have taken place in the years 2000, 2001 and 2004 against the Northeast insurgents. The desired result of this policy was seen when pro-Indian Awami League government in Bangladesh came in power. During its regime, the pro-Awami League government forced the insurgent outfits to leave their territory.

As a result, the United Liberation Front of Assam and National Democratic Front of Bodoland, had set up a number of bases in southern Bhutan during 1996 to 2001 for operational convenience. These insurgent groups began to attack on selected targets in Assam using the territory of Bhutan. In 2003, there were thirty camps in Bhutan, of which ULFA had thirteen, the NDFB had twelve and the Kamatpur Liberation Organisation (KLO) had five camps. These camps were scattered across the dense jungles of southern Bhutan, adjacent to Assam and West Bengal.[33] The geographical proximity of the jungles to these states allowed the insurgents to move easily in the states where they could continue their rebellious activities.

Thus, Government of India made an appeal to the Bhutanese authority to take military action against Northeast insurgents who were present in the territories of Bhutan.[34] In response to this appeal, the then Home Minister of Bhutan Lymp Thinely Gyamstsho had two rounds of talks with ULFA respectively on

20th November 1998 and 7th May 1999.[35] In the second round, Paresh Barua, Army Chief of ULFA, agreed to reduce the number of camps but expressed his inability to leave Bhutan before the end of 2000.[36] In the third round of talks, along with Paresh Barua and his Chairman, Arbinda Rajkhowa was also invited. The talks in the third round were successful. Later, the Home Minister had similar talks with Ranjan Dimary of NDFB; however, Dimary refused to leave by giving security reasons.[37] Consequently, the Bhutanese National Assembly (BNA) at its 78th session in July 2000 called Royal Bhutanese Army (RBA) to initiate its military operation against these insurgent outfits; however, it was not ready for Indo-Bhutan joint operations.[38] However, Bhutan government showed its willingness for joint operation against the Northeast insurgent outfits operating from their land because in the month of December 2000, the NDFB initiated violence in Bhutan and Bodo dominated areas.[39]

5.2.4 Operation All Clear

On 15th December 2003, the 'Operation All Clear' was initiated to wipe out Northeast insurgent outfits, such as, ULFA, NDFB and KLO from the Bhutanese territory. In this operation, about 6,000 soldiers of the Royal Bhutan Army and the Royal Bhutan Guards were involved.[40] The RBA concentrated its counter- insurgency operation where most of the camps of insurgent outfits were located. RBA successfully eradicated most of the bases and captured many top and middle ranking leaders.[41] RBA handed over many of the ULFA leaders to the Indian army; however, a large number of insurgent leaders could not be detained. In December 2003, more than 450 insurgents, including some senior leaders, surrendered to the RBA and about 120 insurgents and 44 RBA personnel were killed.[42] The intensity of military operations was very severe that the insurgents' outfits were forced to ask for a ceasefire. In this CION, a huge arsenal of weapon and sophisticated communication equipments were seized from the insurgents. Approximately more than five hundred AK-47/56 assault rifles and 328 other assorted weapons were recovered. These weapons included rocket launchers and mortars, along with more than 1,00,000 rounds of ammunitions.

Besides, an anti-aircraft gun was also found at the General Head Quarter (GHQ) of the ULFA.[43]

According to Lt. Gen J. S. Verma, the role of Indian army in the operations was very restricted. He admitted that the Indian army had provided only logistical support, which included sealing the international border, taking the injured to Indian hospitals, capturing those insurgents who tried to escape into Indian territory and killing those who had shown resistance.[44] ULFA suffered a lot due to the counter-insurgency operations carried out by security forces against them. However, in the following time, ULFA implemented recruitment campaign effectively. They provided two thousand rupees to each trained cadre in addition to food and shelter.[45]

After the Bhutan operation All Clear, ULFA cadres were shifted to Kachin province of Myanmar with its old supporter NSCN (K)[46] and established its base at Manabhum of Lohit district in Arunachal Pradesh. Manabhum was merely twenty-five kilometres away from the ULFA's battalion, which was located at the border with Myanmar. Therefore, Manabhum became the insurgents' preferred hub for the coordination and launching their operations. To put check on these activities of the outfit, the second mountainous division of the army, which was based near the eastern Assam district town of Dibrugarh, conducted regular offensive operations in the dense jungles adjacent to Arunachal Pradesh.[47] These offensive operations had been given code names. 'Operation Blazing Khukri' was one of these code names. The operation was conducted at the border of Manabhum during 5th to 10th April 2007. This operation was followed by next operation namely, 'Operation Blooming Orchid.' This operation was carried out inside the Manabhum during 27th April to 1st May 2007. This operation successfully destroyed two ULFA camps.[48] However, the ULFA dominated the Assam-Arunachal Pradesh border, which made available a safe place for carrying out insurgent activities in the state. Even though, the security forces carried out a regular CION in this area, it made limited impact. The reason for this restricted success was that many cadres of the insurgent outfits were merely moving inside the Arunachal Pradesh or into Myanmar by crossing the international border and returning back immediately after the army had vacated their base in the forest.[49]

The security forces have been continuously deployed in small CIONs in the state. These CIONs are commonly known as semi-permanent CIONs. The forces have carried out the counter-insurgency operations mostly against insurgent outfit like ULFA. The security forces had killed and had arrested many cadres of the outfit in these counter-insurgency operations. During January 2007 to February 2008, 350 cadres had surrendered to the authorities.[50] Later, ULFA changed its strategy[51] (*see Annexure IV*), which compelled the security forces to carry out more offensive CIONs. They developed some significant amendments in the CION tactics. Elements of these amendments executed by the Army, Police and Paramilitary Forces are as follows :[52]

1. According to intelligence agencies observation, the insurgent groups had been using those students who had failed in school and college. Therefore, these agencies began to keep a close watch on school and college dropouts. The profiles of such students and unemployed youth in this area are increasingly being maintained by the police and intelligence agencies.[53]

2. The enforcement and intelligence agencies have kept a close watch on front organisations, supporters and facilitators, who may provide the links to approach and hire armed force to execute bomb or grenade attacks. The arrest of Lachit Bordoloi, leader of the Manab Adhikar Sangram Samity, a 'human rights' front, is significant for his links with ULFA.[54]

3. The security forces to carry out a well-coordinated offensive CION to displace ULFA cadres from their established camps and areas of operation to newer areas. This operation aimed at hitting both the group's work and its nature.[55]

4. According to intelligence agencies, the ULFA cadres have been pushed by military operations to Nagaland and East Karbi Anglong, where they have not been able to establish

their bases and local support networks, which has affected their ability to strike adversely.[56]

5. According to intelligence agencies, such attempts of dislocating ULFA units have forced different units of the outfit to come together. This has resulted in lack of coordination to some extent and it has affected command structures of the outfits because cadres of different units are not prepared for working together.[57]

6. The ULFA's bond with the Khaplang group of the National Socialist Council of Nagaland (NSCN-K) has become weak. According to intelligence agencies, this had compelled the ULFA to look for other locations to set up their base outside Myanmar, where they had earlier secured safe place under the protection of NSCN-K. This dislocation had made them more helpless as they had to face intensified operations of security forces.[58]

7. The ULFA have set up their semi-permanent camps in Arunachal Pradesh. Counter-insurgency forces are focusing their attention on these areas and are putting pressure on New Delhi to remove the lacunae in the legal framework that does not allow the Army to move more than 20 kilometres beyond Assam's borders, into Arunachal Pradesh.[59]

Furthermore, the emphasis was given on improvement of intelligence gathering and efforts to ensure non-violation of human rights during CIONs. On 17th March 2008, the then Chief of the Army's Kolkata-based Eastern Command, Lt. Gen. V. K. Singh, had met Assam Chief Minister Tarun Gogoi, who had headed the Unified Command in the State, and made an agreement on the following vital points:[60]

1. That intelligence gathering must be improved;

2. That security forces should be told in no uncertain terms to avoid any excesses while carrying out CIONs.[61]

In response to the ethnic conflict in 2012, a large number of security personnel were deployed in Bodoland Territorial Council (BTC) districts and neighbouring minority-dominated Dhubri to control the outbreak between Bodos and minority immigrants. Ministry of Home Affairs (MHA) monitored the situation in Assam on a daily basis. MHA also provided additional 68 companies of Central Armed Police Forces (CAPFs) in the violence-affected areas in addition to 117 companies of CAPFs, which were already deployed in the State of Assam. Moreover, 127 police pickets have been set up in the sensitive areas to infuse a sense of security among the affected people.[62]

Moreover, central government has deployed Central Armed Police Forces (CAPFs) to aid the State authorities for carrying out counter-insurgency operations and providing security for vulnerable institutions and installations.[63] Also, the units of Central Para-Military Forces (CPFs) and army have been deployed to help the civilian authorities in the state with a charge of 10 per cent of the normal charges.[64] The Central Government has also taken initiatives to give financial assistance under the schemes, such as, Modernisation of Police Force (MPF), Reimbursement of Security Related Expenditure (RSRE) to the state.[65] The scheme like Modernisation of Police Force emphasises on strengthening the local police forces and intelligence agencies.[66] These attempts have been made to reduce the State Government's dependence on the army and CPFs. The purpose of this is also to maintain internal security, law and order situation and to create a secured environment with the help of local administration and population. Thus, under this scheme, the central government has been giving aid to procure modern equipment for surveillance, communications, forensic science laboratories, modern weaponry, vehicles, computerisation, training infrastructure and construction of police infrastructure, such as, housing, police stations, outposts and barracks.[67] Under this scheme, all the states from the region receive 100 per cent assistance from the centre.[68] Accordingly, since the financial year 2000 -01 to 31st March 2014, the state of

Assam has received a sum of total Rs 1852.629 crore as a financial aid.[69] The State-wise statement of funds released in cash/kind under scheme for MPF since 2000-01 onwards is indicated at *Annexure V*. The centre has also been giving financial assistance through the scheme like reimbursement of the expenditure related to security for raising additional forces like India Reserve Battalions (IR Bns) for the state. At present, total 51 IR Bns have been sanctioned for the Northeast states, out of which, 48 IR Bns have been raised so far.[70] In the state of Assam, 9 IR Bns have been raised.[71] In addition to these, statues like Village Defence Parties (VDPs), Village Guards (VGs) and Special Police Officers (SPOs) have been created to assist the state police in providing security to the development projects and for intelligence gathering.[72] The State Government has been paying honorarium to VDPs, VGs and SPOs at various rates and Central government has been sharing this expenditure under the scheme of Security-Related Expenditure. In this scheme, the honorarium per VDP, VG and SPO has been confined up to Rs 500, which has been increased up to Rs 1,500 since 8 December 2010.[73] The centre also shares the burden of the state under this scheme, which has incurred for the purpose of CIONs, includes the following activities:

1. The logistics provided to the Central Armed Forces (CAFs) or army deployed in the State;

2. Relief packages to the victims of insurgent violence;

3. Expenditure incurred on Petrol, Oil and Lubricants (POL) in CIONs upto 75 per cent;

4. The expenditure is being reimbursed, which has been incurred on maintenance of designated camps established for the groups with whom the Central Government/State Governments have entered into an agreement for the suspension of operations.[74] In the year 2013-14, upto 31st March 2014 the state of Assam received Rs 159.18 crore under this scheme. In the previous year 2012-13, it was Rs 108.96 crore.[75] Accordingly, since the financial year

2000 - 01 to 31st March 2014, the state of Assam has received a sum of total Rs 1263.8 crore as a financial aid. State-wise details of assistance released to North east states under the RSRE scheme during the last ten years are at Annexure VI.

While strengthening forces through financial aid to put check on the activities of the insurgents, the efforts have been made to seal the borders through fencing of the borders and constructing the patrol roads. Similarly, the attempts have also been made to put check on in and out routes, concealed routes and hideouts at the borders of the region to prohibit the access of the region to the insurgents. The initiatives were also taken for the management of Indo-Bangladesh, Indo-Bhutan and Indo-Myanmar border.

5.2.5 Construction of Border Roads and Fencing along the Border

The Government of India began the programme of fencing of the border and construction of the roads adjacent to the border shared with Bangladesh in two phases. The total length of Indo-Bangladesh border approved for fencing is 3,359.59 kms, out of which about 2,823.046 kms of fencing has been completed.[76] Similarly, the total length of the border roads sanctioned for construction is 4,407.11 kms., out of which 3,697.47 kms. of border patrol roads have been constructed.[77] *See Table 5.1* for the phase-wise progress of fencing and roads.

5.3 Management of International Border

5.3.1 Management of Indo-Bangladesh Border

Besides fencing and construction of the border roads at the Indo-Bangladesh border, there are 802 Border Out Posts (BOPs) on Indo-Bangladesh border, which are useful for maintaining supreme command over the border. Moreover, on 16 February 2009, the Government has sanctioned a proposal for the construction of additional 383 BOPs on the Indo-Bangladesh border[78] with an intention to reduce the distance among the BOPs for effective border management. The government has

Table 5.1
Phase-wise Progress of Fencing and Roads

Fencing (Length in km.)

Name of State	*PHASE I*		*PHASE II*		*TOTAL (PH.I+PH.II)*	
	Sanctioned	*Completed*	*Sanctioned*	*Completed*	*Sanctioned*	*Completed*
W. Bengal	507	507	964.00	729.15	1471.00	1236.15
Assam	152.31	149.29	76.72	74.94	229.03	224.29
Meghalaya	198.06	198.06	264.17	148.60	462.23	346.66
Tripura	-	-	848.00	782.46	848.00	782.46
Mizoram	-	-	349.33	233.54	349.33	233.54
Total	**857.37**	**854.35**	**2502.22**	**1968.69**	**3359.59**	**2823.04**

(Contd.)

(Contd. Table 5.1)

Border Roads (Length in km.)

Name of State	*PHASE I*		*PHASE II*		*TOTAL (PH.I+PH.II)*	
	Sanctioned	*Completed*	*Sanctioned*	*Completed*	*Sanctioned*	*Completed*
W. Bengal	1770	1616.57	0.00	0.00	1770.00	1616.57
Assam	186.33	176.50	102.42	83.56	288.75	260.06
Meghalaya	211.29	211.29	320.00	169.04	531.29	380.33
Tripura	545.37	480.51	637.00	512.27	1182.37	992.78
Mizoram	153.40	153.06	481.30	294.67	634.70	447.73
Total	**2866.39**	**2637.93**	**1540.72**	**1059.54**	**4407.11**	**3697.47**

Source : Ministry of Home Affairs Annual Report 2013-2014, p. 43.

taken this decision with a view to provide all necessary infrastructures for the accommodation, logistic support and the combat functions of the BSF troops deployed on Indo-Bangladesh border.[79]

5.3.2 Management of Indo-Bhutan Border

On Indo-Bhutan border, 150 BOPs have been established[80] in the States of Sikkim (6), West Bengal (50), Assam (69) and Arunachal Pradesh (25) and 14 battalions of Sashastra Seema Bal (SSB) along this border have been deployed as border guarding force to improve the security environment along this border.[81]

5.3.3 Management of Indo-Myanmar Border

On Indo-Myanmar border, 46 battalions of Assam Rifles have been deployed for counter-insurgency operations and guarding the border. Out of these, 31 battalions are for counter-insurgency and 15 battalions are for border guarding role. Presently, these border-guarding battalions have been deployed along Indo-Myanmar border to put check on infiltration, smuggling of arms, ammunition, drugs, fake currency notes etc.[82]

5.4 Surrender and Rehabilitation Policy

The central government has been implementing this scheme since April 1998. The aim of this scheme is to take insurgents away from the path of violence by giving incentives and benefits to those who are ready to surrender and promise that they would not participate any more in violent activities. The efforts have also been taken to encourage misguided youths to come in the main flow, who have joined the insurgent outfits and now find themselves trapped. Under this scheme, the centre has given a 100 per cent grant to the state for the surrender and rehabilitation programme.

Only the armed cadres have been allowed to surrender under this plan. Under the give up and gain criteria, the insurgents were given incentives for the surrender of their weapons to the authorities.[83] The incentives given to the armed cadres were Rs 25,000 for per rocket launcher or sipper rifle; Rs 15,000 for AK 47/

AK 56 assault rifle; the rates are similarly prescribed for pistols, grenades, rockets, remote control devices, explosive materials.[84]

Since the year 1998, the scheme has been revised in the years 2000, 2006, 2009, 2010, 2011 and 2012. As per revised guidelines, surrender would get following incentives:[85]

1. An immediate grant of Rs 1.5 lakh is to be given to each surrendered cadre that would be kept in a bank in the name of surrendered as fixed deposit for a period of three years. This money could be utilised as guarantee/margin money against loan to be availed by the surrendered from the bank for self-employment;

2. Increase in stipend from Rs 2,000 to Rs 3,500 per month to each surrendered w.e.f. 01.12.2009 for a period of one year. The State Governments may consult Ministry of Home Affairs, in case the support to beneficiaries is required for more than one year; and

3. Provisions have been made for vocational training to the surrendered for self-employment.[86]

Mr Saikia, the then Chief Minister of Assam, during his tenure from 1991 to 1996 had proposed and implemented this policy in the state. He had successfully managed to split ULFA and encouraged ULFA cadres to surrender before the authorities.[87] In the subsequent years, it has been believed that many of the ULFA cadres have been surrendered to the Indian authorities. The two Bodo peace accords have also led the surrender of Bodo insurgent outfits namely, BVF and BLTF in the years 1993 and 2003 respectively. Later, the cadres from the insurgent outfits like DHD (J) and KLNLF, which were active in Karbi Anglong and North Cachar Hill areas, had surrendered in 2009 and 2010 respectively.

5.5 Peace Initiatives taken in the State of Assam

In the mid 1990s, soon after the first army operation against the ULFA, the Government of India had extended its first peace offer to ULFA and had expressed its willingness to hold talks in any location. However, the ULFA regarded such kind of offer of negotiations as a clever means by the government to disarm the ULFA and to create a split within the outfit. The authorities had made following attempts to establish peace with ULFA during the second army operation. This time the government was engaged in dialogue with the help of interlocutors consisting mainly of local contacts from the central administrative services and journalists.[88]

It is believed that the ULFA leaders also met secretly with the Chief Minister and discussed about the terms of future dialogues between them.[89] Arvinda Rajkhowa, along with five of his colleagues, was believed to have written a letter to the then Prime Minister Rajiv Gandhi in which he expressed his willingness to enter into some form of negotiations with Government of India and agreed to

1. accept the Constitution of India for the resolution of the Assam problem;
2. abandon the path of violence; and
3. surrender ULFAs arms at an appropriate time.

In return, the same "Compromise Group" requested the government to

1. withdraw military units;
2. stop arresting ULFA members indiscriminately;
3. withdraw the ban on the ULFA and Armed Forces (Special Powers) Act of 1958, which had been fastened on parts of Assam; and
4. transfer all ULFA members arrested by the police all imprisoned ULFA supporters.[90]

Consequently, in January 1992, the Assam police and the Intelligence Bureau (IB) had taken a five-member ULFA team led by its general secretary Golap Baruah alias Anup Chetia to New Delhi. They had talks with the then Home Minister S. B. Chavan and had a round of discussions with the then Prime Minister P. V. Narasimha Rao. Anup Chetia who had been arrested by the Calcutta police a month earlier, was in custody of the Security Forces (SFs) when he was taken to Delhi for talks. As a result, Narasimha Rao agreed to call a ceasefire, promised to avoid violence and to find a negotiated political solution to the insurgency.[91]

The ULFA team returned to Assam and began to seek the options of their supporters. The government also accepted the request of ULFA leaders to allow them to travel to Dhaka to persuade Paresh Baruah to accept the proposed agreement. However, Baruah warned them strictly for dealing with the enemy when the team went to Bangladesh to bring him for the round of talks with Delhi. In 1998, the Assam government made fresh attempt to break the dead lock. A lawyer and a senior Assam police official were sent to London for scheduled meeting with ULFA's Chief Paresh Baruah and others. The News of the initiative was leaked to the local media and the meeting did not take place. Since 2001, ULFA has declared that it believes in a solution to its problems through talks and three pre-conditions for a possible dialogue with New Delhi. These are -

1. Talks outside India;
2. Talks under the supervision of the UN; and
3. Talks to be concentrated on their core demand of sovereignty.

The then Chief Minister of Assam, Prafulla Kumar Mahanta, had declared that he would be ready to resign if it helps in bringing the ULFA for talks with New Delhi. He further said that his government had no objections if the centre held talks with the rebels anywhere outside India. In the month of January 2001, the decision was taken for the final talks. However, a representative of the Ministry of Home Affair made the conflicting public statements on the sovereignty issue at Guwahati and later at New Delhi, which put the ULFA on the defensive track and as a result, this initiative collapsed. In early March 2001, the state government had urged the centre to declare a cease-fire against insurgent outfits in the entire region in order to make a way for peace. After an initial assurance from the Union Minister for Home Affairs that the centre would actively consider such cease-fire, the option was rejected by ULFA on the grounds that Bhutan, Bangladesh and Myanmar were carrying out operations against the insurgents, and it would slow down if India announced a cease-fire.[92]

In 2003, after the RBA's military cooperation, ULFA made another peace offer to GoI with the same pre-conditions. This time, the GoI accused ULFA for initiating peace talks because GoI had observed that ULFA was offering peace talks only when the outfit was under pressure due to the military operation with an intention to give the outfit time to regroup. In November 2004, Indira Goswami, Professor at Delhi University and renowned Assamese litterateur, urged New Delhi to hold talks with insurgents. She met the then Prime Minister Manmohan Singh on 16 November 2004, and handed over a memorandum drafted in consultation with academics from Delhi University. Both Goswami and GoI consulted legal experts for an interpretation of 'Sovereignty' and its place in the Indian Constitution. Goswami also consulted Soli Sorabji, the then Solicitor General of India. As the Telegraph (Calcutta) had reported, "Legal opinion seems to be that there could be various kinds of sovereignty, some of which are not against the constitution. Economic sovereignty is a possibility, for instance."[93] She appealed to Prime Minister Manmohan Singh to initiate a process of dialogue on ULFA's demand for sovereignty of Assam. However, the Prime Minister urged the insurgent groups to avoid violence. He also observed in Dispur on 22 November that violence and peace talks could not go on simultaneously.[94] In December 2004, ULFA leaders rejected the first peace offer made by the Prime Minister Office; but Goswami had not given up the hope.[95] She realised that it was quite difficult for her to handle, although, she knew clearly from the beginning that her involvement in this issue was restricted to the task of bringing both parties to the negotiation table with an intention to reach a solution. On 8 September 2005, the ULFA appointed an eleven-member delegation namely, People's Consultative Group (PCG) to hold talks with the Indian government.[96] PCG consisted mainly of well-known civil society activists.[97] Some of its members were known as sympathisers of the ULFA or ex-ULFA cadre. These members were Arup Borbora (Lawyer), Lachit Bordoloi, Mukul Mahanta (Engineer), Ajit Bhuyan (Editor), Haider Hussain (Editor, Asomiya Pratidin), Braajen Gogoi (Doctor), Dilip Patgiri (Adviser to the Assam Jatiyabadi Yuba Chatra Parishad), Diganta Konwar (Journalist), and Hiren Sakikia (Sports organiser). Indira Goswami was the Chief interlocutor and Reboti Phukan, a former football player and a childhood friend of ULFA Commander-in-Chief Paresh Baruah, assisted her.[98] The group was instructed to clear the roadblocks and prepare the grounds for direct talks. The group put forward six demands as their conditions during the talks. These demands are:

1. End or suspend army operations against its cadres to initiate talks;
2. Release of its top leaders captured by the security forces;
3. Information about those cadres captured during "Operation All Clear" in Bhutan in 2003";
4. Third party involvement for peace talks;
5. Holding talks in world fora like United Nations (UN) and;
6. Demand for a sovereign and independent Assam.[99]

On 25 October 2005, the PCG and the Indian government held their first round of talks. The second meeting between PCG and government was held on 7 February 2006, while the last meeting held in June 2006. In response to the demands made by PCG on suspension of army operations, the then defence minister Pranab Mukharjee stated that there was no question of halting army operations because no ceasefire accord has taken place and individualistic proposals to hold dialogues with the banned outfit could not bring about ceasefire before ground rules are framed.[100] However, later in August 2006, the central government unilaterally announced ceasefire with the outfit. Moreover, lately, on the demand of release of its top leaders federal, the government responded positively and agreed to release five senior ULFA leaders.[101] However, after the three rounds of talks between PCG and government, the negotiations broke down in September 2006. This was because, after a period of six weeks, the government called off the ceasefire and resumed military operations on the ground that the ULFA had not kept its promise. Hence, on 27th September 2006, the PCG had withdrawn from the negotiations protesting against the central government's decision to resume the military operations against the outfit.[102] The following are some factors, which prevented a possible face-to-face meeting between ULFA and the GoI.

1. New Delhi was asking ULFA to name its negotiating team. ULFA said the team could not be named unless the five senior leaders are freed.

2. New Delhi was asking ULFA to give its consent for the talks in writing. ULFA responded by saying that the government must also state in writing that it would discuss the group's key demand of 'Sovereignty'.

3. ULFA demanded to know locations of its 14 cadres, who were missing after Bhutanese military attack in December 2003, and why the authorities have remained silent on this matter.[103]

Meanwhile the state government also took measures to initiate direct negotiations with the ULFA. The Assam government announced an offer of safe passage on 7th January 2006 for a span of 14 days, wherein the state government allowed the ULFA cadres to meet their family members with prior intimation to the concerned authorities. However, the ULFA expressed its willingness to avail of such offers by calling it a political trick.[104]

Such an offer was not an exception; the state government made a similar offer to the ULFA's top leaders to meet the then Prime Minister P. V. Narasimha Rao. In 1999, the AGP government had proposed ten-day safe passage, where around 250 insurgents had responded.[105] The government did not refuse the possibility of holding peace dialogues during the army operations in the state, even though peace dialogues have been deadlocked due to the resumption of army operations on 24 September 2006, and the PCG have rejected to continue the talks. In the month of January 2007, Prime Minister Manmohan Singh offered a safe passage to ULFA leaders for direct negotiations.

However, the outfit did not respond in the positive manner. Later, the arrest of top ULFA leaders in 2009 paved the way for talks.[106] The ULFA also finally gave up its earlier preconditions of holding talks in third country, including sovereignty as an issue on its agenda, and having the UN as an observer during the talks.[107] The ULFA leaders called on Union Home Ministry and subsequently the Union Secretary on 10th February 2011 at New Delhi. Shri P. C. Haldar was appointed as a representative of GoI for peace talks with ULFA.[108] Later on 5th August 2011, ULFA submitted its broad charter of demands to the Union Home Minister. On 29th June 2012, Union Home Secretary reviewed the status of talks between a representative of Government of India and ULFA Leaders.[109] A year later once again meeting was held to review the progress made in talks between then Union Home Secretary R. K. Singh, representatives of government of Assam and ULFA leaders on 26th June 2013.[110] However, in spite of such attempts, Paresh Baruah, Commander-in-Chief of ULFA is out of the peace talks till date. Meanwhile, the central government also showed the willingness for the talks with other insurgent outfits in the state, which are ready to give up violence. The government also made it clear that if there is a split group in future, then Government will not consider them for the talks.[111] Accordingly, the central government has entered into the agreement of Suspension of Operations (SoO) with NDFB (P), and ULFA.[112] On 24th May 2005, NDFB (Progressive) signed an agreement of SoO with Government of India and Government of Assam, which came into effect since 1st June 2005. Today, the NDFB is engaged in peace talks with the central government and Shri P. C. Haldar was appointed as a representative of GoI for peace talks with NDFB (Progressive and Ranjan Daimary). Accordingly the meetings were held between Shri P. C. Haldar and representatives of NDFB (P) on 12th September 2013 and 20th February 2014 to discuss the demands of NDFB.[113] Meeting also review the functioning of SoO and extended the period upto 30th September 2014.[114] On 10th September 2013 and 23rd October 2013, meetings of Joint Working Group with NDFB were held at Guwahati to finalise the agreed ground rules of SoO agreement.[115] The SoO with agreed ground rules signed with NDFB on 29th November 2013, at Guwahati.[116] According to this agreement the outfit had to deposit all the weapons possess with them to the government.[117]

The United People's Democratic Solidarity (UPDS) led by Shri Horensing Bey, General Secretary also came forward and expressed its willingness to give up violence and to seek solution to its problems peacefully within the framework of Indian Constitution. The SoO agreement with UPDS came into effect from 1st August 2002. The SoO agreement of agreed ground rules signed with UPDS had been revised with stringent conditions and it was valid up to 30th April 2011.[118] Central government on 25th November 2011, signed a Memorandum of Settlement (MoS) with the United People's Democratic Solidarity (UPDS) of Karbi in Assam. As a result of this MoS, Autonomous Council in Karbi Anglong area received special package for speedier socio-economic development of the area.[119] Later the organisation dissolved itself in December 2011.[120] Similarly, The SoO agreement with DHD came into effect from 1st January 2003. The agreement had been extended with stringent conditions and it was valid up to 30th June 2011.[121] On 8th October 2012, DHD and DHD (Joel/Black Widow) signed a Memorandum of

Settlement (MoS) with the Central Government and the Government of Assam. The MoS provided an enhanced autonomy to the Autonomous Council of North Cachar Hills in Assam and it also offered a special package for speedy socio-economic and educational development of the area.[122]

5.6 Political / Diplomatic Initiatives

Political initiatives and military operations are undertaken alongside to achieve long-lasting results. In the context of Northeast region insurgencies, the Government of India and the state government have taken political initiatives at two levels, internal and external (Strategic). At the internal level, negotiations have resulted in accords that have granted greater political and economic autonomy to the tribal-dominated areas, such as, Karbi Anglong and North Cachar Hills districts in Assam. Later, the Bodoland Territorial Autonomous District (BTAD) consisting of the four districts of Assam, namely, Chirag, Kokrajhar, Baska and Udalguri, was formed. It has been included in the sixth schedule. The BTAD is governed by BTC.

As, ULFA and NDFB of Assam has been received moral and material support from the neighbouring countries i.e. Myanmar, Bangladesh and Bhutan, at the external level, political and diplomatic steps are taken to deny safe havens to the insurgents in neighbouring countries. Since 1998, India's foreign policy has been strengthening her strategic ties with all these neighbouring countries with an intention to reduce the involvement of neighbouring countries in the internal affairs of the region in particular and India in general. The then Central Home Secretary brought out the issue before the Bangladesh Government during his visit. He made an appeal that the soils of Bangladesh should not be used in anti-India activities. Thereafter, a joint action committee was formed. Later, the committee had its meeting at Dhaka and New Delhi for the mutual interest. During these meeting, there was a discussion about the security problems of both the countries. As a part of line of action in this direction, the Home Secretary again visited Dhaka during 21st to 23rd November 1998 and discussed the security issues, illegal infiltration, border crossing by the insurgents and anti-social elements.[123] In the light of such crucial aspects regarding the protection of borders, on the 22nd December 1999, Home Minister of Bangladesh also visited New Delhi,[124] wherein the matters relating to mutual interest and defence issues were discussed.

Recently, after signing a deal with Dr Manmohan Singh, Sheikh Hasina, Prime Minister of Bangladesh, during her visit to India, reiterated to fight jointly against terrorism and not to allow Bangladesh land to be used by militant groups. Her solid stand on the issue of terrorism has reduced the insurgent acts to a great extent and the remarkable decline in violence on the border is enough indication of it.[125] Home Secretary G. K. Pillai and his counterpart Abdus Sobhan Sikadar signed the agreements after delegation-levels talks. There were three treaties related to security issues: (1) Agreement on mutual legal assistance in criminal matters; (2) Agreement on combating international terrorism; and (3) Agreement on transfer of guilty persons, which would help New Delhi to ask for the banishment of insurgents who have taken shelter in Bangladesh.[126]

In October 2004, Senior General Than Shwe, Head of the military leadership and the state democratic peace committee of Myanmar had paid a six-day official visit to India. It was just because of the greater understanding shown by India towards the military leadership of Myanmar. The Government of India entered into an agreement with the Myanmar for peace and defence in the border areas. There were a number of meetings at national and state levels. The MOU signed between the two nations on the security issues included of tightening the noose of all the insurgent outfits operating in the Northeast from outside India.[127] During their talks, Prime Minister of India, Manmohan Singh, expressed serious concerns about these groups, and General Shwe assured him that he would not allow Myanmar to be used for anti-India operations.[128] He further said that Myanmar was willing to become more offensive against these insurgent groups involved in anti-India operations, and strengthen the vigilance along the border shared with India.

The two countries decided to exchange operational intelligence and personnel too.[129] Since then Myanmar Government is providing help in controlling the insurgent activities in the Northeast. As a result, increased cooperation between Indian and Myanmar security forces movements of insurgent outfits has been restricted. Government of India also made a request to the Government of Thailand to discourage anti-India activities of the insurgents, as many insurgent groups of Northeast were procuring arms and ammunition illegally from Thailand.[130]

5.8 Economic/ Development Initiatives

In the view of the strategic significance, Assam and ultimately the Northeast region has been given the status of special category states. The central government has been trying to open the ways to accelerate economic growth in the region. A number of special schemes and programmes have been evolved considering the strengths and requirements of the region. In this context, it is important to state that the government has given special attention to the economic development of the region from eighth five-year plan onwards. The central government has also been announcing special economic packages for socio-economic development of Northeast region from time to time. Some of the important initiatives taken by the government are North East Council, National Development Council, Non-Lapsable Central Pool of Resources, Department of Development of North Eastern Region (DoNER), Look East Policy, Bangladesh, India, Myanmar, Sri Lanka, and Thailand Economic Cooperation (BIMSTEC), Mekong Ganga Cooperation (MGC).

5.9 Sum Up

1. Counter-insurgency measures incorporate military as well as non-military measures. Both types of measure are required to combat insurgency. The Government of India along with Assam State Government have been using both military and non-military counter insurgency (CI) measures to control and eradicate the rebellious activities being carried out by the insurgents in Assam and the Northeast region as well. It seems that both types of measures are essential

to fight against insurgency in the state and the region. The central Government, along with its military and non-military operations, has been making strategic attempts by revising its foreign policy and thereby improving the relations with foreign countries in order to isolate the insurgent outfits and rule out their existence from the neighbouring countries, thus, compelling the insurgent groups to surrender before it. The Central and State governments have succeeded largely in their efforts to take down the insurgent outfits through its various operations and tactical practice like peace talks with insurgent groups and socio-economic development programmes.

2. Thus, it can be said that since the inception of CI operations in the state in 1990, it has been a progressive journey on the part of central and state governments. Both governments have been considerably successful in bringing down the insurgency in the state through its various operations that have been carried out from time to time in last few years.

3. On the one hand, both central and state governments, to curb insurgency in the state of Assam, mostly relied on the use of force against various insurgent outfits. While on the other, governments kept on talking with these insurgent outfits to establish peace in the region; however, while having peace talks with them, the important leaders of the ULFA and NDFB were out of the peace talks. The anti-talk group formed by these leaders are now engaged in committing violence in the state. Therefore, the question arises that whether the talks with these surrendered outfits would establish peace in the state.

References

1. US Joint Publication 1-02, Department of Defense Dictionary of Military and Associated Terms, 12 April 2010, p. 102.

2. Rajesh Kapoor, Revolutionary in Military Affairs and Counter Insurgency in India, Centre for Land Warfare Studies, Working Paper 2, (2010), p. 35.
3. The Need for a Strategic Response to Insurgency and Terrorism, IDSA Issue Brief (New Delhi), 26 November 2010, p. 2.
4. H. K. Barpujari, Northeast India: Problems, Policies and Prospects Since Independence (New Delhi, 1998), p. 81.
5. The outfit requested a huge amount from tea gardeners on the ground of economic development viz. Tata Tea, Mac Leod Russell, Mac Neil Magor and it has been reported that were all paid. However, Unilever having seven gardens in the Doom Dooma region referred the matter to the higher authorities in London. This was brought to the notice of the Indian High Commissioner, and Kuldip Nayar, an eminent journalist by the company and the latter request to the then government to take strong action against insurgents. *Ibid.*, p. 83.
6. Queen's University of Belfast School of Law, Emergency Law Database, available online at http://www.law.qub.ac.uk/humanrts/emergency/india/ind1.htm; accessed on 02.02.04.
7. Barpujari, n. 4, p. 83.
8. Uttam Sengupta, "Assam: State of Strife", India Today (Noida) 31 December 1990, p. 23.
9. The Sentinel, 16 February 2005.
10. *Ibid.*
11. Chandra Bhushan, Terrorism and Separatism in Northeast India, (Delhi, 2004), p. 134.
12. Emergency Law Database, n. 6.
13. Ved Prakash, Encyclopaedia of North East India (New Delhi, 2007), p. 634.
14. The Sentinel, n.9.
15. Chandra Bhushan, n. 11, p. 135.
16. Sanjib Baruah, India Against Itself: Assam and the Politics of Nationality (New Delhi, 1999), p. 158.

17. Wasbir Hussain, "Multi Force Operations in Counter Terrorism: A View from the Assam Theatre", available online at www.satp.org/satporgtp/publication/faultlines/volume9/Article2.htm, accessed on 11.11.10.

18. *Ibid.*

19. *Ibid.*

20. *Ibid.*

21. *Ibid.*

22. *Ibid.*

23. *Ibid.*

24. *Ibid.*

25. *Ibid.*

26. *Ibid.*

27. *Ibid.*

28. *Ibid.* and Assam Tribune, 22 January 1997.

29. Ibid.

30. Jadeep Saikia, "Autumn in Springtime: The ULFA Battles for Survival", Fault Lines (New Delhi), Vol. 7 (November 2000), p. 35.

31. Subir Bhaumik, "Insurgency in India's North East: Conflict, Co-option and Change", available online available online at http://www.eastwestcentre.org/fileadmin/stored/pdfs/EWCWwpolo.pdf accessed on 11.11.10.

32. *Ibid.*

33. Dipankar Banerjee and Bidhan S. Laishram, "Bhutan's Operation All Clear: Implications for Insurgency and Security Cooperation", IPCS Issue Brief, No. 18, January 2004, available online at www.ipcs.org/pdf_file/issue/IB18-OperationAllClear.pdf accessed on 11.11.10.

34. Prakash, n.13, p. 476.

35. *Ibid.*

36. *Ibid.*

37. *Ibid.*

38. *Ibid.*

39. *Ibid.*, p. 477.

40. Bhashyam Kasturi, "Bhutanese Army Action against Militants" Indian Defence Review (New Delhi), Vol. 19, no. 2, (April-June 2004), p. 81.

41. V. K. Nayar, Crossing the Frontiers of Conflict in the North East and Jammu and Kashmir: From Real Politik to Ideal Politik (Delhi, 2005) p. 34.

42. Kasturi, n. 40.

43. *Ibid.*

44. *Ibid.*

45. Renaud Egreteau, "Instability at the Gate: India's Troubled Northeast and Its External Implications", available online, http://egreteau.com/images/Documentries%20PDF/CSH%200P%20_%N%BO16.pdf accessed on 28.01.10.

46. *Ibid.*

47. Wasbir Hussain, Assam: Impotent Counter Insurgency, available online at http://www.satp.org/satporgtp/sair/Archives/5_48.htm#assessment2 accessed on 17.11.10.

48. *Ibid.*

49. *Ibid.*

50. Wasbir Hussain, Assam: Counter-insurgency Rejig, available online at http://www.satp.org/satporgtp/sair/Archives/6_37.htm#assessment2 accessed on 17.11.10.

51. Earlier ULFA were engaged in kidnappings, selective killings and direct gun-battles with security forces. These activities were their regular tactics to create a terror and for fund generation. But later they have shifted their strategy to secure its cadres from security forces by avoiding direct combat with them. They started to hire the cadres for depredation activities. Security officials in Assam have described this new trend as 'outsourcing' by the ULFA, with the objective of inflicting maximum damage with minimum loss to the group itself. Wasbir Hussain, Assam: Counter-insurgency Rejig, available online at www.satp.org/satporgtp/sair/Archives/6_37.htm#assessment2 accessed on 17.11.10. see *ANNEXURE IV*

52. *Ibid.*

53. *Ibid.*

54. *Ibid.*

55. *Ibid.*

56. *Ibid.*

57. *Ibid.*

58. *Ibid.*

59. *Ibid.*

60. *Ibid.*

61. *Ibid.*

62. Annual Report, Ministry of Home Affairs, Government of India (2012-13), p. 12.

63. Annual Report, Ministry of Home Affairs, Government of India (2011-12), p. 25.

64. Annual Report Ministry of Home Affairs, Government of India, (2009-10), p. 14.

65. Annual Report Ministry of Home Affairs, Government of India, (2013-14), p. 311.

66. *Ibid.*
67. *Ibid.* p. 27.
68. *Ibid.*
69. Annual Report, n.65, p. 311.
70. *Ibid.*, p. 20-21.
71. *Ibid.*
72. Annual Report n.63, p. 26.
73. *Ibid.*
74. Annual Report, n. 65, p. 21.
75. *Ibid.*
76. *Ibid.*, p. 43.
77. *Ibid.*
78. Annual Report, n.63, (2011-12), p. 51.
79. *Ibid.*
80. Annual Report, n.65, p. 49.
81. Annual Report, n.63, (2011-12), p. 72.
82. *Ibid.*
83. Annual Report Ministry of Home Affairs, Government of India, (2008-09), p. 14.
84. Ajai Sahani and J. George, "Security and Development in India's Northeast: An Alternative Perspective", Fault lines, Vol. 4, (February 2000), pp. 43-67.
85. Annual Report, n.62, p. 15.
86. *Ibid.*
87. In 1992, middle level cadres of ULFA surrendered to government authorities. These surrendered cadres were allowed to keep their weapons to defend themselves against their former colleagues

and were offered bank loans without any liabilities. This loose group, now called Surrender ULFA (SULFA).

88. Samir Kumar Das, "Conflict and Peace in India's Northeast: The Role of Civil Society", available online at www.eastwestcenter.org/fileadmin/stored/pdfs/PSo42.pdf accessed on 11.11.10.

89. *Ibid.* it seems that by middle of 1991, ULFA was divided on the question of whether to enter into dialogue with the Indian government. According to Budhbar it was possible to indentify the moderates and extremists on this crucial question. In an interview with Budhbar, Raju Baruah the then chief of ULFA's Nalabari unit observed: "There has been no change in our position on freedom (Swadhinata). The struggle will continue the question of compromise with treacherous state or its representatives is absurd". On the other hand, there were reports that have five leaders under the leadership of Arbinda Rajkhowa acquiesced to the Constitution of India and signed what Parag Kumar Das termed "a treaty of compromise" with the Government of India. See Budhbar 30 October 1991, 8 January 1992 and 23 January 1992.

90. *Ibid.*

91. Ajai Sahani, "Survey of Conflicts and Resolution in India's Northeast", available online at www.satp.org/satporgtp/publication / faultlines/volume12/Article3.htm accessed on 18.07.10.

92. *Ibid.*

93. Available online at www.telegraphindia.com/1050222/asp/frontpage/story_4408414.asp accessed on 18.07.10.

94. Responding to Singh's categorical rejection of ULFAs sovereignty demand, Paresh Baruah interpreted the Prime Minister's commitment as unsurprising and completely in tune with the earlier "Colonial Policy" followed by his predecessors. Both Baruah and Goswami maintained that the latter was talking with the Prime Minister in her own private capacity and initiative, but Baruah lauded her effort to bring the issue of sovereignty in to the agenda.

95. Sometimes in early 2005, Indira Goswami met Prime Minister Singh to request the start of a dialogue between ULFA leaders and the government. Despite a series of blast in Assam apparently set off by ULFA, Goswami wrote to the Prime Minister to issue a fresh call to ULFA for peace talks. During her visit to Guwahati jail on 1st January 2005, she met three prominent ULFA leaders, Vice Chairman Pradip Gogoi, Political Adviser Bhimakanta Buragohain, and Publicity Secretary Mithinga Daimari. She requested that they talk to the government with an open minded. In the past, the GoI invited ULFA for talks, but most of the requests were turned down. After telephonic conversations with some top ULFA leaders, Goswami is believed to have submitted a letter to the Prime Minister's office justifying the need to discuss the issue of sovereignty. The leader does not included two of ULFA's earlier demands that peace be held in another country and under UN supervision. Goswami seems to have convinced the government to discuss the issue of sovereignty. In an interview with Nava Thakuria, she observed "The issue of sovereignty per se should not seen as a precondition...I understand that he (PM) will have to find out some middle path and some solution after consulting all parties and experts. However, without the sovereignty issue, the ULFA leaders are unlikely to come." In fact, Arbinda Rajkhowa reportedly requested that she continue to push for peace despite the earlier setbacks in December 2004. Goswami's non-political past and immense respectability made her acceptable to both the government and ULFA ranks. Her humanist and apparently non political commitment literally catapulted her into the rough and tumble world of peace politics. As she argued "The government should listen to the boys why have they taken to the path of violence? They are our boys, with guns in their hands. We have maintained the armed struggle for the last quarter of a century. So we cannot simply ignore them.

96. Anup Kumar Deka, "ULFA and the Peace Process in Assam", IPCS Special Report, 21 May 2006.

97. This was first time that ULFA involved individuals from civil society in the peace process. It also seemed to realise the necessity of involving the larger civil society in the peace process so that the issue of sovereignty would discussed across diverse social

constituencies although once nominated, it became apparent that the PCG could hardly act independently. Moreover, the formation of such a group gives ULFA more room to manoeuvre, because it does not have to take direct part in talks with the government, despite several invitations to do so. The PCG provides ULFA with advantage of not needing to make a commitment, diversions and most obviously, a wide negotiating space.

98. Anup Kumar Deka, n. 96.

99. *Ibid.*

100. Samir Kumar Das, n.88.

101. The Statesman (Culcatta), 11 August 2006.

102. Pushpita Das and others, "Dealing with ULFA's Terror", available online at www.idsa.in/indiastrategiccomments/ Dealingwith ULFA'sTerror_GSingh_220107 accessed on 23.01.10.

103. Wasbir Hussain, "So near, yet So far in Assam", Thelka 30 September 2006.

104. Anup Kumar Deka, n. 96.

105. *Ibid.*

106. When Rajkhowa was trapped by security forces in Bangladesh and handed over to India in December 2009, the only way left for him was to seek a respectable solution through peaceful negotiations. However, Rajkhowa was first produced before court in Guwahati, he said he had not surrendered and that it was not acceptable to hold talks with handcuffs on. A year later, as former IB chief P. C. Haldar held several rounds of informal discussions with him inside the Guwahati jail, the government agreed not to oppose the bail petitions of the ULFA leaders. They were released on the bail to come on the negotiation table.

107. Anup Kumar Deka, n. 96.

108. Annual Report, n. 69, p. 14.

109. Annual Report, n. 62, p. 12.

110. Annual Report, n. 65, p. 16.

111. Annual Report, n. 62, p. 12.

112. *Ibid.*

113. Annual Report, n. 65, pp. 16-17.

114. *Ibid.*, p. 17.

115. Annual Report, n. 65, p. 17.

116. *Ibid.*

117. *Ibid.*

118. Annual Report, n. 69, p. 16.

119. Annual Report, n. 65, p. 16.

120. *Ibid.*

121. Annual Report, n. 69, p. 16.

122. Annual Report, n. 62, p. 13.

123. Chandra Bhushan, n.11, p. 178.

124. *Ibid.*

125. The Sentinel, 14 Jan. 2010.

126. Delhi, Dakha move closer, impacts to boost security, Indian Express posted online Shubhajit Roy, 12 Jan 2010.

127. Prakash, n.13, p. 481.

128. *Ibid.*

129. *Ibid.*

130. Bhushan, n.11, p. 178.

6

Impact

Introduction

"...*there are no winners in...conflicts...There are only victims and the results can be measured only in human terms...their very humanity can be measured only in human terms...This very humanity is assaulted and violated, and the onslaught leaves the survivors scarred both in mind and soul.*"

Temsula Ao, Naga Academic and Writer.

While discussing about insurgency, one cannot set aside the impact of insurgency. In this chapter, the attempt has been made to understand the impact of insurgency and counter-insurgency on the state of Assam, Northeast region and India. It would be rather paradoxical to study separately the impact of insurgency movement and counter-insurgency operation because it consists of social, economic, political and military aspects. Therefore, the descriptive and analytical approach has been followed in this chapter while studying the impact of insurgency. For this purpose, the chapter has been divided into (1) Social Implication: (a) psychological aspect, (b) displacements, (c) implication on community; (2) Economic Implication; (3) Political Implication; (4) Military Implication; (5) Strategic Implication; (6) Implication of Environment. Northeast region has witnessed more violence in the last sixty years than any other part of the country. The violent activities of several insurgency movements have created internal instability and terror in the Northeast region. The fatalities caused by insurgency in the Northeast region have gradually increased from about 492 in the year 1992 to 21,628 in 2014. A crucial aspect of violence in the region has been frequent ethnic clashes, which has resulted in heavy loss of life and property. These have also led to large displacements. The prevailing law and order situation has made it difficult for the journalists to work in the region. Ethnic violence has continued in the state due to various issues like racial and regional conflicts, discrimination in the availability of resources and opportunity of development, wherein the state finds itself pulled in different directions and finds no solutions to it. Thus, protest rallies, public curfews and blockade by the students with an active support of insurgents have become inevitable part of life in the state.

6.1 Social Implications

The act of insurgency in the state of Assam has resulted into the loss of lives, which has long-term consequences. Even though, the peace process has begun with ULFA and the Suspension of Operations (SoO) with other insurgent outfits in the state, the situation in Assam is quite frightening because of the nature and degree of the violence that has eroded civil society. Almost every day the insurgents are killing young people in mysterious circumstances. Many of them are innocent citizens. Hence, violence related to insurgency has contributed largely towards the shrinking of the democratic space of civil society. The insurgent outfit has not left democratic space and the average citizen finds no way to appeal against the insurgent violence.[1] Such acts attempts to establish that the state is incapable to protect the civil society from the insurgent violence. Hence, the cautiousness lies in supporting the insurgents.

Moreover, the prolonged Counter Insurgency Operation (COIN) on a large-scale has imposed heavy restrictions on the fundamental rights and civil liberty of the local population in the state. The widespread barricade operations, curfews, protests are disturbing the routine life of the people. During COIN, there has been a prolonged interference in the traditional local self-governance institutions of tribal communities, which has been disturbing the day-to-day life of the people in the state. The forces involved in counter-insurgency operations are mostly unfamiliar with local culture, customs, norms and they care little for peoples' sensibilities and unintentionally hurt the feelings and sentiments of the people, and at times leave deep scars on the mindset of the local communities.[2]

During insurgent violence by insurgents and counter-operations by the security forces, the common people have to face the violation of human rights, which makes their life vulnerable. The constant violation of human rights upsets the social life, which brings the people of the community together in most cases to form their network and stand against such violent powers whether it is army or insurgent outfit. Often the insurgent outfits, in the name of revolution, perform their violent acts cruelly and the forces oppose these activities by carrying out their armed operations. In both cases, the common people suffer badly and get deprived of their common rights. However, such situation develops certain bonds of the community, and begins interacting among themselves on an unprecedented scale. In case of Assam, insurgent outfits have been carrying out their insurgent acts to get back their sovereignty, and the governance of their land. Therefore, the role of this kind of acts in favour of constructing a community can never be doubted.

Sometimes, the sense of denial is so acute and intense that it makes the community of the people to encourage and gradually support the insurgent elements. While the people of Assam thoroughly disliked the army's action involving the violation of human rights. According to Prof. Hiren Gohain, "they are not eager to support widespread extortions and killings by the ULFA 'in the name of revolution'.

6.2 Psychological Implication

The killing of non-tribal in Assam has created social unrest and the complexity of the issue to resolve. This situation has forced various incidents of violence to take place followed by propaganda. Thus, the common people have restricted their movement due to the fear of insurgents as well as security forces. The curfews, bandhs and strikes, which are often found in the Northeast region in general and in Assam in particular, have paralysed the good social atmosphere. Such social atmosphere is not suitable for proper economic and social development. Under such circumstances, the quality of education gets affected as such worse situation put a deep impact on the minds of the youths residing in the disturbed areas. Unemployed youths become victims of this worse situation and subsequently, they join insurgent outfits due to frustration. Most of these youths die who join insurgents' outfits, and those who return home, fail to live normal social life. Moreover, as far as the drug addiction and other related practices are concerned, the insurgency has a greatest influence especially on the minds of the youths of the Northeast region. Most of the youths in the region are acting as the agents of foreign dealers in Narco-terrorism.

In such circumstances, the women suffer most, as they are very much dependent upon the men for their varied social, economic and domestic needs and requirements. In such social environment, the women go through greater psychological stress due to non-assurance of the lives of the men in their family. The women usually are aware about the prevailing situation, which makes them more vulnerable, anxious and frightened due to constant violence and terror around them. Mostly, they are extremely worried for the safety of their family members. One finds that women in a widespread insurgency environment tend to form extreme and imprecise view regarding the situation, personalities and the issues involved. Sometimes, women extensively become victim of dominance and arrogance. The people who witnessed the killing, rape suffer from trauma. They could become mental patients. For example, after witnessing killing and torture, the guard of Thaligram–Pathimara Tea Estate one day fired on a road passer who was going to his home with a stick. The guard saw his stick as rifle and he fired.[3]

Hence, the psychological impact due to insurgency cannot be underestimated.

Consequently, many people who have been caught for firing both insurgents as well as security forces are seeking psychiatric help to overcome the extreme mental distress resulted from violent activities. Those who have survived the trauma of violent activities have ended up with what psychiatrists' term as Post Traumatic Stress Disorder (PSTD) in acute, mild or moderate form. According to psychiatry in the Guwahati medical college, "Post Traumatic Stress Disorder (PSTD) is a form of reactive psychosis. In such a state, a patient often experiences a flashback phenomenon which results in paroxysm or sudden action like beginning to throw whatever is laying around, scream, palpitation or breathlessness, finally ending up with chronic depression. He feels victims of insurgency are found to be confronting an impossible situation in which social norms fail." According to him, there was no way the orphan could go back to the normal family environment when his parents were alive. In this context, the physical and psychological damage to children who witnessed killing, rape or sexual abuse at the time of insurgency and COIN is very serious.

Psychiatrists say the consciousness of children has been affected by the prevailing situation, as their friends are constantly exposing them to the shocking stories of terrorism. The children often frame stories in their minds since their imagination runs wild, they think that victims would be their family members. As a result, a child undergoes crying spells which the parents are unable to recognize."[4] It is relevant to mention that, during Bodo-Santhal clashes in Kokrajhar, and Bongaigaon districts in 1998, 102 children were killed and thousands were displaced in Assam.[5] A report prepared by UNICEF on the impact of insurgency and conflict on children in Assam has focused on the status of more than 70,000 children in different camps of Kokrajhar.[6] It has reported the existence of 76 relief camps during 1998, due to continuous ethnic violence. There were 2,54,787 inmates sheltered in the camps, of which 74,103 were children. The report further revealed that 1,257 children were orphaned during the violence. The health of most of the children in the relief camps was very poor with 27.07 per cent of them suffered from diarrhea, malaria, typhoid worms and malnutrition.[7] Education is also being disrupted by armed violence.

6.3 Displacements

Every insurgent outfit represents a particular ethnic group who claims over land and territory has often led to violent conflict among communities. Such violent incidents have not only claimed several human lives but also displaced several thousands from their homes thereby disturbing their livelihood for the years. The largest forced displacement movements have occurred in the state of Assam.[8] The largest displacement situation in the state has arisen from the conflict between Bodos and Santhals. This conflict erupted in the early 1990s and caused the displacement of an approximate 2,50,000 persons. In the month of December 2005, about 1,10,000 people had remained in the relief camps in Assam's Kokrajhar and Gossaigaon subdivisions, which shows a decrease of 40,000 people since 2003. However, the displaced persons have not been able to return to their villages, as the Bodo communities have occupied their villages. Today, they are landless and poor.[9] In recent years, the Karbi Anglong and North Cachar Hills districts of Assam have been the major regions of ethnic violence. Thousands of civilians have been dislocated mainly due to fight among Karbi, Kuki and Dimasa insurgent groups. In October 2005, there were clashes between the rival Karbi and Dimasa tribes, which continued until the end of the year. As a result, 50,000 people from both tribes were displaced and they took shelter mainly in public buildings situated in safe areas.[10] Moreover, communal violence between the Assamese and foreigners, mostly the immigrants from Bangladesh, has led to widespread displacement. During the year 2005, the angry mobs had driven out thousands of Muslims of Bengali origin from the state because according to Assamese they were illegal migrants from Bangladesh.[11] Major waves of displacement have also occurred due to violence against seasonal workers, mainly from Bengal. In November 2003, communal violence displaced at least 18,000 people who took shelter in about 40 camps inside and outside Assam.[12]

6.4 Implication on Community

While studying the implication of the impact with community it seems apparently that the continuous migration of Muslims from Bangladesh to the region has altered the demographic pattern in the entire Northeast region, which has made the situation worst. Although, the increasing percentage of minority population was a disturbing factor for the government, the quality of its governance and its attitude towards the Muslims has also made a big difference. Banks are unwilling to give loans to Muslim entrepreneurs. Their children were deprived of admission to the best schools and Muslim girls from Bangladesh were smuggled into the markets of flesh trade. The insensitivity of administration has alienated the minorities from the mainstream. For instance, names of the lakhs of Muslims were deleted from the voters list. The attacks by Bodo insurgents to unsettle the refugees from Char lands created fear and deep sense of insecurity among the minority community. On the contrary, this fear has strengthened the Muslim Fundamentalist groups from Bangladesh and insurgent outfits, especially in Assam.[13] Therefore, outfits like Muslim United Liberation Front of Assam (MULFA), Muslim United Liberation Tigers of Assam (MULTA), Harkat – Ul- Mujahideen (HuM), or Muslim Liberation Army (MLA) have gained importance in Assam. SIMI has gradually spread its base by taking advantage of the situation. The rapid networking of madrassas, the long porous Indo-Bangla border has provided a strong platform for these organisations to express their anger.

6.5 Economic Implications

Security problems created by secessionism and fundamentalism have affected the development[14] process in this region. As a result, it has led threat to the national security of the country. The Siliguri corridor is the gateway to the

Northeastern region and all flows to and from the region pass through this corridor into Brahmaputra Valley. Therefore, any disturbance in Brahmaputra Valley and/or its adjoining hills brings the activities in the whole of the Northeast region to an inactive position. Similarly, the impact of insurgency in one state also affects the neighbouring states.

The economy of any region depends upon its infrastructural base i.e. transport facilities, communication network and secured social environment. As far as the economy of the Northeastern region is concerned, the region has already weak infrastructure especially, its transport system. The rebellious activities of the insurgents damage rail tracks, cause accidents leading to loss of life and property, create terror among the travellers and create terrible threat for the entire system. Similarly, vehicles on the state and national highways are often attacked, passengers and transport workers are killed or wounded and sometimes kidnapped for money; and their goods are looted. The insurgents' attack on the transport route forces the region to suffer from geographical isolation on one hand and the region faces ravages from nature in the form of floods and landslides during monsoon on other hand. In 1990s, Bodo insurgent outfits had destroyed public property such as, roads, bridges, and schools on a large-scale. The next important target of the insurgents is the resource-based industries like petroleum and tea that form the core of the modern organised sector in the region.[15] The attacks of the insurgents on tea and petroleum plants has conveyed negative signal to the prospective investors. Moreover, such insurgency situation would also seriously hamper the potential of using gas reserves of the region.[16]

The insurgency has also created serious problems for development of the internal areas. In other words, rural-urban economic interaction in the hilly and internal areas of the Northeast region has deal with a number of hurdles. The insurgency has provoked the problem to such an extent that the development workers of both the Government and NGOs have become completely discouraged from going to the hilly and rural areas, as they have to face constant extortions and threats of kidnapping or death. Consequently, insurgency is pushing the backward areas of the region to the darkness of greater underdevelopment. The insurgency has been acting as a retarding force making constant damages to the rural poor; especially to the indigenous people whose should be given support.[17] Moreover, the quality of developmental work has been deteriorating due to insurgency. In several instances, insurgency act has delayed the timely execution and completion of development projects leading to increase of the cost. Sometimes, projects have been stopped due to insecurity, for example, the 201 kms long Silchar-Lumding Broad Gauge Conversion project in Assam.[18] This project was sanctioned in 1996 with a budget of Rs 648 crore.[19] The project was halted due to an incessant violence carried out by Dimasa insurgents of the Dima Halam Daogah (DHD) and its opponent the Black Widow who kidnapped and killed the workers engaged in this project.[20] According to its earlier target, the project was to be completed up to 2006; however, the deadline was revised to 2009, which resulted in the cost escalation to Rs 1,823 crore.[21] Moreover, many times, the resources allocated for the plan and non-plan expenditures have not been utilised for the purpose they were allocated for. It has been observed that the corrupt bureaucrats have drawn off the huge economic packages provided by the central and the state governments for this region in the name of being seized by the insurgents. In this context, it would be right to say that the corruption in this area is so uncontrolled that even 15 per cent of these funds could not reach to the grassroot level. The Government of India's Comptroller and Auditor General (CAG) report says that the funds provided to the states under the head of plan expenditure have not been properly utilised in stipulated period. Further, there were irregularities in utilisation of these funds because of the absence of proper plans and programmes due to mismanagement. Because of all these incidences, the youths of this area feel that the central government gives them step-motherly treatment.[22]

In Assam, the illegal trade of PDS quota in the state has generated Rs 60 lakhs per month. In actual practice, ULFA and

SULFA do not provide any security of food to the common people and they divert the entire PDS quota of the state to open market.

Similarly, 70 per cent of the funds for the rural development go to the treasury of the ULFA.[23] The same situation prevails in more or less amount in all other states of the region. Thus, under the above circumstances, rural development, food security and developments in other fields are very difficult to take place in the region. Consequently, the economic condition of the Northeast region has remained poor.

The insurgency has made an adverse effect on Tea Industry. The Tea Industry in Assam has suffered the most during the past few years. The incidences of extortion of money from the owners of tea gardens and killings of the officials of tea gardens have been common during this period. As a result, different industries and professionals are moving away from the region due to security reasons. All these occurrences have led to the under-utilisation of the resources and under-development in the region. In order to survive, almost every industry or business in most of the parts of the Northeast region makes regular contributions to insurgent outfits to avoid extortion, ransom or protection money. Even a company as huge and powerful as the Tata has been making the payments to the outfits. Such 'insurgency tax' is the biggest hindrance for the investment in the area.[24] In addition, the absence of law and order, militarisation and widespread corruption make any investment in the area highly risky. For example, in Assam, the insurgents have forced a large number of businesses and shops to shift to particular areas, such as Nagaon, because of extortion from insurgents. Even a few World Bank projects have delayed due to extortion demands and kidnapping by the ULFA. Moreover, most of the industries gathered into Assam/Meghalaya are either producing high excise duty items like cigarette, pan masala, IMFL, cosmetics or high power consumption units like aluminum and alloy steel are mainly present in Meghalaya owing to the state government concession in power sector. In this context, it may be stated that if in the future, the concessions are withdrawn or power tariffs are revised, then these industries are likely to close down. Investors, entrepreneurs and industrialists were not even willing to visit the area because of this unpredictability. As a result of the disturbed situation, businessmen and foreign firms are hesitant to make any big economic plan and invest in this region.[25] Hence, the level of investment has gone down in this region due to the sense of insecurity among the investors. For instance, the budget for industrial investment in the region from August 1991 to December 1994 was worth Rs 2,224 crore, whereas the budget in a single state like Maharashtra during the corresponding period was Rs 67,978 crores.[26]

It is relevant to mention that if law and order situation in the region is not sound, the capital of such disturbed region would be used in other region where law and order situation is sound. The same situation exists in the state of Assam. The capital moved from the districts like Dibrugarh, Tinsukia and Kamrup to other safe areas. Assam has witnessed a massive flight of merchant capital to the nearby state of West Bengal, more precisely to Siliguri and Alipar during the last two decades. According to the report of West Bengal commercial tax department 2001-02, the sales tax revenue was Rs 5,984 crores from the Siliguri sub-division alone. Moreover, the capital of Assam has also been diverted to the states of Rajasthan, Maharashtra and New Delhi. Similarly, in the state of Assam, credit deposit ratio of the bank is much lower than other parts of India because entrepreneurs do not like to invest in this region due to internal disturbances. The banking sector transfers nearly Rs 5 crores from this region to other regions for the sake of investment.[27] According to the report of a committee on Integrated Rural Development Programme (IRDP) in the Northeastern states, "a rise in insurgency in Assam is responsible for non-development, particularly in rural areas, which has resulted in a shift of capital from the rural areas to urban areas as the rural area is less secured than urban".[28] Business transactions do not take place at night time in many hilly areas of the Northeast region due to insecurity. This reduces trade, savings and investment in the region.

In the Northeast region, the natural economic development of the region has almost taken a back seat. During last several years, the government has been spending a large amount of national wealth for internal security of the region to control the armed violence. In other words, the central and state governments have been spending huge amount of money in the COIN, which could be spent for economic development of the state in particular and the region in general. Hence, it imposes additional financial burden on the state and the central government. It has been observed that in situations of armed violence, the state resources are often redirected to achieve political goals. However, funds spent for counter-insurgency operations have remained beyond public scrutiny. This further encourages state corruption.[29]

6.6 Political Implications

The political parties from the region and the insurgent outfits are reportedly to have developed a relation amongst them. Thus, it has gradually affected the political life and development prospects of the region. In this context, according to Nani Gopal Mahanta, "The ULFA and political parties have a symbiotic relationship." He further says, "The ULFA play the most dominating role not just in the state's politics, but also in the state's economy, and the ULFA determines to a great extent which party or combination should come to power". For instance, when Prafulla Kumar Mahanta, Chief Minister of Assam, decided to take firm action against ULFA in 1998, ULFA pulled him down from the power by using its influence during election. Whenever Assam goes into election phase, political parties tactfully convince the ULFA for its support. After the election, especially 1996 and 2001, all the parties had turned around and accused each other of using the ULFA to come into power. For example, former Chief Minister of Assam Prafulla Kumar Mahanta said, "The Congress led government could not crack down on the ULFA because it captured power in 2001 with their support." He further added, "Tarun Gogoi is riding on a tiger, and he cannot come down from it and recalling how armed rebels threatened traditional non-Congress voters in 2001". Again, the

AGP and other opposition parties have blamed the Congress for using the ULFA for its advantage in the 2006 elections.

ULFA's determination had seen in past when they almost openly appealed for the ouster of the party in 1996 when the Congress government of Hiteswar Saikia went tough on the rebels. But as Prafulla Mahanta decided to get tough, the result was an attack on his convoy in Guwahati. A massive crackdown that the regional party's government carried out on the insurgents continues to hound it; the AGP is still in the ULFA's bad books. There were numerous attacks on candidates and supporters of the AGP and its allies including the BJP, and the Congress was back in power. That was in 2001.[30]

6.7 Military Implications

The militarization of the state has adversely affected the everyday life of the ordinary citizens. The major portion of 60,000 strong Assam Police Force is engaged in the personal security arrangements of the political leadership and even of the bureaucracy including the police itself. The commandos, who are raised and trained to fight against insurgents, have been diverted to what is commonly called VIP security. Thus, the politicians and public servants protect themselves; the common citizen is left exposed to extortion and violence. Detection and prevention of crime or traffic control with which a common person is immediately concerned had become the first casualty. In this context, it would not be wrong to state that, though the ratio of police per thousand people is high in the Northeast states compared to other states of India, the Northeast states lack in tight police administration. The police are not efficient enough to create mutual beliefs between the original residents and the outsiders. It has been observed that many times the police administration remains partial while registering FIR; eventually FIR against the insurgents is almost stopped. The traders have a feeling that it is beneficial for them to continue their trade in these states by satisfying the insurgents. The situation is still worse regarding filing a report against insurgents. If any one dares to file a report, the insurgents immediately come to know it and thus the security of the reporter and his family is endangered.

Moreover, if an honest police officer arrests an insurgent, the insurgents kill him. For example, the then Superintendent of Police (SP) of Dibrugarh was killed after the release of three ULFA activists in 1990. In the same way, in 1996, Shri Ravikant Singh, S.P. of Tinsukhiya was killed along with four persons. The incidences like these have spread a wave of demoralisation among the police force, which is still increasing. Eventually, the police stood in dilemma and avoided direct action against insurgents. According to statistical report, about 600 policemen were killed during the last decade.

The fact is that some policemen had direct relations with the insurgents, who were responsible for the lives of some police officers, has come to light.[31] Hence, the armed forces have been deployed for internal security of the state, as the state police are unable to deal with such violent situation. However, it has been observed that there are two distinct processes while analysing the military accumulation in the region. First, there is militarisation of the local ethnic population by the forces who are sympathetic to their individual cause and, second, the region's militarisation is objectively understood as the state's military build up to counter-insurgency. The state's military establishment requires land to settle and the resources for consumption. The local population with the military establishment thus shares the little non-forest land that this region has and its produce.[32]

Moreover, the increased military presence increases land isolation in the nature and consequently the use of land moves from productive to non-productive purposes.[33] The military presence in the region has also caused the alienation of common masses of the region. Many times the Northeast region was declared as a 'Disturbed Area' under the Armed Forces Special Power Act of 1958 (AFSPA). The use of AFSPA and Disturbed

Area Act has proven that the voice of civil society would no longer be the central force, as the state has moved far away from its goal of ensuring a democratic state. Several army operations were conducted in the region to flush out the extremists in order to end a reign of terror since the security forces were assigned for internal security duties. Because of which, anybody could be arrested without referring to police authority. Moreover, the countless 'encounter deaths' that have been taking place in Assam, have given the state a clear terrorist image and further eroded the reliability of the state. In this sense, it would be right to say that the constant deployment of security forces has caused meaningless violation of human rights and threatened the security of the common people.

The army's prolonged involvement in COIN has several other major disadvantages as well. The deployment of army for internal security duties adversely affects the army's preparation for its main task nation's security. In addition, due to the causalities being suffered almost daily affect the morale of the army personnel and it also imposes an extra burden on the defence budget. The financial costs of sustaining a successful CI campaign are awesome. It was estimated in 1998 that the army spent approximately Rs 2,500 crores out of its annual budget on COIN. This was about 13 per cent of the army's 1997-98 budget of Rs 19,000 crores approximately. The outcome was that the army spent almost 57 per cent of its budget on pay and allowances, about 40 per cent on the maintenance of equipment and the reload of ammunition and other essential stores being consumed for COIN. Furthermore, only three per cent were kept for modernisation, including capital acquisitions. Even the expenditure on the Rashtriya Rifles, amounting to approximately Rs 500 crores annually, was incurred from the army's budget for many years.[34] Thus, the army can hardly afford such high expenditure on COIN from its budget neglecting its operational efficiency for its primary task that is being significantly spoiled. As the Defence Minister informed in

Indian Parliament, the army's modernisation programme has been adversely affected by its prolonged and continued involvement in CI duties.

6.8 Strategic Implications

The insurgent outfits from Northeast have become successful to establish the contacts with the neighbouring countries. It is an age-old history, which has been discussed in earlier chapters. With this point of view, it would not be wrong to state that, the bilateral bitterness between India and Pakistan have created different political flows in Bangladesh. Prime Minister Khaleda Zia is supposed to be close to Pakistan. However, Sheikh Hasina, the leader of opposition, is known for her desire to improve relations with India.[35] The regime of Begum Khaleda is seen to be ignoring the presence of HUJI and other terrorist organisations on the Bangladeshi territory. In this sense, the political instability and the growth of Jihadi terrorist organisations, particularly in Bangladesh, have created terrible threat to the Northeast. In addition, the growth and internationalisation of organised criminal organisations with powerful political support and a strong network of well-funded institutions for the communal mobilisation of the people through a growing complex of madrassas has become a very dangerous syndrome in the country.

According to a senior Border Security Force official, "Islamic fundamentalists and Jihadi elements from Bangladesh were infiltrating the Northeast in the name of studying religion". Moreover, the IG of BSF said that the Jihadi elements entered Assam but subsequently some of them went to Meghalaya as well. In view of this, the BSF has reviewed its intelligence sharing among other security agencies and identified susceptible spots. The ISI has a strong presence in Bangladesh, which is strongly supported by DGFI. Even certain outfits of the country have links with ISI. The ISI has now adopted a strategy to bring all armed groups of the region under a 'single umbrella' instead of helping them individually. There is definitely a pressure from the ISI on both Jihadi and insurgent outfits for a 'intensive action' in the Northeast parts of the country. The experience of Bangladesh suggests that the antagonism between India and Pakistan is spreading far and wide. Countries in the neighbourhood are being pulled into this fire.

6.9 Impact on the Environment

There are significant points that need to be noted while analysing the impact of armed insurgency on the environment of the region. First, the insurgency directly affects the environment through harmful acts, like disturbing the eco-system by clearing of forest areas to set up camps, burning crops and houses during search operations. Second, the claims over the land and other natural resources by insurgents also lead to environmental imbalance. According to the Report of Forest Department of Assam, the Mahamaya and Kachugaon forest reserve of Dhubri and Kokhrajar districts respectively, which constitute the most important forest areas in the Northeast region for bio-diversity conservation, are now on the edge of destruction due to the meaningless devastation made by anti-social elements. These forests are famous for their rare species of flora and fauna. These forest reserves have been gradually destroyed due to the government's attitude of issuing permit indiscriminately.

On the one hand, Bodos claim that they protect forest reserves and its resources; while on other hand, they have caused extensive damage to the dense forest in lower Assam. The robbers with Naga insurgents, Bodos, ULFA insurgents have also destroyed the forest reserve and sanctuaries in various states. For example, in the Manas Tiger Reserve in Assam, which is used as a hiding place for the insurgents, the Bodos are indulged in destruction of forest resources and they have endangered animals like Tigers, Rhino and Elephants. Most of the hideouts and training camps of the insurgents are located in Jungle areas. With every COIN, the insurgents have to clear more jungle areas as their safe heaven.[36]

6.10 Sum up

1. The insurgency in the state of Assam has made its impact on all aspects of life of the region in general and the state in particular. It has disturbed the social, economic and political life of the region. Moreover, insurgency-related violence has contributed largely towards the shrinking of the democratic space of the civil society. Thus, it can be concluded that the insurgency has endangered the life of common citizen in the state and the Northeast region.

References

1. Udayon Misra, "Shrinking Democratic Space and the Role of Civil Society", in Imdad Hussain, ed., Guwahati Declaration and The Road to Peace in Assam (New Delhi, 2005), pp. 97-98.

2. Ashish Sonal, Terrorism and Insurgency in India (New Delhi, 1994), p.116.

3. Yugashanka, 12 November 2002.

4. Sabir Nishant, "Terror Plague", Eastern Panorama (Shillong), Vol. IX, No. 1, November 2000, p. 17.

5. Mandy Turner and Binalaksmi Nepram, "Impact of Armed Violence in Northeast India: A Mini Case Study for the Armed Violence and Poverty Initiatives", Centre for International Cooperation and Security, University of Bradford, November 2004.

6. *Ibid.*

7. *Ibid.*

8. Monika Mandal, "Internal Displacement in India: Status, Condition and Prospects of Return" available online at http://www.mcrg.ac.in/rw%20files/RW33/3.IDP_Monika.pdf accessed on 29.08.11.

9. *Ibid.*

10. *Ibid.*

11. *Ibid.*

12. *Ibid.*

13. Krishna Gopal, "Islamic Fundamentalism in Bangladesh and its role in North east Insurgencyt," in Dipankar Sengupta and Sudhir Kumar Sing, ed., Insurgency in North-East India: The Role of Bangladesh (New Delhi, 2002), p.191.

14. Economic development is considered to the foundation of society. Hence, security and economic development have a symbiotic relationship, without security there can be no economic development and without economic development security has no meaning. Development is an over-arching term encompassing economic growth through agricultural improvement, industrialisation and national-integration. Anything that comes in the way as hindrance of such development is a threat to the national security.

15. P. R. Bhattacharjee and Purusottam Nayak, "Vicious Circle of Insurgency and Underdevelopment in Northeast India, available online at http://www.freewebs.com/pnayak/research_papers/33p.pdf accessed on 02.01.11.

16. *Ibid.*

17. *Ibid.*

18. M. Amarjeet Singh, "Insurgency and Development in India's North-East States: A Study of Assam", in Rakhee Bhattacharya and Sanjay Pulipaka, Perilous Journey: Debates on Security and Development in Assam, ed., (New Delhi, 2011), p.170.

19. *Ibid.*

20. *Ibid.*

21. *Ibid.*

22. Chandra Bhushan, Terrorism and Separatism in North – East India (New Delhi, 2004), p. 209.

23. P. C. Dutta, "Problems of Ethnicity and Security in North East India" in S. K. Agnihotri and B. Dutta Ray, Perspective of Security Development in North East India (New Delhi, 2005) p. 118.

24. G. Sachdeva, Economy of the North-East: Policy, Present Conditions and Future Possibilities (Delhi, 2000), pp. 225-6.

25. Jayanta Madhab, "Unbounding the Frontier: Enabling the Northeast", Dialogue (New Delhi), Vol. 7, No. 3, pp. 69-70.

26. See Wsbir Hussain, "Contemporary North East Indian; Problems and Prospectus" in J. P. Singh and others ed., Trends in Social Science and Humanities in North East India (New Delhi, 1998).

27. Jayanta Madhb, "North East: Crisis of Identity, Security and Underdevelopment", Economic and Political Weekly (Mumbai), Vol. 34, No. 06, (06-12 February 1999), pp. 320-22.

28. Ministry of Rural Development, Government of India, "Report of the Committee on Credit related Issues under IRDP in Northeastern States", 2000.

29. G. Das, "Armed Struggle in Nagaland: Tactics, Strategies and its Ramifications for Economic Development", in C. J. Thomas, ed., Dimensions of Development in Nagaland (New Delhi: 2002), p. 33.

30. India Express (Mumbai), 14 January 2007.

31. Bhushan, n. 22, pp. 212-15.

32. Mohammed Asif, "Development Initiative and the Concomitant Issues of Displacement and Improvement in the Northeast States, in Kailash Agrawal, ed., Dynamics of Identity and Intergroup Relations in Northeast India (Shimla, 1999), p. 56.

33. *Ibid.*

34. Gurmeet Kanwal, "Internal Security Challenges" Indian Defence Review (New Delhi), Vol. 21, No. 4, (October- December 2006), pp. 76-79.

35. The rivalry between Begum Khaleda and Sheikh Hasina is largely based on domestic issues. It has its roots in the history of Bangladesh in the last 20 years and the conflict of egos between the two women leaders. They had collaborated in the agitation to restore democracy during General Irshad's period. They fell apart

as soon as they had to compete for power. Therefore, it would not be appropriate to ascribe their rivalry to either India or Pakistan. Nevertheless, once the bitterness of the Khaleda-Hasina competition was established, it is argued that Pakistan and India offered sympathies and support to them on a competitive basis. See Chapter Three: Vulnerabilities, available online at www.strategicforesight.com/finall settlement/vulnerabilities2.pdf accessed on 27.08.11.

36. Neparam, Binalakshmi, South Asia's Fractured Frontier: Armed Conflict, Narcotics and Small Arms Proliferation in India's Northeast (New Delhi, 2002), pp. 167-68.

7

Conclusion and Recommendations

7.1 Findings of the Present Study

Since twentieth century, there has been a conceptual shift in the concept of national security. Earlier, this concept was based on state centric military oriented security, according to which, territorial boundary of a nation has to be protected from external aggression by means of war. Thus, the efforts have always been taken to improve the military capability of the country in order to protect the country. However, in the late Twentieth century, the concept of national security has transformed from the state centric military oriented security to security of groups and individuals. This has been observed when it was argued that the concept of national security needs a holistic approach, which would cover the wider areas of national security, such as, environment, food, social, political and cultural rights of individuals. At the same time, it has been widely accepted that the military capability is essential in pursuit of national security when and where required.

Today, the key objective of national security is not only to protect the country from external aggression but also to maintain peace and harmony within the country by fulfilling the aspirations of the people and checking the internal security threats to the country originating within the country itself. However, geo-strategically important Northeast region of India, which is a union of eight states, with having abundant of natural resources has been suffering from insecurity since the independence of the country. There are many complex sets of issues, which ended into insurgency, are responsible for constant disorder in the region. The roots of this constant chaos are found in the historical and geographical aspects of the region. The policies formulated by British, partition of the country, the succesive Indian governments' policies made a negative impact on the people of this region. This is because borders were closed at the time of partition of the country. The close borders and the emergence of new countries across the borders have cut the age-old railway, road and cultural links of this region. The gravity of this impact was multiplied when the then Indian leadership followed the British policy of keeping tribal people of the hills aloof from plain politics, who are ethnically, culturally and linguistically diversed. This further helped to sow the seeds of insurgency in the region.

During post-independence era, revolt was broken out in Naga Hills, which later ended into the insurgency movement. It was the first incidence of insurgency erupted in the region. Since then, the insurgency movement at different points of time has engulfed many other parts of the region. Today, with some exceptions, the whole region is engulfed with insurgency related violence. The causes of insurgency differ from state to state in the region with some exception. Situations in two different states are not alike. It would not be wrong to state that insurgency is an outcome of dissatisfaction, deprivation, frustration and lack of positive response from the state, which ultimately alienated the inhabitants of this region. It is relevant to mention that until 1962, the region could not receive any attention from the central government. However, after the Indo-China war, many administrative changes had taken place in the region and breakup of undivided Assam is an outcome of one of such changes. The economic capability of these states has not been taken into consideration while breaking up undivided Assam and carving out states from Assam. Hence, these states have been dependent on the central transfer of resources. The huge natural resource potential has yet to be fully utilized for the development of this region. The economy of this region is still primarily agrarian; however, there has been no sufficient development in the agricultural sector. The condition of the industrial sector of this region is poor, whereas service sector has been enriching. The funds generated by service sector have come from the public administration. Infrastructural development in this region is also poor. The demography of this region has been witnessing a constant increase in the growth rate of the population since the early twentieth century. The population of this region is heterogeneous. It is due to the migration that had taken place in the early centuries and in the nineteenth and twentieth century's. Later, demographic transformation became the cause of concern as it was identified as one the reasons of insurgency movement.

The term 'insurgency' has been defined as an armed struggle against the authority by group of people to fulfill their aspirations. However, nowadays insurgents are often mistaken with terrorists because their method of operation is similar with the terrorist. They attempt to project themselves like extremist group. Thus, violence and extremism have become the main tools of insurgency in achieving political and economic power. Insurgent outfits have not only been fighting against the Indian security forces but they have also been fighting against the communities from mainland of Indian states and within the region. For example, Bodo - non-Bodo conflict in Assam, anti-Chakma movement in Arunachal Pradesh, anti-outsider movement in Meghalaya, Naga-Kuki and Kuki-Paite clashes in Manipur, Tripuri-Bengali conflict in Tripura.

Insurgency took place in the state of Assam due to various factors, such as, emergence of Assamese nationalism, economic exploitation, political distortion and illegal migration in the state. Assam was geographically a large state in the region before reorganization of the Northeast region. The newly emerged middle class of this undivided Assam wanted to restrain the influence of Bengali-speaking people and to rule over the minority classes of undivided Assam such as Bengalis, Bodos, Khasis, Mizos, Nagas and Chakmas. Thus, attempts were made to gain such control by playing language politics. They also encouraged the Muslim rice cultivators and peasants from East Pakistan to settle in Assam with a condition that they should declare Assamese language as their mother tongue. However, in the 1971, the Bengali-speaking immigrant Muslims refused to declare Assamese as their mother tongue. This language politics had disturbed other minority ethnic communities. Later in 1972, reorganization of the region limited the influence of Assam. Consequently, Assamese middle class and rural masses felt threatened because of the changing demography and transfer of land ownership to the Bengali migrants. They also noticed economic exploitation that was taking place in the state. They had raised the issue of economic exploitation through the protest at oil refinery. Also, Assamese initiated a mass agitation against the illegal migrants with a feeling of economic exploitation, linguistic issue and a fear that the Assamese would one day become foreigners in their own land. This mass agitation ended with Assam accord in 1985.

The success of Assamese students' leaders in sustaining prolonged campaign and acquiring the political power had inspired other student movements in the state. Thus, the situation became worse than before. The emergence of Muslim Fundamentalist Organizations (MFOs) added a new dimension in the insurgency of Assam. Thus, Assam witnesses insurgency on ethnic and communal lines. There are some dangerous insurgent groups in Assam, such as, ULFA, BdSF – NDFB, BVF - BLTF, DHD, UPDS, MULFA and MULTA. The ULFA, which was formed in 1979, had emerged as a prominent insurgent outfit in the state and began to run a parallel administration in many parts of Assam. The ULFA advocated decentralization of ethnic communities to ensure that they have accepted the broad goals of Assamese nationalism. The ULFA had promised to implement scientific socialism to build Assamese society after the liberation from Indian colonial rule. Due to the growing influence of ULFA, law and order of the state was collapsed in the state. Other insurgent outfits are prominent in their respective areas, such as, Bodo Insurgent outfits in Bodo dominated area, DHD in North Cachar Hills and Karbi Anlong districts, UPDS in Karbi Anlong districts and Muslim Fundamentalist Organisations (MFOs) like MULFA and MULTA are prominent in Muslim-dominated areas. They have formed an alliance with other insurgent outfits within and outside the state and the region to act against India.

All outfits from the state have maintained close nexus among them for the operational purpose. In addition, they have maintained close contacts with the neighbouring countries for arms and training. These outfits have generated the funds through extortion, kidnapping, robberies etc. The insurgent outfits from the state, like other insurgent outfits from the region, have diluted their original agenda and lost the support of local population. However, over the years, insurgencies in the region have sustained and multiplied due to varied factors. Some of the important contributory factors are criminalisation of insurgency, drug trafficking and small arms proliferation, and criminalisation of politics. Moreover, the countries like Bangladesh and Pakistan have played very significant role by providing aid and support in the form of safe sanctuaries, training facilities, weapons and financial and moral support to the insurgent outfits in the state. Besides Pakistan and Bangladesh, the role of neighbouring countries like Bhutan and Nepal has remained supplementary. These two nations have provided safe shelter as well as transit facilities to the insurgent outfits of the state. The insurgency in the region has claimed 21,628 lives including civilians, security forces and insurgents since 1992.

Both central and state governments have been taking counter insurgency measures to contain the insurgency from Assam. In Assam, while tackling with the insurgency, during the initial period army was continuously deployed to counter the ULFA. Later BVF was used against the ULFA. However, it has gained little due to lack coordination among the security forces and due to lack of coordinated policy of the government. At the same time, peace initiatives and surrender and rehabilitation policies were introduced to curb the insurgency in the state. Presently all the major insurgent groups from the state are under the ceasefire agreement but violence still persists. It is because important leaders of those groups did not accept ceasefire agreement and formed another insurgent group. Therefore, although the central government had initiated negotiation with them, the anti – talk groups were engaged in violent activities. Moreover, talks at diplomatic level were initiated with the neighbouring countries for not assisting Indian insurgent outfits. In spite of such diplomatic attempts, many insurgent outfits in the state received help and support from the neighbouring countries like Bangladesh and Pakistan. Number of reserved battalions was augmented. Modernization programme of the forces was undertaken and efforts were taken for the management of international borders. While taking these initiatives, army has been continuously deployed in small counter insurgency operations. Moreover, various development initiatives were also taken with a viewpoint that the development would help to restrain the insurgency problem form Assam and the Northeast region. These initiatives include the establishment of Northeast Council, Ministry of Development of Northeast Region and formation of Look East policy. Though, the central government of India has been spending a lot of money and a lot more is likely to flow to the Northeast region, the desired result is not appropriate with the money spent. This is due to the fact that money was drained off by the corrupt politicians, bureaucrats and insurgents.

The insurgency in the state of Assam has made its impact on all modes of life in the region in general and in the state in particular. It has disturbed social, economic and political life of the region. Moreover, the insurgency-related violence has largely shrunk the democratic space of the civil society

7.2 Conclusion of the Study

The conclusion of the study consists of the process of verification of the claim, the supportive data and the validation of the hypotheses stated in the beginning of the study.

1. The army had been continuously deployed during the initial period while dealing with the insurgency. However, it has gained a little due to lack of coordination among the security forces and due to lack of coordinated policy of the government. Political interference has affected the efficiency of the security forces adversely in dealing with the insurgents. In this context, a role of the army was to create a situation that could bring the insurgent outfits for the negotiation resulting in a ceasefire declaration and peace talks. However, peace initiatives did not produce any desired results as the prominent leader of insurgent outfit like ULFA and NDFB were remain away from the peace talks. Hence, these leaders acted against the state. Moreover, huge funds have been provided for the development in the state. However, very little development could take place in the state due to malpractice of corrupt politicians, bureaucrats and the insurgents.

On the basis of the supportive data presented in the fifth chapter of the present study, it can be concluded that the first hypothesis stands validated. The validated first hypothesis is therefore confirmed as below:

- The continued dependence on the security forces for the maintenance of law and order in the state of Assam, and short-term peace settlement for narrow political gains has not produced the desired results.

2. It has been observed that the external powers, which are contrary to India, have always taken a special interest in the Northeast region. They have taken advantage of the ethnic, religious and linguistic diversities of the region in general and in Assam in particular while giving support to the insurgents to destabilize the country. Although, the neighbouring countries like Bangladesh, Nepal, Bhutan, Myanmar except Pakistan, have apparently stopped helping the insurgent outfits in the state; at one point of time, they had played a significant role in assisting the insurgent outfits

in the Northeast region. They have provided sanctuaries, training, funds, arms and ammunition to the insurgent outfits in order to achieve their desired goals. Pakistan's Inter Services Intelligence (ISI) is the prominent agency, which searches for the disturbed groups of insurgents. In the month of February 2000, the Ministry of Home Affairs, in a booklet "Bleeding Assam" has accused Pakistan's ISI for offering training to the Northeast insurgent outfits. Besides Pakistan and Bangladesh, the role of neighbouring countries like Bhutan and Nepal is mostly of supportive nature. These two nations have provided safe heavens as well as transit facilities to the insurgent outfit of the state. Recently, it has been reported that the leaders of anti-talk outfits, such as, ULFA are asking help from China. Up till now, Pakistan is helping the insurgent outfits in the Northeast region in general and in Assam in particular.

This supportive evidence verifies the validity of the claim made in the second hypothesis. The validated hypothesis is stated below:

- The neighbouring states of the Northeast region of India have not ceased the violence as a state policy against India.

7.3 Recommendations

Some necessary steps have been suggested at micro and macro level to control violence and establish and maintain peace in the state and the Northeast region. Some of these steps are mentioned and explained below:

Steps to be taken at Micro Level

1. Win Hearts and Minds

The central and state governments must take confidence-building steps and establish trustworthiness among the tribal people of the Northeast region. Moreover, while taking any efforts to restore peace, the government must protect and promote the historical rights and political identity of the indigenous people of Assam.

2. Dealing with Ethnic Groups

There should not be settlement policy while dealing with ethnic groups. Dealing with one underground group at a time would merely create distrust among the ethnic communities, which would develop a feeling that the centre is following divide, and rule policy in the region.

3. Observation of religious activities at border areas

It should be made mandatory to seek the district authority's approval for establishing any religious institution at the border areas and keep continued vigilance on the border to prohibit illegal activities.

4. Role to be played by private sector

Private sector from the region must take the responsibility to carry out community welfare activities and provide financial support to social and educational institutions, besides generating employment for the youth of the state.

Steps to be taken at Macro Level

1. Good Governance

Good governance is essential for the implementation of drawn policies to establish harmony in the region. There should be proper decision-making and implementation of those decisions should be in a transparent, accountable and in participatory manner.

2. Development

The government should form a comprehensive policy to ensure security and development in the region. Moreover, there should be optimal utilization of natural resources of the region and dissemination of the developmental activities in the rural areas. The feeling of negligence can be removed through development that would bring the region reasonably to the same level of development as in the rest of the country.

3. Opening of Border

India needs to open and develop its border trading routes, which would gradually create a regional economy that would go beyond international borders. Moreover, India needs to put more emphasize on her 'Look East' policy, which could bring about the market access and trade with the neighbouring countries.

4. Enhanced cooperation with neighbours

India must develop her strategic relations with her neighbours and look for full cooperation from the governments of Bangladesh, Myanmar and other countries for effective check on the movement of insurgents through borders. India should also create barriers for smuggling of drugs through international borders with the help of neighbouring countries.

5. Education

The universities of the region must ensure the balance between quality and quantity education, as more and more technical work-force would be required to exploit available resources.

6. Counter Insurgency Force

The employment of the army for internal security duties or CION must be reduced and the role of paramilitary forces to tackle internal security problems should be upgraded. Education on human rights and constitutional rights must also be given to the security forces.

ANNEXURE I

Distribution of Area, Population, Decadal Growth and Density of Northeast Region of India

Ref: Chapter Two: 2.4

State	*Area in Sq. Km.*	*Population (Person)*	*Decadal Growth Rate (2001-2011)*	*Density Per Sq. Km.*
Arunachal Pradesh	83743	1383727	26.03	17
Assam	78438	31205576	17.07	398
Manipur	22327	2570390	12.05	115
Meghalaya	22429	2966889	27.95	132
Mizoram	22081	1097206	23.48	52
Nagaland	16579	1975802	-0.58	119
Sikkim	7096	610577	12.89	86
Tripura	10486	3673917	14.84	350

Source: NEDFi Databank available online at http://databank.nedfi.com/content/general- information, accessed on 06.04.14 and http://www.dataforall.org/dashboard/censusinfoindia_pca/ accessed on 1.1.15

ANNEXURE II
Decadal Variations in Population 1951-1961 to 2001-2011
Ref: Chapter Two: 2.4

Years –States	*1951- 1961*	*1961-1971*	*1971-1981*	*1981-1991*	*1991-2001*	*2001-2011*
Arunachal Pradesh	N.A	38.91	35.15	36.83	27.00	26.03
Assam	34.98	34.95	23.36	24.24	18.92	17.07
Manipur	35.04	37.53	32.46	29.29	24.86*	24.50
Meghalaya	27.03	31.50	32.04	32.86	30.65	27.95
Mizoram	35.61	24.93	48.55	39.70	28.82	23.48
Nagaland	14.07**	39.88	50.05	56.08	64.53	-0.58
Sikkim	17.76	29.38	50.77	28.47	33.06	12.89

(Contd.)

(Contd. Annexure II)

Years –States	*1951- 1961*	*1961-1971*	*1971-1981*	*1981-1991*	*1991-2001*	*2001-2011*
Tripura	78.71	36.28	31.92	34.30	16.03	14.84

* The population of Manipur State of Senapati district by sex includes the estimated population of Mao Maram, Paomata and Purul sub-divisions of Senapati district for 2001.

* While working out decade variation, the population of 74,392 and 59,883 under Tuensang and Mon district respectively for 1961 census have not been taken into account as the area was censuses for the first time in 1961.

Source:

Arunachal Pradesh: available online at http://www.censusindia.gov.in/2011census/PCA/A2_Data_Tables/12%20A-2%20Arunachal%20Pradesh.pdf accessed on 21.08.14.

Assam: available online at http://www.censusindia.gov.in/2011census/PCA/A2_Data_Tables/18%20A- 2%20ASSAM.pdf accessed on 21.08.14.

Manipur: available online at http://www.censusindia.gov.in/2011census/PCA/A-2_Data_Tables/14%20A- 2%20Manipur.pdf accessed on 21.08.14.

Meghalaya: available online at http://www.censusindia.gov.in/2011census/PCA/A-2_Data_Tables/17%20A- 2%20Meghalaya.pdf accessed on 21.08.14.

Mizoram: available online at http://www.censusindia.gov.in/2011census/PCA/A-2_Data_Tables/15%20A- 2%20Mizoram.pdf accessed on 21.08.14.

Nagaland: available online at http://www.censusindia.gov.in/2011census/PCA/A-2_Data_Tables/13%20A- 2%20Nagaland.pdf accessed on 21.08.14.

Sikkim: available online at http://www.censusindia.gov.in/2011census/PCA/A-2_Data_Tables/11%20A- 2%20Sikkim.pdf accessed on 21.08.14.

Tripura: available online at http://www.censusindia.gov.in/2011census/PCA/A-2_Data_Tables/16%20A- 2%20Tirupura.pdf accessed on 21.08.14.

ANNEXURE III

Fatalities in insurgency related violence in Northeast region of India since 1992 to 31st March 2014

Ref: Chapter Three: Table 3.1

States	*Heads*	*1992*	*1993*	*1994*	*1995*	*1996*	*1997*	*1998*	*1999*	*2000*	*2001*	*2002*	*2003*
ASSAM	Civillians	80	74	173	170	302	285	531	214	366	264	193	182
	Security Forces	34	24	35	73	87	85	72	77	65	59	26	12
	Insurgents	19	33	63	27	62	167	180	212	327	283	308	207
Arunachal Pradesh	Civillians	0	1	3	3	4	9	2	3	7	40	7	7
	Security Forces	0	2	0	0	1	1	2	0	3	12	4	1
	Insurgents	0	0	0	0	0	0	1	3	24	11	21	31
Manipur	Civillians	84	266	189	183	117	233	87	89	93	70	60	50
	Security Forces	30	91	98	64	65	111	62	64	51	25	54	27
	Insurgents	51	66	63	74	93	151	95	78	102	161	125	128
Meghalaya	Civillians	0	0	4	7	3	3	5	5	12	24	28	35
	Security Forces	0	0	0	0	4	0	14	17	7	8	14	7
	Insurgents	0	0	0	0	0	1	1	0	17	8	24	37

(Contd.)

(Contd. Annexure III)

States	Heads	1992	1993	1994	1995	1996	1997	1998	1999	2000	2001	2002	2003
Mizoram	Civillians	0	0	0	0	0	0	0	0	2	4	0	0
	Security Forces	0	0	0	0	0	4	0	0	5	7	0	1
	Insurgents	0	0	0	0	0	0	0	0	0	1	0	0
Nagaland	Civillians	34	62	110	80	144	104	26	26	13	25	16	13
	Security Forces	33	43	26	25	48	38	14	4	4	2	54	27
	Insurgents	29	68	56	108	112	218	72	118	84	76	125	128
Tripura	Civillians	59	148	206	178	140	205	214	240	453	239	150	207
	Security Forces	18	28	22	34	31	50	25	41	16	31	46	39
	Insurgents	21	7	10	45	18	19	26	22	45	42	22	50
Total Fatalities													
	Civillians	257	551	685	621	710	839	865	577	946	666	454	494
	Security Forces	115	188	181	196	236	289	189	203	151	144	198	114
	Insurgents	120	174	192	254	285	556	375	433	599	582	625	581
Total Cumulative Fatalities Year Wise		492	913	1058	1071	1231	1684	1429	1213	1696	1392	1277	1189

(Contd.)

(Contd. Annexure III)

States	Heads	2004	2005	2006	2007	2008	2009	2010	2011	2012	2013	2014	Total Cumulative Fatalities State Wise
ASSAM	Civillians	194	173	164	287	245	152	53	18	27	35	22	4204
	Security Forces	17	7	32	27	18	22	12	14	5	5	1	809
	Insurgents	104	74	46	122	110	194	109	46	59	52	20	2824
Arunachal Pradesh	Civillians	6	3	0	12	3	3	2	6	5	2	2	130
	Security Forces	2	1	0	5	0	0	0	0	0	1	0	35
	Insurgents	35	16	4	25	6	19	11	21	14	7	5	254
Manipur	Civillians	62	158	96	130	137	81	33	26	21	28	2	2295
	Security Forces	38	50	28	39	16	19	6	10	8	5	3	964
	Insurgents	112	202	187	219	364	336	108	28	65	25	4	2837
Meghalay	Civillians	17	1	6	9	1	3	4	12	36	30	10	255
	Security Forces	8	0	0	1	2	0	0	8	1	7	0	98
	Insurgents	22	23	2	14	7	6	14	11	16	21	6	230
Mizoram	Civillians	0	2	0	2	0	1	0	0	0	0	0	11
	Security Forces	1	0	0	0	4	0	0	0	0	0	0	22
	Insurgents	3	4	0	6	0	0	0	0	0	0	0	14
Nagaland	Civillians	42	28	29	44	70	16	0	7	8	11	0	908
	Security Forces	38	1	2	1	3	0	0	0	0	0	0	363
	Insurgents	112	70	116	109	140	15	5	8	66	33	3	1871

(Contd.)

(Contd. Annexure III)

States	Heads	2004	2005	2006	2007	2008	2009	2010	2011	2012	2013	2014	Total Cumulative Fatalities State Wise
Tripura	Civillians	67	28	14	14	10	8	2	1	0	1	0	2584
	Security Forces	46	11	14	6	3	1	2	0	0	0	0	464
	Insurgents	51	21	22	19	13	1	0	0	2	0	0	456
Total Fatalities	Civillians	388	393	309	498	466	264	94	70	97	107	36	10387
	Security Forces	150	70	76	79	46	42	20	32	14	18	4	2755
	Insurgents	439	410	377	514	640	571	247	114	222	138	38	8486
Total Cumulative Fatalities Year Wise		977	873	762	1091	1152	877	361	216	333	263	78	21628

Source:

1. Insurgency related killings in Assam 1992-2015, available online at http://www.satp.org/satporgtp/countries/india/states/assam/data_sheets/insurgency_related_killings.htm, accessed on 1.07.15.
2. Insurgency related killings in Arunachal Pradesh 1992-2006, available online at http://www.satp.org/satporgtp/countries/india/states/aunachal/data_sheets/insurgency_related_killings.htm, accessed on 1.07.15.
3. Insurgency related killings in Manipur 1992-2015, available online at, http://www.satp.org/satporgtp/countries/india/states/manipur/data_sheets/insurgency_related_killings.htm, accessed on 01.07.15.
4. Insurgency related killings in Meghalya 1992-2015, available online at, http://www.satp.org/satporgtp/countries/india/states/meghalaya/data_sheets/insurgency_related_killings.htm, accessed on 1.07.15.
5. Insurgency related killings in Nagaland 1992-2015, available online at, http://www.satp.org/satporgtp/countries/india/states/nagaland/data_sheets/insurgency_related_killings.htm, accessed on 1.07.15.
6. 152 Insurgency related killings in Tripura 1992-2015, available online at, http://www.satp.org/satporgtp/countries/india/states/tripura/data_sheets/insurgency_related_killings.htm, accessed on 1.07.15.
7. Insurgency related killings in Mizoram 1992-2015, available online at, http://www.satp.org/satporgtp/countries/india/states/mizoram/data_sheets/insurgency_related_killings.htm, accessed on 1.07.15 and Ministry of Home affairs Annual Reports, (Governemtn of India, 2006-2014).

ANNEXURE IV
Tactical Shift of ULFA

Some of the principal tactical shifts the ULFA has undergone include the following:

- In the past, the group used to recruit cadres and send them for prolonged military training at their bases in Bhutan, Myanmar or Bangladesh. The long absence of certain youths from a particular village or localities, and their reappearance after a considerable gap, made it easier for the security and intelligence machinery to ascertain if they were ULFA members and to keep tabs on them. However, in the wake of the loss of ULFA's staging and training facilities in Bhutan, following the Bhutanese military crackdown in December 2003, and the comparatively better cooperation from the military *junta* in Myanmar, the ULFA is sending fresh cadres for short-term training, mostly within Assam and along the Arunachal Pradesh-Myanmar border.
- This strategy of sending recruits for short training courses has reduced the span of absence from their homes, and has lessened the possibility of suspicion being aroused in the minds of informers or the intelligence community.
- Until 2000, the ULFA was engaged in shootouts with the Security Forces (SFs), but such direct engagement between the rebels and the troopers have now become a rarity. The ULFA clearly finds the costs of direct confrontations disproportionate with any calculable returns.
- The new strategy adopted by the ULFA includes hiring youths, even students, who do not have any criminal records

or do not figure in the scan list of the security forces, to lob grenades or plant improvised explosive devices (IED) at public places. These 'stealth attacks' constitute a zero risk to the rebel group in terms of potential loss of trained manpower.

- This 'outsourcing' of tasks has been confirmed by the Police even in ULFA strongholds in the eastern Tinsukia and Dibrugarh Districts as recently as in March 2008. The Assam Police intelligence chief, Inspector General of Police, Khagen Sharma, told this writer that there were several confirmed cases where the ULFA had hired people outside the group to ferry and plant bombs.

Source: Wasbir Hussain, Assam: Counter-insurgency Rejig, available online at http://www.satp.org/satporgtp/sair/Archives/6_37.htm#assessment2 accessed on 17.11.10.

ANNEXUER V

Modernisation of Police Force Funds Released in Cash/Kind to North-eastern States under Scheme for Modernisation of State Police Forces during the period from 2000-01 to 2010-11

(Position as on 31.03.2014)

Name of the State	*2000-01*	*2001-02*	*2002-03*	*2003-04*	*2004-05*	*2005-06*	*2006-07*	*2007-08*	*2008-09*	*2009-10*	*2010-11*	*2011-12*	*2012-13*	*2013-14*	*Total in crores*
Arunachal Pradesh	6.53	5.21	10.61	8.06	9.13	7	11.53	11.71	14.72	11.5	10152	0.2274	178	8.49	10434.7174
Assam	59.03	58.8	32.11	36.89	41.37	56.68	52.18	88.12	68.12	60.79	48.11	0.379	1193	57.05	1852.629
Manipur	10.61	8.57	12.22	17.52	15.24	16.97	14.09	32.06	39.24	27.44	26.48	22.659	432	20.64	695.739
Meghalaya	7.89	8.43	5.43	5.32	7.58	6.57	8.59	15.41	10.82	9.73	8.33	0.0758	170	8.12	272.2958
Mizoram	9.31	9.15	13.64	8.51	7.45	6	10.48	10.98	12.69	11.48	1940	10.9392	216	11.94	2278.5692
Nagaland	9.35	19.39	25.83	23.29	13.09	17.52	22.68	30.72	38.43	31.5	33.61	0.1516	486	29.02	780.5816
Sikkim	3.89	3.76	1.83	0.95	5.9	2.43	3.46	4.42	6.12	4.72	2.09	0.0758	90	4.79	134.4358
Tripura	20.2	13.92	15.92	19.89	11.17	11.83	11.34	8.85	20.66	22.92	23	0.0758	355	16.95	551.7258
Total	**126.81**	**127.23**	**117.59**	**120.43**	**110.93**	**125**	**134.35**	**202.27**	**210.8**	**180.08**	**12233.6**	**34.5836**	**3120**	**157**	**17000.6936**

Source: Annual Report, Ministry of Home Affairs, Government of India (2010-11), p. 290 and Annual Report, Ministry of Home Affairs, Government of India (2013-14), p. 311.

ANNEXURE VI

State-wise Details of Assistance Provided to Northeastern States under Security Related Expenditure (SRE) During the Period from 2000-01 to 2013-14 (Position as on 31.03.14)

State	*2000-01*	*2001-02*	*2002-03*	*2003-04*	*2004-05*	*2005-06*	*2006-07*	*2007-08*	*2008-09*	*2009-10*	*2010-11*	*2011-12*	*2012.13*	*2013-14*	*Cumulative Total (amount released from 2000-01 to 2013-14)*
Assam	63.97	92.86	68.01	50.80	75.40	63.91	90.86	75.61	108.60	60.56	92.04	153.04	108.96	159.18	1263.8
Nagaland	7.50	12.71	22.42	19.17	26.49	24.83	25.55	21.97	33.13	41.23	79.81	83.11	69.36	42.50	509.78
Manipur	14.18	7.75	7.64	4.00	9.44	33.65	13.60	14.45	21.58	27.26	27.28	28.88	20.62	25.01	255.34
Tripura	15.00	27.70	29.85	34.33	36.17	27.00	18.24	16.47	45.04	11.85	21.12	39.25	11.32	42.18	375.52
Arunachal Pradesh	1.00	1.90	0.95	2.47	1.35	1.35	1.28	3.02	5.45	7.17	16.57	17.90	50.74	4.53	115.68
Meghalaya	3.21	0.60	8.35	1.92	1.56	13.17	3.91	5.88	6.24	1.93	3.16	27.82	-	16.60	94.35
Total	104.86	143.52	137.22	112.69	150.41	163.91	153.44	137.40	220.04	150.00	239.98	350.00	261.00	290.00	2614.47

Source: Annual Report, Ministry of Home Affairs (Government of India), (2012-13), p. 215 and (2013-14), p. 310.

Bibliography

Government Documents

1. India, the Annual Report of Ministry of Home Affairs (2003-2004 to 2013-2014).

2. India, the Annual Report of Ministry of Development of North Eastern Region (2004-2005 to 2009 – 2010).

3. India, Basic Statistics of NER 2002.

4. India, Census of India 2001, 2011.

5. India, Economic Survey of Assam (Directorate of Economics and Statistics, Government of Assam 2005-2006).

6. India, Eleventh Five Year Plan 2007-2012, Inclusive Growth, Planning Commission of Government of India (Oxford University Press 2008).

7. India, Report of the committee on Credit related Issues under IRDP in Northeastern States (Ministry of Rural Development, 2000).

8. India, Result Framework Document for Ministry of Development of North Eastern Region (2010-2011).

9. India, Report on Illegal Migration into Assam by Governor of Assam S. K. Sinha to the President of India on 08.09.98.

10. India, Second Administrative Reforms Commission (State and District Administration Fifteen Report, April 2009).

11. India, Second Administrative Reforms Commission, Capacity Building for Conflict Resolution: Friction to Fusion (State and District Administration, Seventh Report, (Government of India, February 2008).

12. India, Statistical Profile of Scheduled Tribes in India, (Ministry of Tribal Affairs, 2010).

13. India, Human Development Report of Assam (Department of Planning and Development, Government of Assam 2003).

Memorandum

1. All Bodo Students Union (ABSU), Bodo Peoples' Action Commiittee (BPAC), the text of the Memorandum submitted by ABSU, BPAC HQ. Kokrajhar (Assam) to Honorable Prime Minister of India Shri Vishwanath Pratap Singh and Honorable Union Home Minister of India Mr. Mufti Mohammed Sayeed, December 1989.

2. All Bodo Students Union (ABSU) the text of the Memorandum submitted by ABSU, HQ. Kokrajhar (Assam) to Honorable Prime Minister of India Shri H. D. Devegowda, July 1996.

3. All Bodo Students Union, Why Separate State of Bodoland (Demand and Justification), HQ. Kokrajhar, Assam.

Books

1. Aggarwal, S. Kailash, (ed.), Dynamics of Identity and Inter-group Relations In NorthEast India (Shimla: The Deputy Secretary Indian Institute of Advanced Study, 1999).

2. Agnihotri, S.K., Ray, B. Datta, (ed.), Perspective of Security and Development in North-East India (New Delhi: Concept Publishing Co., 2005).

3. Ahmed, Jaynal Uddin, (ed.), Development Vision of North East India (New Delhi: Concept Publishing Company, 2010).

4. Anand, V. K., Conflict in Nagaland (New Delhi: Chanakya Publications, 1980).

5. Ao, Lanunungsang, A., From Phizo to Muivah: The Naga National Question in Northeast India (New Delhi: Mittal Publications, 2002).

6. Aosenba, The Naga Resistant Movement (New Delhi: Regency Publications, 2001).

7. Banerjee, Dipankar, Myanmar and North East India (New Delhi: Delhi Policy Group, 1997).

8. Barpujari, H. K., ed., The Comprehensive History of Assam: Medieval Period (Guwahati, Publication Board Assam, 1992), Vol. 1.

9. Barpujari, H. K., Northeast India: Problems, Policies and Prospects: Since Independence (New Delhi: Spectrum Publications, 1998).

10. Baruah, Sanjib, Durable Disorder: Understanding the Politics of Northeast India (New Delhi: Oxford Press, 2005).

11. Baruah, Sanjib, India Against itself: Assam and the Politics of Nationality (New Delhi: Oxford University Press, 1999).

12. Bhattacharya, S. R., Tribal Insurgency in Tripura, (New Delhi: M.C Mitta Inter- India Publications, 1989).

13. Bhattacharjee, Chandana, Ethnicity and Autonomy Movement (New Delhi: Vikas Publishing House, 1996).

14. Bhattacharya, Rakhee and Pulipaka Sanjay, (ed.), Perilous Journey: Debates on Security and Development in Assam (New Delhi: Manohar Publications, 2011).

15. Bhattacharya, Hiranya Kumar, The Silent Invasion: Assam Versus Infiltration (Guwahati: Spectrum Publications, 2001).

16. Bhattacharya, Sanjukta Banerji, Das, Rochona, ed., Perspectives on India's Northeast (Calcutta: Bibhasa, 1998).

17. Bhaumik, Subhir, Insurgent Cross Fire: Northeast India (New Delhi: Lancer Publishers, 1996).

18. Bhushan, Chandra, Terrorism and Separatism in Northeast India (Delhi: Kalpaz Publication, 2004).

19. Bhuyan, B.C., Political Development of The North East (New Delhi: Omsons Publications, Part I and II, 1989).

20. Chakraborty, Kiran Shankar, Das Gurudas, Human Development Experiences of Northeast India (New Delhi: Akansha Publishing House, 2007).

21. Chari, P. R., (ed.), Perspective of National Security in South Asia (New Delhi: Manohar Publications, 1999).

22. Das, Gurudas, Purkayastha, R. K., (ed.), Border Trade: North East India and Neighbouring Countries (New Delhi: Akansha Publishing House, 2000).

23. Das, Gautam, "Insurgencies in North-East India: Moving Towards Resolutions", (New Delhi: Pentagon Press, 2013).

24. Das, Samir Kumar, ULFA: A Political Analysis (New Delhi: Ajanta Publications, 1994).

25. Das, Sanghita, North Eastern Insurgency: Problem of Assessment, (New Delhi: Anmol Publications, 2012).

26. Datta, P. S., (ed.), Ethnic Movements in Poly-Cultural Assam (New Delhi: Vikas Publishing House, 1990).

27. Datta, P. S., Autonomy Movements in Assam (New Delhi: Omsons Publications, 1993).

28. De, Sibopda, Illegal Migrations and the North-East: A Study of Migrants from Bangladesh (New Delhi: Anamika Publishers and Distributors (P) Ltd., 2005).

29. Deb, Bimal J., (ed.), Development Priorities in North East India (New Delhi: Concept Publishing Company, 2002).

30. Dev, Nirendra, The Talking Guns: North East India (New Delhi: Manas Publication, 2009).

31. Dhar, Pannalal, Ethnic Unrest in India and Her Neighbour (New Delhi: Deep and Deep Publications, 1998).

32. Dutta, Anuradha and Bhuyan Rtan, (ed.), Genesis of Conflict and Peace: Understanding Northeast India: Views and Reviews (New Delhi: Peace Studies and OKDISD, 2007) Vol. I.

33. Ghosh, Parth S, Unwanted and Uprooted: A Political Study of Migrants, Refugees, Stateless and Displaced of South Asia (New Delhi: Samskriti, 2004).

34. Ghosh, Subir, Frontier Travails: Northeast: The Politics of a Mess (New Delhi: Macmillan, 2001).

35. Gokhale, Nitin, Kashyap, Samudra Gupta, Legal Protection to Illegal Migrants (Mumbai: Rambhau Mhalgi Prbodhini, 2004).

36. Gopalkrishnan, R., Ideology, Autonomy and Integration in the North-East India (New Delhi: Omsons Publications, 1990).

37. Gopalkrishnan, R., Insurgent North-Eastern Region of India (New Delhi: Vikas Publising House Pvt. Ltd., 1995).

38. Gopalkrishnan, R., Saikia, J., Development Challenge in India: Assam in 21st Centaury (New Delhi: Omsons Publications, 2001).

39. Gopalkrishnan, R., Socio-Political Framework in North-East India (New Delhi: Vikas Publishing House Pvt. Ltd., 1996).

40. Haque, Mahfuzul, Ethnic Insurgency and National Integration A Study of Sectoral Ethnic Problem in South Asia (New Delhi: Lancers Books,1997).

41. Hazarika, Joyshankar, Geopolitics of North East India (New Delhi: Gyan Publishing House, 1996).

42. Hazarika, Niru, Ethnic Autonomy Question in Northeast India: Searching for an Answer (Guwahati and Delhi: Spectrum Publication, 2005).

43. Hazarika, Niru, Profile of Youth Organisations in North East India (Assam: V. V. Rao Institute of Micro Studies and Research, 1998).

44. Hazarika, Sanjay, Rites of Passage-Border Crossings, Imagined Homelands, India's East and Bangladesh (New Delhi: Penguin Book Publishers, 2000).

45. Hazarika, Sanjay, Strangers in the Mist: Tales of War and Peace from India's Northeast (New Delhi: Viking Publishers, 1994).

46. Horam, M., (ed.), The Rising of Manipur including other North-eastern States, (New Delhi: Manas Publications, 2000).

47. Horam, M., Naga Insurgency (Delhi : Cosmo Publications, 1988).

48. Hussain, Monirul, Class, Ideology and Identity (Manak Publications and Har-Anand Publication, 1993).

49. Hussai, Imdad, (ed.), The Guwahati Declaration and The Road to Peace in Assam (New Delhi: Akansha Publishing House, 2005).

50. Hussain, Monirul, The Assam Movement: Class, Ideology and Identity (New Delhi: Konark Publications, 1993).

51. Kar, M., Muslims in Assam Politics (New Delhi: Omsons Publications, 1990).

52. Karna, M. N., (ed.), Social Movements in North East India (Delhi: Indus Publishing Company, 1998).

53. Kotwal, Dinesh, Dynamics of Unending Violence in Assam (New Delhi: Institute of Defence Studies and Analysis, 2000).

54. Krishnarao, K. V., Prepare or Perish: A Study of National Security, (New Delhi: Lancer, 1991).

55. Kumar, B. B., Tension and Conflict in Northeast India (New Delhi: Cosmo Publications, 1995).

56. Mackenzie, Alexander, The North East Frontier of India (New Delhi: Mittal Publications, 2001).

57. Maitra, Kiranshankar, The Noxious Web: Insurgency in the Northeast (New Delhi: Kanishka Publishers, Distributors, 2002).

58. Marwah, Ved, Uncivil Wars: Pathology of Terrorism in India (New Delhi: Harper-Collins Publications, 1995).

59. Misra, Udayn, The Transformation of Assamese Identity: A Historical Survey, (Shillong, North East India History Association 2001).

60. Misra, Udayon, The Periphery Strikes Back: Challenges to the Nation-State in Assam and Nagaland (Shimla: Indian Institute of Advanced Study, 2000).

61. Mukherjee, J. R, Insurgency in India's Northeast (London: Anthem Press, 2005).

62. Nag, Sajal, Contesting Marginality: Ethnicity, Insurgency and Sub nationalism in North-East India (New Delhi: Manohar, 2002).

63. Nag, Sajal, Nationalism, Separatism, and Secessionism (Jaipur: Rawat Publications, 1999).

64. Narahari, N. S, Security Threats to the Northeast India (New Delhi: Manas Publications, 2002).

65. Nayar, V. K., Crossing Frontiers of Conflict in the Northeast and Jammu and Kashmir. (Delhi: Shipra Publications, 2005).

66. Nayar, V. K., Threat from Within: India's Internal Security Environment (Lancer Publishers, 1992).

67. Neog, D, New Light on History of Asamiya Literature, (Guwahati, 1962).

68. Neparam, Binalakshmi, South Asia's Fractured Frontier: Armed Conflict, Narcotics and Small Arms Proliferation in India's Northeast (New Delhi: Mittal Publications, 2002).

69. Nuh, V. K., Struggle for Identity in North-east India: A Theological response (New Delhi: Spectrum Publications, Guwahati: 2001).

70. O'Neil, Bard E. Insurgency and Terrorism: Inside Modern Revolutionary Warfare, (New York, Brassey, 1990).

71. Pakem, B., (ed.), Insurgency in North-East India (New Delhi: Omsons Publications, 1997).

72. Pakem, B., (ed.), Regionalism in India with Special Reference to North East India (New Delhi: Har-Anand Publications, 1993).

73. Pakem, B., Nationality, Ethnicity and Cultural Identity in North-East India (Guwahati: Omsoons Publications, 1990).

74. Paranjpe, Shrikant, ed., India's Internal Security: Issues and Perspectives (Delhi: Kalinga Publication, 2009).

75. Prakash, Ved, Encyclopedia of North-East India, Vol. I to V (New Delhi: Atlantic Publishers and Distributors (P) Ltd., 2007).

76. Prasad, Rajendra, ed., India's Security in 21st Century: Challenges and Response (New Delhi, 2002).

77. Rafiabadi, H. N., Assam from Agitation to Accord (New Delhi: Genuine Publications and Media, n.d.).

78. Raghavan, V. R., (ed.), Comparative Security: Perspectives from India's Regions (New Delhi: Delhi Policy Group, 2002).

79. Ram, Samay, Tackling Insurgency and Terrorism (New Delhi: Manas Publication, 2004).

80. Raha, M. K. and Ghosh, Alok Kumar, ed., North-East India: The Human Interface, (New Delhi: Gyan, 1998).

81. Rammohan, E. N., Insurgent Frontiers: Essay from the Troubled Northeast (New Delhi: India Research Press, 2005).

82. S. L. Barua, A Comprehensive History of Assam, (New Delhi: Munshiram Manoharlal, Reprint 1997).

83. Sachdeva, Gulshan, Economy of the North-East: Policy, Present Conditions and Future Possibilities (Delhi: Konark Publisher 2000).

84. Saikia, Anil, Goswami, Homeswar, Goswami, Atul, Population Growth in Assam 1951-1991: With Focus on Migration (New Delhi: Akansha Publishing House, 2003).

85. Saikia, Jaideep, Terror Sans Frontiers: Islamist Militancy in North East India (New Delhi: Vision Books, 2004).

86. Schuman, Frederick, 'Insurgency', Encyclopedia of Social Science, (New York, 1967).

87. Sen, Gautam, ed., Conceptualizing Security for India in 21st Century (New Delhi: Atlantic, 2007).

88. Sengupta, Dipankar, Singh Sudhir Kumar, (ed.), Terrorism in South Asia (Delhi: Authors Press, 2004).

89. Sengupta, Dipankar, Singh, Sudhir Kumar (ed.), Insurgency in Northeast India: the Role of Bangladesh (New Delhi: Author Press, 2004).

90. Sharma, S. C., Insurgency or Ethnic Conflict (New Delhi: Mangum Business Associates, 2000).

91. Sing, Chandrika, North-East India: Politics and Insurgency (New Delhi: Manas Publications, 2004).

92. Sing, Sudhir Kumar, Sengupta, Dipankar, (ed.), Insurgency in North East India: The Role of Bangladesh (Delhi: Author Press, 2004).

93. Sonal, Ashish, Terrorism and Insurgency in India (New Delhi: Lancer Publishers Pvt. Ltd., 2006).

94. Sonwal, Paramananda, (ed.), Insurgency and Economic Development in Northeast India (Guwahati: DVS Publishers, 2007).

95. Tarapat, Drug Abuse and Illicit Trafficking in North Eastern India (New Delhi: Vikas Publishing House, 1997).

96. Tarapat, Phanjoubam, Insurgency Movement in Northeastern India (New Delhi: Vikas Publishing House Pvt. Ltd., 1993).

97. Thomas, C. Joshua, Dimensions of Displaced People in Northeast India (New Delhi: Regency Publications, 2002).

98. Thomas, C. Joshua, Engagement and Development: India's Northeast and Neighbouring Countries, (New Delhi: Akansha Publishing House, 2006).

99. Vas, E. A., The Search for Security: Controlling Conflict and Terrorism, (Dehradun, 1989).

100. Verghese, B. G, India's Northeast Resurgent (New Delhi: Konark Publishers Pvt. Ltd., 1996).

Articles in Journals and Periodicals and Magazines

1. Banerjee, Sumanta, "India's Home Front", Economic and Political Weekly (Mumbai), Vol. 39, No. 40, 2-8 October 2004, pp. 4404-06.

2. Baruah, Sanjib, "Territoriality, Integrity and Rights in the North-East India", Economic and Political Weekly (Mumbai), Vol. 43, No. 12 and 13, March 22 - April 04, 2008, pp. 15-19.

3. Baruah, Sanjib, "The Problem", Seminar, (New Delhi), No. 550, June 2005, pp.12-16.

4. Chattopadhyay, S. S., and Habib, Haroon, "Challenges in the East", Frontline (Madras), Vol. 23, No. 1, 14-27 January 2006, pp. 11-23.

5. Chaudhari, Kalyan, "Tea Terror", Front Line (Madras), 17 October 1997.

6. Das, Pushpita "Management of India-China Border in Eastern Sector", World Focus (New Delhi), Vol. 27, No. 8, August 2006, pp. 13-14.

7. Datta, Sreeradha, "Northeast Turmoil: Vital Determinants", Strategic Analysis (New Delhi), Vol. XXIII, No. 12, March 2000, pp. 2123-33.

8. Editorial, "Elusive Identities", -EPW-17 December 2005, p. 5351).

9. Fernandes, Walter, "Limits of Law and Order Approach to the North-East", Economic and Political Weekly (Mumbai), Vol. 39, No. 42, 16-22 October, 2004, pp. 4609-11.

10. Gogoi, Dilip "Northeast India – Gateway to Southeast Asia", South Asia Politics (New Delhi), Vol. 6, No. 7, November 2007, p. 15.

11. Gohain, Hiren, "A Question of Identity: Adivasi Militancy in Assam", Economic and Political Weekly (Mumbai), Vol. 42, No. 49, 8-14 December 2007, pp. 13-16.

12. Gohain, Hiren, "Of Human Rights and Wrongs", Economic and Political Weekly (Mumbai), Vol. 43, No. 14, 05 -11 April 2008, pp. 13-15.

13. Gohain, Hiren, "Once More on Ethnicity and North East", Economic and Political Weekly (Mumbai), Vol. 43, No. 21, 24-30 May 2008, pp. 18-21.

14. Gohain, Hiren, "Violent Borders: Killings in Nagaland-Assam", Economic and Political Weekly (Mumbai), Vol. 42, No. 52, 11-17 August 2007, pp. 3280-83.

15. Goswami, Namrata, Miklian, Jason, "India's Violent Internal Dissent", Economic and Political Weekly (Mumbai), Vol. 43, No. 21, 24-30 May 2008, pp. 21-22.

16. Govind, Sunita, "Congress acts for foreigners", Organizer (New Delhi), Vol. LVII, No. 33, 26 February 2006, p. 4.

17. Gujaral, I. K., "India's Demographic Feature", Mainstream (New Delhi), Vol. XXXVI, No. 6, 30 January 1999, pp. 9-13.

18. Gupta, 'Youthful take over' India Today, 15 January 1986.

19. Hiranandani, G. M., "Low Intensity Conflict Revisited", Indian Defence Review (New Delhi), Vol. 22, No. 3, July-September 2007, pp. 122-23.

20. Huda, Noorul, "On Supreme Court's Verdict on IMDT Act-II", People's Democracy, (Weekly Organ of the Communist Party of India (Marxist), Vol. XXIX, No. 38, p. 3 and 15.

21. Hussain, Monirul, "Tribal Movement for Autonomous State in Assam," Economic and Political Weekly (Mumbai), Vol. XXI, 8 August 1987, p. 1332.

22. Hussain, Monirul, "Food Security and the North East", Economic and Political Weekly (Mumbai), Vol. 39, No. 41, 9-15 October 2004, pp. 4515-16.

23. Hussain, Monirul, "State, Identity Movements and Internal Displacement in the North East", Economic and Political Weekly (Mumbai), Vol. 35, No. 51, 16-22 December 2000, pp. 4519-23.

24. Kamath, M. V., "ULFA: Time to Deal with Firmly with Terror", Organizer (New Delhi), Vol. LXI, No. 27, 10 January 2010.

25. Kamoj, Anil, "Border Management: Bangladesh, Nepal, Bhutan", World Focus (New Delhi), Vol. 27, No. 8, August 2006, p. 24.

26. Kamoj, Anil, "Complexities of the Twin Hill District of Assam", Dialogue (New Delhi), Vol. 7, No. 3. pp.108-115.

27. Kanwal, Gurmeet, "Internal Security Challenges" Indian Defence Review (New Delhi), Vol. 21, No. 4, October-December 2006, pp. 76-79.

28. Kapur, Amrit, "Demographic Invasion", Indian Defence Review (New Delhi), Vol. 23, No. 2, April-June 2007, pp. 98-02.

29. Kartha, Tara, "Tools of Terror: Light Weapons and India's Security", Strategic Analysis (New Delhi, 1999).

30. Kharat, Rajesh, "Bhutan: Coping with ULFA", Economic and Political Weekly (Mumbai), Vol. 39, No. 17, 24-30 April 2004, pp. 1661-1663.

31. Kotwal, Dinesh "Insurgency in Assam: The Demographic Dimensions", Strategic Analysis, (New Delhi), Vol. XXV, no. 2, (May 2001), p. 318.

32. Kasturi, Bhashyam, "Bhutanese Army Action against Militants" Indian Defence Review (New Delhi), Vol. 19, No. 2, April –June 2004, p. 81.

33. Madhab, Jayanta, "Unbounding the Frontier: Enabling the North East", Dialogue (New Delhi), Vol. 7, No. 3, p. 64.

34. Madhab, Jayanta, "North East: Crisis of Identity, Security and Underdevelopment", Economic and Political Weekly (Mumbai), Vol. 34, No. 06, 6-12 February 1999, pp. 320-22.

35. Mall, Jagdamba, "Demographic Invasion of North-East", Organizer (New Delhi), Vol. LV, No. 10, 19 September 2004, p. 14.

36. Misra, Udayan, "ULFA: Beginning of the End", Economic and Political Weekly, Vol. XLIV, No. 52, 26 December 2009, p. 13.

37. Misra, Udayon, "Adivasi Struggle in Assam", Economic and Political Weekly (Mumbai), Vol. 42, No. 51, 22-28 December 2007, pp. 11-14.

38. Misra, Udayon, "Targeting the Innocent in Assam", Economic and Political Weekly (Mumbai), Vol. 42, No. 4, 27 January-2 February 2007, pp. 273-275.

39. Patra, Soumyajit, Samita, Manna, "Integrative Reconciliation: Mothers in the Naga Movement", Economic and Political Weekly (Mumbai), Vol. 43, No. 10, 8-14 March 2008, pp. 21-23.

40. Prabhakara, "The Bodo Question", Frontline (Madras) Vol. 19, No. 15, 20 July – 2 August, 2002.

41. Prabhakara, M. S., "Assam Updating Past", Economic and Political Weekly (Mumbai), Vol. 42, No. 4, 27 January-2 February, 2007, pp. 271-272.

42. Prabhakara, M. S., "Degrees of Separatism", Frontline (Madras), Vol. 23, No. 18, 9-22 September 2006, pp. 11-23.

43. Prabhakara, M. S., "In the Name of Tribal Identities", Frontline (Madras), Vol. 22, No. 24, 19 November to 2 December 2005, pp. 35-39.

44. Prabhakara, M. S., "Talking about Talks", Economic and Political Weekly (Mumbai), Vol. 41, No. 09, 4-10 March 2006, pp. 777-80.

45. Puri, H. K., "Fifty Years of India's Demographic Future", Mainstream (New Delhi), Vol. XXXVI, No. 11, 7 March 1998, pp. 13-19.

46. Ram Krishnan Venkitesh, "Dealing with Delhi", Frontline, (Madras) Vol. 14, No. 20, 4-17 October 1997.

47. Ranganathan, Maya, Chowdhury, Roy S., "The Nation on the Net", Economic and Political Weekly (Mumbai), Vol. 43, No. 29, 19-25 July 2008, pp. 61-67.

48. Rathore, Raunaq, "Terrorism and Indian Ambivalence", Indian Defence Review (New Delhi), Vol. 23, No. 2, April-June 2008, pp. 97-99.

49. Roy, Sanjay, "Conflicting Nations in North-East India", Economic and Political Weekly (Mumbai), Vol. 40, No. 21, 21-27 May 2005, pp. 2176-181.

50. Sabir Nishant, "Terror Plague", Eastern Panorama (Shillong), Vol. IX, No. 1, November 2000, p. 17.

51. Sachdeva, Gulshan "Demystifying Northeast", Dialogue, (New Delhi), Vol.7, No. 32, 2006, pp. 70-74.

52. Sahoo, Prasanta , "Bangladesh in the Fry Plot", World Focus (Delhi), April 2007, Vol. XXVIII, No. 4, pp. 145-46.

53. Saikia, Jaideep, "Autumn in Springtime: The ULFA Battles for Survival", Faultlines, (New Delhi), Vol. 7, November 2000, p. 35.

54. Shashikumar, V. K., "Rattle and Human in Nagaland", Indian Defence Review (New Delhi), Vol. 23, No. 2, April-June 2008, pp. 79-84.

55. Sengupta, Uttam, "Assam: State of Strife", India Today, 31 December 1990, p. 23.

56. Singh,Udai Bhanu, "Challenges to Border Management in India-Myanmar Relations", World Focus (New Delhi), Vol. 27, No. 8, August 2006, pp. 31-32.

57. Sing, Anil Kumar, "Insurgency in India: Internal and External Dimensions", Akrosh (New Delhi) Vol. 7, No. 25, (October 2004).

58. Singh, Amarjeet, "Challenges Before Bodo Territorial Council", Economic and Political Weekly (Mumbai), Vol. 39, No. 8, 21-27 February 2004, pp. 784-85.

59. Sinha, S. K., "Violence and Hope in India's Northeast", Faultlines (New Delhi), Vol. 10, 2002.

60. Sinha, S. P., "Insurgencies in North East India: An Appraisal", Akrosh (New Delhi), Vol. 3, No. 7, April 2000, pp. 40-61.

61. Talukadar, Sushanta, "Routing out Distress", Frontline (Madras), Vol. 25, No. 3, 2-15 February 2008, pp. 38-41.

62. Talukadar, Sushanta, "Violence in the Hills", Frontline, Vol. 22, No. 23, 5-18 November 2005, p. 40.

63. Talukadar, Bharali, Ratna, "State of Denial", Frontline (Madras), Vol. 25, No. 17, 16-29 August 2008, pp. 49-53.

64. Talukadar, Sushanta, "Chance for Peace", Frontline (Madras), Vol. 25, No. 07, 29 March – 11 April 2008, pp. 33-35.

65. Talukadar, Sushanta, "Communal Inferno", Frontline (Madras), Vol. 25, No. 22, 25 October – 07 November 2008, pp. 28-32.

66. Talukadar, Sushanta, "On the Boil", Frontline (Madras), Vol. 25, No.18, 30 August - 12 September 2008, pp. 36-38.

67. Talukadar, Sushanta, "Shock of Assam", Frontline (Madras), Vol. 25, No. 24, 22 November – 05 December, 2008, pp.118-23.

68. Talukadar, Sushanta, "Unrest in the Hills", Frontline (Madras), Vol. 25, No. 2, 5- 18 January 19 to February 1, 2008, pp. 31-33.

69. Talukadar, Sushanta, "Violence in the Hills", Frontline (Madras), Vol. 22, No. 23, 5-18 November 2005, pp. 38-40.

70. Tripathi, Purnima S., "North-eastern Dream", Frontline (Madras), Vol. 25, No.12, 7-20 June 2008, pp. 38-40.

71. Upadhyay, Archana, "Terrorism in the North-East: Linkages and Implications", Economic and Political Weekly (Mumbai), Vol. 41, No. 48, 2-8 December 2006, pp. 4993-99.

72. Verma, Bharat, "Democracy and Security", Indian Defence Review (New Delhi), Vol. 22, No. 4, October-Dcember 2007, pp. 3-4.

73. Verma, Bharat, "The Danger", Indian Defence Review (New Delhi), Vol. 22, No. 3, July-September 2007, pp. 3-4.

Thesis:

1. Chakraborty, "Demographi Dimensions of National Security" (A Thesis Submitted to the National Defence College, New Delhi 2005).

2. Katoch, Dhruv C, "Viable Strategy to Fight Insurgency in the North East" (A Thesis Submitted to the National Defence College, New Delhi 2004).

3. Singh, S K, "Economic Dimensions of National Security", (A Thesis Submitted to the National Defence College, New Delhi 2004).

News Papers:

1. The Assam Tribune (Guwahati)

2. The Hindu (Madras/New Delhi)

3. The Indian Express (New Delhi/Mumbai)

4. The Pioneer (New Delhi)

5. The Sentinel (Guwahati)

6. The Statesman (Kolkata/New Delhi)

7. The Times of India (New Delhi/Mumbai)

8. The Telegraph (Kolkata)

9. The Nagaland Post

Webliography

1. A-2, Decadal variation in population since 1901, Assam, available online at http://www.censusindia.gov.in/2011census/PCA/A-2_Data_Tables/18%20A- 2%20ASSAM.pdf accessed on 21.08.14.

2. Ajai Sahni, "Survey of Conflicts and Resolution in India's Northeast", available online at http://www.satp.org/satporgtp/publication/faultlines/volume12/Article3.htm, accessed on 24.09.10.

3. Aminesh Roul, "ULFA Violence Continues despite Counter Terror Operations in India's Northeast", available online at www.counterterrorismblog.org/2007/01 accessed on 17.11.10.

4. Bethany Lacina, "Does Counter Insurgency Theory Apply in Northeast India?", (Indian Review), Vol. 6, No. 3., July-September, 2007.

5. Concept paper for the Task Force for Recommending A Regional Plan for the Northeastern Region Including Sikkim, available online at http://necouncil. nic.in/ writerddata/mainlinkfile/ Concept% 20Paperfor%20the%Tas k%Force%20for%20 Recommending %20A%20Regional %20Plan% 20for%20the %20NER%20including%20Sikkim.pdf accessed 01.06.2011.

6. Charles Chasie and Sanjoy Hazarika, "The States Strikes Back: India and the Naga Insurgency", Policy Studies paper 52, (Washington, 2009).

7. David Kilcullen "Three Pillars of Counter Insurgency" Speech delivered at the U.S. government counter insurgency conference, Washington D. C. p. 2, available online at www.au. af.mil/au/awc/awcgate/uscoin/3pillars_of_ coounter insurgency.pdf accessed on 06.09.12.

8. Dima Halim Daogah, available online at Indianarmy. nic.in /Site/FromTemplete/frmTempSimple WithTwo Para.aspx? Mnld=x25YGCOG KvK=&ParentID=KDe+m3KVGiw= accessed on 17.11.10.

9. Dima Halim Daogah, Terrorist Group of Assam, available online at http://www.satp.org/satporgtp/countries/india/states/assam/terrorist_outfit/dhd.ht m, accessed on 18.11.10.

10. Dipankar Banerjee and Bidhan S. Laishram, "Bhutan's Operation All Clear: Implications for Insurgency and Security Cooperation", IPCS Issue Brief, No. 18, January 2004, available online at http:www.ipcs.org/pdf_file/issue/IB18-Operation AllClear.pdf accessed on 11.11.10.

11. Directorate of Economics and Statistics, Government of Assam, Profile of the State, available online at http://www.ecostatassam.nic.in/ accessed on 01.08.11.

12. Dhruv Katoch, "Viable Strategy to Fight Insurgency in Northeast", National Defence College Thesis available online at http://ndc.nic.in/pdf/44-katoch.pdf accessed on 19.01.10.

13. Government of Assam, available online at http://www.assam govt.nic.in/glance.asp accessed on 11.05.10.

14. Human Development Report 1993, available online at http://www. undp.org/en/reports/global/hdr1993/ accessed on 11.11.10.

15. Human Development Report 1994, available online at http://undp. org/en/reports/global/hdr1994/ accessed on 11.11.10.

16. Indian Army Doctrine, Part 1, 2004, available online at http://ids. nic.in/Indian%20Army%20Doctrine/indian army doctrine_1 .doc, accessed on 01.09.12.

17. India–Myanmar Relations, available online at http://mea.gov.in /Portal/ForeignRelation/myanmar-july-2012.pdf, accessed on 18.10.12.

18. "ISI Activities in Assam" available online at www.satp.org/satporgtp/countries/india/states/assam/documents/papers/isi_activiti es.htm accessed on 19.09.2010.

19. Jason Abbott, "Burma and India: the New Geopolitical Reality" available online at http://www.nl-aid.org/continent/south-asia/burma-and-india-the-new-geopolitical- reality/, accessed on 18.10.12.

20. Jasjit Singh, "Vision for Peace in 2020" available online at http://planningcommission.gov.in/reports/genreo/bkpap2020/22_be2020.doc accessed on 26.10.09.

21. Javed Umbreen, "The Changing Trends of Security: Influences on South Asia", available online at http://pu.edu.pk departments/doh_journal/Previous%20issues/umbreen %20javed. pdf accessed on 26.10.09.

22. K. Hrishikeshan, "Assam Agony: The ULFA and Obstacles to Conflict Resolution, available online at www.satp.org/satporgtp/publication/faultlines/volume12/Article2.htm accessed on 24.09.10.

23. Mandy Turnur and Binalakshmi Nepram, "The Impact of Armed Violence in Northeast India: A Mini Case Study for the Armed Violence and Poverty Initiative", Centre for International Studies, University of Bradford, November 2004.

24. Management of Indo-Myanmar Border available online at http://mha.nic.in/hindi/sites/upload_files/mhahindi/files/pdf/BM_MAN-IN- MYAN(E).pdf, accessed on 18.10.12.

25. M. Biswanath Sinha, "Report on Northeast India: The Development Paradigm", available online at http://www.dorabjit atatrust.org/norheast/pdf/ReportNE.pdf , accessed on 01.07.11.

26. M. Amarjeet Singh, "Resolving the Bodo Militancy", available online at http://www.idsa.in/idsastrategiccomments/

Resolving BodoMilitacny_MASingh_2 01008_M. Amarjeet Singh, accessed on 30.10.10.

27. M. Amarjeet Singh, "Growing Fundamentalism in the Northeast", available online at www.idsa.in/idsastrategic comments/Growing Fundamentalisminthr Northeast_MA Sing_190207, accessed on 23.01.10.

28. Militant Groups Profile, ULFA, available online at http:// www. cdpsindia.org/assam_mgp.asp accessed on 11.11.10.

29. Monika Mandal, "Internal Displacement in India: Status, Condition and Prospects of Return" available online at http://www.mcrg.ac.in/rw%20files/RW33/3.IDP_Monika.pdf accessed on 29.08.11.

30. Namrata Goswami, "Illegal Migration into Assam", IPCS Issue Brief, 14 January 2010, available online at http:// www.idsa.in/issuebrief/Bangladesh:Illegal Migration into Assam_ ngoswami_ 140110, accessed on 03.10.10.

31. National Democratic Front of Bodoland – Terrorist Group of Assam, available online at www.satp.org/satporgtp/ countries/india/states/assam/terrorist_outfits/ndfb.htm, accessed on 17.11.10.

32. North East Resources Databank, NEDFi Databank, available online at http://databank.nedfi.com/content/generalin formation accessed on 09.06.11.

33. North East Resources Databank, NEDFi Databank, available online at http://databank.nedfi.com/content/forest-2, accessed on 05.07.12.

34. North East Resources Databank, NEDFi Data Bank, available online at http://databank.nedfi.com/content/ general-information-0 accessed on 04.01.15.

35. NDFB Home Page, available online at www.oocities.com/ ndfb2001 accessed on 14.01.11.

36. P. G. Rajamohan, "Fundamentalism and the ISI in the North Insurgency", available online at http://www.ipcs.org/article/terrorism/fundamentalism-and-the-isi-in- northeast-insurgency-1090.html, accessed on 25.01.11.

37. Pushpita Das and others, "Dealing with ULFA's Terror", available online at http://www.idsa.in/indiastrategic comments/Dealingwith ULFA's Terror_GSingh_2 20107 accessed on 23.01.10.

38. Queen's University of Belfast School of Law, Emergency Law Database, available online at http://www.law.qub.ac.uk/humanrts/emergency/india/ind1.htm; accessed on 02.02.04.

39. R. Upadhyay, "Northeast Violence – An Overall View", available online at www.saag.org/papers17/paper1700.html, accessed on 08.02.08.

40. R. N. Prasad, "Sixth Schedule and Working of the District Councils in North- Eastern States", Dialogue (October-December, 2004), Volume 6 No. 2, available online at www. asthabharati.org/Dia_Oct04/ R.N.Pras.htm accessed on 9.06.11.

41. P. R. Bhattacharjee and Purusottam Nayak, "Vicious Circle of Insurgency and Underdevelopment in Northeast India, available online at http://www.freewebs.com/pnayak/research_ papers/33p.pdf accessed on 02.01.11.

42. Rajesh Joshi, "Pawar's Time of Reckoning", available online at http://www.outlookindia.com/article.aspx?200790.

43. Renaud Egreteau, "Instability at the Gate: India's Troubled Northeast and its External Implications", available online at http://egreteau.com/images/Documentries%20PDF/CSH%200P% 20_%n%BO16. pdf accessed on 28.01.10.

44. Subir Bhaumik, "Insurgency in India's North East: Conflict, Co-option and Change", available online at http://www. east

westcentre.org/fileadmin/stored/pdfs/EWCW wpolo. pdf accessed on 11.11.10.

45. Samiir Kumar Das, "Conflict and Peace in India's Northeast: The Role of Civil Society", available online at www. east westcenter.org/fileadmin/stored/pdfs/PSo42.pdf accessed on 11.11.10.

46. Sunil Nath, "Assam the Secessionist Insurgency and the Freedom of Minds", Available online at http://www.satp. orgtp/publication/faultlines/volume13/Article2.htm accessed on 24.09.10.

47. Saswati Choudhury, "Towards Sub-regional Cooperation: India's Northeast and Bangladesh", available online at http:/ /mpra. ub.unimuenchen.de/34991/1/Sub_ regional_ ccooperation- NEI_and_Bangladesh.pdf accessed on 27.07.12.

48. Swaran Rajgopalan, "Peace Accords in Northeast India: Journey Over Milestones", available online at http://www. eastwestceentre.org/fileadmin/stored/pdfs/PS046.pdf, accessed on 17.11.10.

49. Time Line 2000, available online at www.axom. faithweb. com/timeline/, accessed on 17.11.10.

50. The Telegraph, Available online at www.telegraphindia.com/ 1050222/asp/frontpage/story_4408414.asp accessed on 18.07.10.

51. United States, Counter Insurgency Guide, (Bureau of Political-Military Affairs, United States, January 2009), available online at www.state.gov/ documents/organisation/ 119629. pdf accessed on 26.08.12.

52. ULFA's home page-available online at www. geocities. com/ Capito Hill/Congress/7434/ulfa.htm#ULFA'sAIM&OBJECTI VES accessed on 15.05.10.

53. United Liberation Front of Assam, available online at http:/ /www. satp.org/satporgtp/countries/india/states/assam/ terrorist_ outfits/ulfa.ht m accessed on 17.11.10.

64. Virendra Sahai Verma, Dnaces with Dragons, available online at http://www.thehindu.com/opinion/op-ed/dances-with-dragons/article3800096.ece, accessed on 18.10.12.

65. Vijendra Singh Jafa, "Administrative Policies and Ethnic Disintegration Engineering Conflict in India's North East", available online at http://www.satp.org/satporgtp/publication/faultlines/volume2/Fault2-JafaF.htm accessed on 24.09.10.

66. Walter C. Ladwig (B), Managing Separatist Insurgencies: Insights From North East India, A paper prepared for International Studies Association Annual Conference 16-18 February 2009, New York, available online at http://users.ox.ac.uk/~mert1769/Managing_Separatists.pdf accessed on 06.09.12.

67. Wasbir Hussain, India's Northeast: The Super Highways to Southeast Asia? IPCS Issue Brief, No. 104, June 2009.

68. Wasbir Hussain, "Multi Force Operations in Counter Terrorism: A View from the Assam Theatre", available online at http://www.satp.org/satporgtp/publication/faultlines/volume9/Article2.htm, accessed on 11.11.10.

69. Wasbir Hussain, "Demographic Jitters", available onlne at http://www.satp.org/satporgtp/sair/Archives/3_10.htm#assesment1, accessed on 17.11.10.

70. Wasbir Hussain, Assam: Counter-insurgency Rejig, available online at http://www.satp.org/satporgtp/sair/Archives/6_37.htm# assessment2 accessed on 17.11.10.

71. Wasbir Hussain, "Assam: ULFA's Success or a Counter-Insurgency Faluer?", available online at www.satp. org. satporgp/sair/Archives/3_5html# ASSESS MENT2 accessed on 17.11.10.

72. Wasbir Hussain, Assam: Impotent Counter Insurgency, available online at http://www.satp.org/satporgtp/sair/Archives/5_48.htm#assessment2 accessed on 17.11.10.

73. Identity politics and Social Exclusion in India's North – East, available online at http://www.bangladeshsociology.org/Identity%20politics%20and%20social%20E xclusion% 20in%Indians%20North-East.pdf accessed on 27.08.11.

Index

O

P

R